Male Daughters, Female Husbands

This book is dedicated to
the memory of my mother,
Janet Onuegbunam

Also published by the author:
Afrikan Matriarchal Foundations
(Karnak House, 1987).

Male Daughters, Female Husbands

Gender and Sex in an African Society

Ifi Amadiume

Zed Books Ltd.
London and New Jersey

Male Daughters, Female Husbands was first published by Zed Books Ltd., 57 Caledonian Road, London N1 9BU and 171 First Avenue, Atlantic Highlands, New Jersey 07716, USA, in 1987.

Cover design Andrew Corbett

Printed and bound in the UK by The Bath Press, Avon

British Library Cataloguing in Publication Data

Amadiume, Ifi
  Male daughters, female husbands : gender
  and sex in African Society.
  1. Women——Nigeria——Social conditions
  I. Title
  305.4'2'09669   HQ1815.5

  ISBN 0-86232-594-3
  ISBN 0-86232-595-1 Pbk

Contents

The goddess Idemili symbolized. *Ekwe* titled women dressed in the same fashion.

Ekwe wooden gong which belonged to the *obi* of Eze Okigbo.

Mpata sitting stool of the titled.

Idemili's shrine. All the other deities and spirits are also represented. Idemili towers over them, including her husband—far right of Idemili.

Eze Agba, the priest of Idemili's shrine. He must not pass his loin-cloth between his legs as men normally do, but wear it like a shirt or wrapper.

Preface

This study grew out of a Ph.D. thesis. The primary incentive determining both the subject and method of research was my reaction, as an African woman, to both the interpretation and use of data on African women in the West. At a general level, data first collected within the discipline of social anthropology are now used in wider political debates by all sectors of society in the Western world. With respect to African women, social anthropological data are, with increasing frequency, cited as resulting from the influence of various schools of feminism.

My initial reaction of anger and disbelief came when I was an undergraduate reading social anthropology in Britain in the second half of the 1970s. The ethnography used in the universities was that collected by old 'masters' of anthropology during the colonial period. As the data were gathered selectively, and interpreted and applied according to the point of view and the politics of that period, which had to justify conquest and the subjection of indigenous peoples and their cultures to foreign rule, the material produced was inevitably racist (see Baxter and Sansom (eds.,) 1972, especially Worsley's 'Colonialism and Categories'; Nash's 'Race and Ideology of Race'; Curtin's 'British Images of Africans in the Nineteenth Century'; and Mitchell's 'Myth and Society in Southern Rhodesia').

The personal racism of the two patriarchs of British social anthropology has also been exposed. Worsley, citing Radcliffe-Brown's view of evolution, writes: '"the steady material and moral improvement of mankind from crude stone implements and sexual promiscuity to the steam engines and monogamous marriage" of the high nineteenth-century Western world [Radcliffe-Brown 1952:203]. The relationship of the rest of the world to Europe had to become one of inferiority and backwardness' (in Baxter and Sansom (eds.) 1972:99). Worsley goes on: '"Primitive" now became a label applied indiscriminately to the coloured peoples of the world. Social science grew up reflecting the division of the world: anthropologists largely studied non-Europe . . . sociologists, on the other hand, studied whites' (Baxter and Sansom (eds.) 1972:100). If the second father of British social anthropology, Radcliffe-Brown, believed in Europe's superiority to the rest of the world, the indifference of the first father of British social anthropology, Malinowski, to the people he studied was no less racist. Malinowski said of the Trobrianders, about whom he wrote so many books and who gave him fame, 'I see the life of the natives as utterly devoid of interest or importance, something as remote from me as the life of a dog' (Kuper 1973:28). Later, I shall show the

1

influence of these two shortcomings of social anthropology – the racist division of the world and the indifference to those being studied – in the attitude and politics of Western feminists to Third World women.

If colonialists found it necessary to divide the world into two – their own the 'civilized' and others the 'primitive' – anthropology concretized that view. For this reason, social anthropology has been called the child or handmaiden of colonialism. Several anthropologists have themselves acknowledged the contribution of social anthropology to colonial administration. (See Asad (ed.) 1973, especially Peter Forster's 'A Review of the New Left Critique of Social Anthropology' and Talal Asad's 'Two European Images of Non-European Rule'; Bailey 1944; for the parallel development of anthropology in America, see papers in Hymes (ed.) 1969, especially Dell Hymes's Introduction 'The Use of Anthropology: Critical, Political, Personal'.)

My reaction to the racism in social anthropology was probably mild compared to that of the celebrated African writer, Okot p'Bitek, who was shocked by his experience at Oxford University in 1960. He has called anthropology 'dirty gossip', reminding us that the word 'anthropologist', when it first appeared in Aristotle's *Nicomachean Ethics*, meant one who told anecdotes about men, a gossip (1970:22). He was sufficiently outraged as to protest against the insulting language of social anthropology and its classification of Africans and other non-Western peoples as barbarians, savages, primitives, tribes, etc. The titles of the books he found in the libraries reflected the same racism; for example, *Primitive Culture*, *Primitive Religion*, *The Savage Mind*, *Primitive Government*, *The Position of Women in Savage Societies*, *Institutions of Primitive Societies*, *Primitive Song*, *Sex and Repression in Savage Society*, *Primitive Mentality*, etc. These are standard textbooks for comparative studies in social anthropology; their authors are the patriarchs of social anthropology. They include women who thought and wrote like men. Later anthropologists came to acknowledge the racism and ethnocentrism of the old school of anthropologists, but these books remain on library shelves or the reading lists of the social sciences. They still feed the racist appetite of the West.

If non-Western cultures were described as primitive, barbaric, savage, etc., one can imagine how women in these cultures were presented. To early anthropologists, evolutionists that they were, 'primitive' women stood at the lowest end of the scale, described as no better than beasts and slaves, while the Victorian lady stood at the apex. Evans-Pritchard (1965), a highly acclaimed giant in social anthropology, has referred to such descriptions as 'wild flights of fancy' in his essay 'The Position of Women in Primitive Societies and in our Own'. The racism, class bias and ethnocentrism of old anthropology are well illustrated in the essay. In conclusion, he himself writes, 'taking everything into consideration and on balance, it cannot be said, certainly not without many qualifications, that women are much more favourably situated in our own society than in primitive societies' (1965:54). Yet at no time did he question the validity of the terms 'primitive', 'savages', 'barbarians', that he himself used throughout his essay. Malinowski was no less guilty in his classification of the Trobrianders as savages. Only after writing his volumes, as many anthropologists do, in the fallacious ethnographic present tense, did he admit that the most serious shortcoming of his whole anthropological research in

Melanesia was his failure to take social change into consideration, as the Trobrianders were not unaffected by European influences. As Kuper writes, 'This was a remarkable admission. Malinowski came to see ethnographic reality as not "savage culture" but rather colonial culture in process of rapid change' (1973:48).

Despite the insults heaped on Third World peoples, racism in social anthropology was not the main concern of the Western radical anthropologists and feminists who came later. For the supposedly more 'progressive' element in anthropology, the debate in the 1960s and 1970s revolved around the question of ethnocentrism. By 1960, after 30 years of British social anthropology, the comparative generalizations about societies had given way to particularistic ethnographies. While men like Needham (1971) disputed the universality of given concepts in social anthropology, for example, incest, kinship and marriage, others, such as Leach (1961), questioned the assumption that English language patterns of thought could serve as a universal model. Leach's solution to what he called the 'butterfly collecting' (classification into types and subtypes) and 'tautology' (explaining what is already obvious or needless repetition) of social anthropology was a mathematical one plus feats of 'inspired guesswork'. He regretted the new direction taken by those who had rejected comparative generalizations and had begun instead to write detailed historical ethnographies of particular peoples. According to Leach: 'Instead of comparison let us have generalization; instead of butterfly collecting let us have inspired guesswork' (1961:5). This position suggests the reduction of peoples and their cultural systems to figures on a chess board. This is best illustrated by a quotation from Leach, made in the course of an argument about whether certain peoples knew or did not know the biological facts of conception: 'It would of course clinch the argument if I could show that the rules allow a Lakher male to marry his own divorced mother, but I am afraid that neither the Lakher nor their ethnographer seems to have considered this bizarre possibility!' (Leach 1961:14). To the Lakher this would be an unspeakable thought, indeed sacrilege. This illustrates the disrespect implicit in Leach's 'inspired guesswork'. At no period in the history of the patriarchal cultures of Europe has motherhood been accorded the same status and reverence it has had in African cultures. This, in my opinion, epitomizes the arrogance and insensitivity of 'abstract anthropology', an attitude which unfortunately also permeates the work of most Western feminist theoreticians.

When in the 1960s and 1970s female academics and Western feminists began to attack social anthropology, riding on the crest of the new wave of women's studies, the issues they took on were androcentrism and sexism. (See *Critique of Anthropology – Women's Issue* Vol. 3, Nos. 9 and 10, 1977; E. Ardener 1975; Mathieu 1973; Rosaldo and Lamphere 1974; Reiter 1975.) The methods they adopted indicated to Black women that White feminists were no less racist than the patriarchs of social anthropology whom they were busy condemning for male bias. They fantasized a measure of superiority over African and other Third World women. Black women's critique could not therefore be restricted to the male bias of social anthropology and not challenge White women. Drawing their data from the Third World, especially Africa, works on women produced in Europe and America have shown White women's unquestioning acceptance of anthropology's racist division of the world. In the debates in the West, the Third World supplied the 'raw data' for random sampling, citation and illustration of points. It baffles African women that Western academics and feminists feel no apprehension or disrespectful trivialization in taking on all of Africa or, indeed, all the Third World in one book. It is revealing that most such works have not been written by women from Third World nations; they, instead, tend to write about their particular ethnic group, their country or surrounding region.

Given the racist element of the Western women's movement, it is perhaps not surprising that none of their studies have dealt with the issue of racism. As a result, in the past few years, Black women have begun to expose the racism in the women's movement and to accuse Western feminists of a new imperialism. (For the US, see Hooks 1982; Davis 1982. For the situation in Britain, see Carby 1982; Amos and Parmar 1984.)

P'Bitek (1970) observed that Western scholars were not really interested in African religion as such: 'their works have all been part and parcel of some controversy or debate in the Western world'. The same can be said of female academics and feminists in the West, for even though they used material about Third World women, they were not really interested in the points of view or concerns of those they were writing about. They were preoccupied with themselves and their own rebellion. The issues they were concerned with were in the West, yet the illustrations came from elsewhere. In the introduction to Rosaldo and Lamphere (1974), which to me really set off the feminist debates of the 1970s, we read: 'we have become increasingly aware of sexual inequalities in economic, social and political institutions and are seeking ways to fight them', 'contemporary feminists have only begun to uncover the depth and pervasiveness of our inequalitarian sexual ideology', 'we are searching for ways to think about ourselves.'

This collection of high-powered female anthropologists in the US, reacting to androcentrism in anthropology, got together and organized a lecture course that would focus on women. But already, a conclusion had been reached before the reassessment of material on women. To them, the universal social and cultural inferiority of women was a foregone conclusion: 'sexual asymmetry is presently a universal fact of human life'. This kind of global presupposition is itself ethnocentric. Furthermore, the domestic/public dichotomy which led them to the conclusion that maternal and domestic roles were responsible for the supposed universal subordination of women was a feature of their particular class and culture. These post-doctoral women anthropologists had not de-anthropologized themselves before embarking on their gigantic project of assessing women's condition in societies chosen haphazardly from all over the Third World.

Because they were primarily concerned with themselves and their own needs, their conclusions are necessarily ethnocentric. Hence their call for changes in two directions: one, that men should be made to participate in the domestic spheres of childcare and housework; two, that women should 'participate equally with men in the public world of work'. In short, the demand was for sexual equality in all spheres of life. But as we shall see, Third World women did not identify the same priorities at the recent United Nations End of Decade for Women's Conference held in Nairobi in 1985. As was widely reported, Western feminists used Third World data upon which to base propositions for the West, as if the whole world was represented by the West; exactly as male anthropologists had done earlier!

Rosaldo and Lamphere (1974) succeeded in showing the limitations of employing the simple division of social subjects on the basis of sex as a tool of analysis. Their book sparked off a new departure in women's studies: the question of gender as a cultural construct (see, for example, Oakley 1972; Friedl 1975; MacCormack and Strathern 1980; S. Ardener 1975, 1978, 1981; Ortner and Whitehead 1981).

While high-powered female anthropologists were meeting in the US, their contemporaries were also meeting in the UK. The UK feminists also took trips to the Third World, even though their aims had roots in the West. The preface to Caplan and Bujra (1978), for example, states, 'our aim was to produce a book that would contribute to the growing academic debate on women, and yet at the same time be accessible and relevant to matters of concern to the women's movement.' In Bujra's introductory essay we read that they also wished to contribute 'to the current debate in the women's movement over the notion of "sisterhood"'. Like the other edited works, their essays dealt with partial systems and consequently can present only sketchy, if not inaccurate, pictures of the situation of women in the societies written about. However, unlike their American colleagues, they considered factors which can divide women such as gender, class, status, age and kinship affiliation. Even though their material was drawn from the Third World, none considered the issue of racism, which directly concerns how they view Third World women and how they relate to Black women in the West. Yet racism is a crucial factor in the whole notion of sisterhood, whether for the purpose of female solidarity or for co-operative political action. Otherwise, a concern with the notion of sisterhood becomes reduced to another abstract anthropological inquiry in the true tradition of male anthropology.

Nevertheless, Caplan and Bujra (1978) must be commended for recognizing the more useful study of co-operation between women, especially for political action and solidarity. But, one must question the choice of women in Mathare (Nelson 1978), since the author herself states that the women 'have not learnt to operate effectively as a group in the political arena'. The choice of harassed and powerless beer-brewers using every means to survive reinforces the racist notion that African women prostitute themselves to survive. (For an equally silly book on African women, see Little 1973: that a male university professor could descend to 'dirty gossip' about African women which serves no political purpose baffles the imagination.) Why choose cases of co-operation between middle-class women from elsewhere, but only select the downtrodden when it comes to African data? A picture of Black women as universally deprived only reinforces racism.

Amos and Parmar (1984) have also noted the class characteristic of such studies in their critique of the orientation of the contributors to Caplan and Bujra (1978). They write,

There is no apology for, nay awareness even, of the contradictions of white feminists as anthropologists studying village women in India, Africa, China for evidence of feminist consciousness and female solidarity. Furthermore, one wonders why they find it easier to study middle-class women in India and their organizations to prove that "these women organise to protect class privilege in activities that complement their husbands' objective positions in the class hierarchy" than to study or examine the class position of the majority of the white women in the women's organizations in Western Europe; to examine how these women have different interests and power according to their class, age, race and sexuality and organize accordingly to protect their interests. By adopting the research methods and frameworks of white male academics much academic feminist writing fails to challenge their assumptions, repeats their racial chauvinism and is consequently of less use to us.

It seems to me that what Evans-Pritchard said in 1965 remains true today. He wrote,

I have not been able to discover any book which can be regarded as a sociological study of the status of women in modern English society; indeed I am assured by a recent paper by Mr McGregor of this university [London] on the literature about 'The Social Position of Women in England, 1850–1914' in *The British Journal of Sociology* (1955) that no such study exists. (1965:43–4)

If anthropologists can collapse the whole of Third World women into one book, surely British women will not require more than one book. The big question is, therefore, with what have they been comparing Third World women in their haphazard theoretical formulations?

Among the definitions with implicit ethnocentric assumptions universally applied in Western feminist academic writing are those of motherhood, marriage and the family. Hence their condemnation of other people's customs such as arranged marriage and polygyny as exploitative to women. The implication for Black families in Britain, as argued by Amos and Parmar (1984) and Mama (1984), is that this condemnation feeds false information to the police and the racist state and, therefore, supports legislation and policies which are oppressive and discriminating against Black people in the areas of adoption, fostering, immigration, etc. Wittingly or unwittingly they are playing the same role that male anthropologists played to the colonialists and to the CIA in the USA.

It seems to me, therefore, that to expect Black women to separate racism from feminism or to minimize racism in favour of class, which is the position of socialist feminists and international socialists (see *Review of African Political Economy*, Double Issue No. 27/28, 1984) is adding insult to injury. Socialist and radical feminists argue and theorize about the need for an autonomous women's movement; feminism before socialism; challenging sexism in their mixed socialist organizations; suggesting only an alliance with socialist men (see Barrett 1980). Because they never tackled the question of race, it never occurred to them that their Black sisters would follow the same mode of argument in prioritizing race.

Two acknowledged socialist feminist theoreticians, recently published an article (see Barrett and McIntosh 1985) which indicates that White women may finally be reacting to the angry cries of their Black sisters and consequently acknowledging and dealing with their own racism and ethnocentrism. Barrett and McIntosh are recanting to the extent of reassessing their previous publications and pointing out their errors and omissions *vis-à-vis* Black and other ethnic minority women. Brave and courageous as these two feminists have been, Black women do not wish to inflict a new wave of apologetics on the West, neither are they impressed by a few sketchy, patching-up articles, although these may be a starting-point. My own position is to endorse strongly the call for constructive dialogue.

In terms of reference material for that dialogue, it is unfortunate that most of that on African women which is available to Black women in the West has been collected by White women, written and interpreted from their point of view, embodying all the failings I have illustrated. The distorted view given of the conditions of Third World women is especially dangerous and unsatisfactory in the case of Africa. In the United States, the Caribbean and Britain, for example, where there are communities of peoples of African origin, the constant struggles against racism and oppressive dominant cultures have necessitated a search for roots. This is particularly true of Black women seeking autonomy in creative writing and in formal and informal organizations. Hence, there is a growing curiosity about the 'Motherland' and a constant search for cultural resources.

There are already some indications that Black lesbians are using such prejudiced interpretations of African situations to justify their choices of sexual alternatives which have roots and meaning in the West. Black lesbians are, for example, looking into African women's relationships and interpreting some as lesbian (see Carmen *et al*, 1984). What prejudices and assumptions are they imposing on African material? How advantageous it is for lesbian women to interpret such practices as woman-to-woman marriages as lesbian (see Lorde 1984). Such interpretation of, for example, the cases cited in this book would be totally inapplicable, shocking and offensive to Nnobi women, since the strong bonds and support between them do not imply lesbian sexual practices. In our search for power, or more positive models and images of powerful women, there is a limit to how far facts can be bent or our own wishes and fantasies imposed. Women's politics is consequently becoming more complex.

While it is acceptable that Black women in the West should demand visibility and pose the question that Sojourner Truth sent echoing out of 19th-century America – 'Ain't I a woman?' – African and other Third World women are, on the contrary, saying to anthropologists and Western feminists: Why the interest in us? Why do you want to study African women? It is a very pertinent question which makes the more honest and sensitive female academics nervous each time they present papers on African women to an audience which includes African and other Black women. Once, in such a seminar, I asked a young White woman why she was studying social anthropology. She replied that she was hoping to go to Zimbabwe, and felt she could help women there by advising them how to organize. The Black women in the audience gasped in astonishment. Here was someone scarcely past girlhood, who had just started university and had never fought a war in her life. She was planning to go to Africa to teach female veterans of a liberation struggle how to organize! This is the kind of arrogant, if not absurd attitude we encounter repeatedly. It makes one think: Better the distant armchair anthropologists than these 'sisters'. An African woman, invited to comment on a book about African women written by European women, said that she failed to understand why she was invited to that meeting; that from her reading of the book, the words had already been taken from the camel's mouth; the sister came from North Africa.

It is, therefore, not surprising that the anger and bitterness felt by Third World women are directed more at Western female academics and feminists than at male anthropologists. What Third World women object to includes the imposition of concepts, proposals for political solutions and terms of relationship. These objections have been expressed by a group of African female academics, who, in reaction to the imperialism of Western feminists, formed an association and released a statement. (See Association of African Women for Research and Development 1982.) The widely respected Egyptian writer and feminist El Saadawi has raised similar objections from the point of view of Arab women. Particularly on the question of female circumcision, she makes the cogent point that American and European women are in no position to differentiate themselves from, and feel superior to African and Arab women since they themselves 'are victims of cultural and psychological clitoridectomy' (Preface to El Saadawi 1980).

It is clear from what Third World women are saying that ethnocentrism, racism and imperialism constitute a deep division between White women in the West and women elsewhere. To this must be added the random citation and use of Third World data which are only aspects of other social and cultural factors in their societies. This is exploitative. More seriously, it presents a distorted picture of the conditions of Third World women.

Ironically it is in the face of increasing factionalism and disintegration in the Western women's movement that there has arisen a growing emphasis on a mythical sisterhood. In this quest, the approach of the West, where relationships between women are comparatively underdeveloped, has been arrogant and dishonest. African data have not been approached in order to learn from others who often have more developed concepts of solidarity and women's organization. On the contrary, the persistent intention has been to seek a false solidarity on the basis of what they see as 'common roots of oppression'.

This is exemplified by such scandalous studies as Cutrufelli (1983), which depicts African women as generally oppressed and powerless. She admits the immensity and variety of cultures and geographical areas, in illustrating her points and argument, but nevertheless the whole continent of Africa seems to her to constitute one socio-cultural whole. She starts from conclusions on the effects of either colonialism or the cash economy on 'African marriage', 'African kinship', 'the African woman', etc., and selects one ethnic group to stand for the whole of Africa. Or otherwise, she randomly takes samples from anywhere in East Africa to anywhere in West Africa, Anglophone or Francophone. Even an isolated case reported in a sensationalist journal such as *Drum* is used as an indictment of polygamy (1983:54). This is Cutrufelli's introduction of African women to Italian academics. A well-worded critique of her book from an African woman's point of view was given by Amina Mama (1984). Contrary to Cutrufelli's call for 'oneness', Third World women can ignore historical and cultural differences only at their own peril, in view of the damage already inflicted by colonialism and still being inflicted by neo-colonialism and Western feminist imperialism.

Indeed, a few Western women, disenchanted with their own culture, are now turning to the Third World for a reassessment of 'raw data'. After eavesdropping on Third World women's conversations, they turn self-appointed champions, defenders of our cultural institutions, and are quick to get to publishers before us! Germaine Greer, for example, had been considered the high priestess of women's sexual liberation (Greer 1971). She has now turned full circle to uphold aspects of Third World traditional cultures, which she and other Western feminists had hitherto condemned as primitive and oppressive. These include polygamy, chastity, coitus interruptus, women's traditional medicines, the extended family and the Islamic veil (Greer 1984). Such out-of-context and improper use of data undermines the internal contradictions and political struggles of women within these societies.

Western women have proved, by their inability to consolidate their own women's movement, that they are in no position to tell Third World women what is good for them. The divisions among Western women grow daily, as does their confusion as to where political/economic as opposed to pyscho-sexual solutions are required. Judging from my general experience in the West and work in local government in Britain, the obsession with sexual matters and proselytizing lesbianism (as distinct from lesbians) either dominates or divides women's collectives, groups, organizations and discussions here. The editorial to *Feminist Review*, No. II, June 1982, a special edition on sexuality, states, 'To politicize sexuality has been one of the most important achievements of the Women's Liberation Movement.' These priorities of the West are of course totally removed from, and alien to the concerns of the mass of African women. These basic differences of interest and concern mark yet another great divide between Western and Third World women, which as we have noted was widely reported from the United Nations End of Decade for Women's Conference in Nairobi (1985). Over-generalizing, as world conferences inevitably must, the priorities of Third World women were identified as problems of development, nation-building, internal gender struggles and liberation struggles (see *West Africa*, 22 and 29 July 1985).

Any work by Third World women must therefore be political, challenging the new and growing patriarchal systems imposed on our societies through colonialism and Western religious and educational influences. We cannot afford to be indifferent researchers, glossing over the local struggles in which women in our countries are involved. As well as looking into the socio-cultural systems which guaranteed women power, and making recommendations to their governments, African and other Third World women still have a role to play in exposing the contradictions in their societies, recording their own social history with a view to challenging, where necessary, discrimination against women and positively aiming for more power for women and more egalitarian societies for everyone.

It was, of course, from my knowledge of my own people that I recognized that a great deal of what anthropologists and Western feminists were saying about African women's lack of power was incorrect. It was not enough to shout out in anger at conferences, or to get into heated debates with friends. I decided it was best to go home and, with the help of Nnobi people themselves, write our own social history, especially from the women's point of view. This is why I have conducted this very detailed research in my own home town, where I believe that I have the right to ask questions, act as a spokeswoman and make recommendations for change and improvement. The perspective taken had to be sex and gender because of the uniqueness of the Igbo gender system.

On women in general, Maurice Godelier suggests that there could be as many as 10,000 societies on the globe, of which anthropologists have studied only between 700 and 800. It is even more shocking to learn that 'fewer than fifty serious monographs have been specifically devoted to the relations between men and women' (Godelier 1981). There is a need for material about women, collected and explained by African and other Third World women themselves, from which adequate and suitable theories and methodology can be worked out, as was proposed at the AAWORD workshop on methodology for women's research, held in Dakar, Senegal, in December 1983 (see *Women in Nigeria*, Newsletter, Vol. 2, No. 5, April 1984, p. 9). It is hoped that this book is one such study. It can be argued that because of their plural and multicultural backgrounds as a result of the colonial heritage, Third World women are best qualified to carry out comparative studies and make generalized statements about women's position in their societies. We are, therefore, waiting for invitations and grants from organizations in the West to study Western women, so that we can begin to redress some of the imbalance.

A more acceptable role for Western women has been adopted and argued by Barbara Rogers (1980). This is the monitoring of policies and activities of international development agencies, exposing their ethnocentric bias. In this, they would be working within the culture they know best – their own. Black women are not refusing White women's support and alliance, for there are massive campaigns in which White women can help without leaping into the forefront and usurping a people's struggle and anger. A more inglorious role is in collecting and publishing what Third World women are saying, as if Western women originated the thoughts or arguments. Given the monopoly on resources, this is, unsurprisingly, another form of exploitation; it is stealing words from the horse's mouth!

As a brief note on terminology, I must point out that I have retained the term feminist in spite of the controversy regarding to whom it refers and what is meant by it. The meaning of the word as I have used it is a political consciousness by women, which leads to a strong sense of self-awareness, self-esteem, female solidarity and, consequently, the questioning and challenging of gender inequalities in social systems and institutions. As will be seen from Igbo data, militant feminism, a constant reality for women in traditional Igbo societies, can be said to be a comparatively new phenomenon in the Western world and the monopoly of an élitist few.

Acknowledgements

In expressing my gratitude to Nnobi people, where do I begin to name names, as everyone contributed to this work in one way or another? However, many names are mentioned in this book. I am greatly indebted to my father, Chief Solomon Amadiume, for his encouragement, insight and amazing wealth of knowledge. Had I acknowledged him in the chapters, his name would have appeared on every page. My gratitude goes to my 'wives' and leaders of the Women's Council for their love and support. I cannot describe here the oneness and strength I felt in the midst of these 'matriarchs'. I am also grateful to students of both the boys' and girls' secondary schools in Nnobi for their help in the collection of data. The map of Nnobi produced in this book was compiled from Mr G. C. Egboh's map and that of Mr J. S. C. Okigbo. My thanks go to both men.

On a more personal note, I acknowledge, with a lump in my throat, the love of my mother, Janet Onuegbunam, an Enugu-Ngwuo daughter, who went very far away on a marriage journey to Nnobi. She died at the age of 55. A more beautiful woman to know or to behold, I have yet to meet. She encouraged and supported the education of her daughters, so that our choices might be wider than her own, and it is to her that we owe any feminist awareness that we may claim. I must mention my daughter, Nkemdilim, who was born a few weeks before my mother died, and so tied me to this world after my mother left it. Since then, there has been a newcomer to the family: this is my baby son, Sulaiman, who with his sister, has made living sweet again. Shaikh Hassan Cissé and Madina Kaolack, you are always in my mind. I am extremely grateful to four people who helped me when I was isolated and handicapped due to childcare practices in the West. They are Amina, Maria, Kojo-Seb and Laura. I acknowledge here, in a class by herself, my friend Judy Kimble who died of cancer while still very young. Judy gave me moral and practical support during the writing of this book.

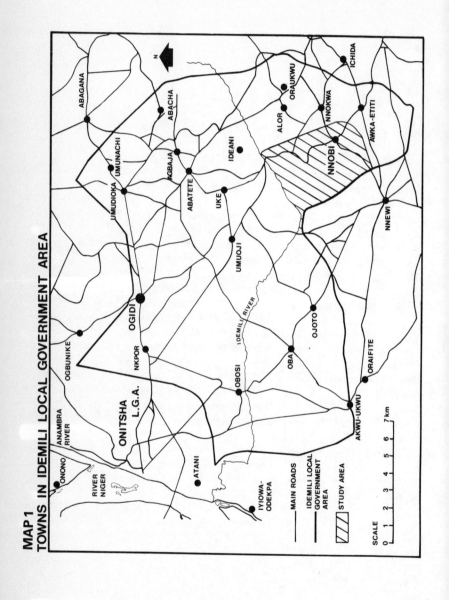

MAP 1
TOWNS IN IDEMILI LOCAL GOVERNMENT AREA

Introduction

Igbo Women and Women's Literature

It will generally be agreed that in the history of anthropological literature, Igbo women of eastern Nigeria were among the first to gain the attention of researchers as a group distinct from Igbo men. This recognition came only after both peaceful and violent mass demonstrations, riots, and finally open war with the British colonial government in 1929. From then onwards, Igbo women were universally recognized as the most militant of women. It is therefore not surprising that data on Igbo women have been cited or included in most important contributions to feminist anthropology (see, for example, Paulme 1963; Rosaldo and Lamphere 1974; Friedl 1975; S. Ardener 1975, 1978; Hafkin and Bay 1976; Caplan and Bujra 1978).

By 1929, the British colonial government finally admitted that it was facing two problems in Igboland: 1) the people as a whole were proving impossible to rule; and 2) the women were rebellious and rioting all over the place, with a militancy unfamiliar to White men. The colonial government consequently sent colonial officials and ethnographers into the field to study indigenous Igbo political systems. Inevitably, the experienced ethnographers were men and studied their fellow men. Early publications were therefore male-biased, general accounts (see Meek 1937; Basden 1938; Forde and Jones 1950). Later, more area-specific studies followed, published nevertheless under general titles (e.g. Uchendu 1965). There were also papers by G. I. Jones in various publications from the 1940s to the 1960s on aspects of Igbo systems (see Bibliography). It is amazing that despite the social and political prominence of Igbo women, none of these studies centred specifically on women.

Later academic contributions were more concerned to correct the general impression that Igbo people had mainly patrilineal descent systems and non-centralized political systems. S. Ottenberg (1968) revealed the dual-descent system of the Afikpo village group, P. O. Nsugbe (1974) stressed the matrilineal system of the Ohaffia, I. Nzimiro (1972) and R. N. Henderson (1972) located centralized state systems in Igbo societies east and west of the Niger.

In addition to publications by M. D. W. Jeffreys from 1935 to 1956, and the archaeologist T. Shaw from 1960 to 1970 on the divine kings of Nri, the anthropologist M. A. Onwuejeogwu published several papers on the same subject.[1] E. Isichei (1976) remains the first and only comprehensive historical account of the Igbo.

Clearly, therefore, the bulk of Igbo studies have not focused on feminist issues or the politics of sex and gender. Much could have been learnt from the two British women who were sent to conduct studies in the southern Igbo provinces, following the 1929 Women's War. Mrs Leith-Ross's study, solely on women, is an account by an inexperienced and untrained wife of a colonial official who describes herself as 'having more experience of the native than scientific training' (1939:44). Her experiences and impressions in a limited Igbo area were published under the ambitious and broad title, *African Women*. It reads more like a diary, full of contradictory statements as a result of her racism.

The 'native' is described as a 'nearly untutored savage', 'not yet enough developed' (1939:44). The same people were, however, capable of a remarkable system of government, as Leith-Ross herself noted: 'So natural did it seem to find autocracy in some form or other wherever one went in Africa that it was impossible even to imagine a democracy so absolute as that of the Ibo' (1939:67); and she writes, 'even now we may not have grasped the genius of the Ibo people' (1939:68). She observed that traditional Yoruba peasants lacked general intelligence or power of thought (1939:112), but the Igbo

have intelligence as we understand it, the power of thought, and the power of reason. Yet their thought is still almost entirely self-centred, their intelligence very limited, flowing along the narrowest channel and mirroring only the slightest facts, their reason so unexercised that it cannot be counted upon. They are dangerous, in that they appear to be so much more advanced than they are. (Leith-Ross 1939:112–13)

In her concluding chapters, which suggest she had become politicized by Igbo women, Leith-Ross applies a different set of adjectives to describe them: 'this rare and invaluable force, thousands upon thousands of ambitious, go-ahead, courageous, self-reliant, hardworking, independent women . . .'; and then, 'their startling energy, their power of organization and of leadership, their practical common sense and quick apprehension of reality' (1939:337). But, of course, as a Victorian puritan she disapproved of the money-making zeal of Igbo women: 'the rich woman she aspires to be will be worth nothing if she is not also a virtuous woman so that, dying, she will not need to sigh: "All my fires have been of grass . . ."' (1939:350). Filling the very important post of colonial adviser on women's education in the massive area of Northern and Southern Nigeria, she suggested to the colonial government the creation of a post of Woman Secretary of Women's Affairs in place of the Woman District Officer which was proposed for the Owerri province after the Women's War.

Green (1947), unlike Leith-Ross who travelled through three Igbo provinces, studied a tiny village of 360 inhabitants and from this reached generalized conclusions about all Igbo people. Both studies provide a glimpse into aspects of women's political organizations and activities in the villages mentioned. However, both books are misleading as a reference source for the political and ritual status of Igbo women of the hinterland. Indeed, as a result of her use of both books, Mba's (1982) knowledge of the hinterland is limited, hence her incorrect assessment of the ritual and political roles open to women in traditional Igbo systems.[2]

The uniqueness of the Igbo gender system was first referred to by Leith-Ross (1939); it seemed abnormal to her as a result of her Western perspective. Although her book on Igbo women of the Owerri province is neither objective nor theoretical, a few observed impressions are stated between lines of blatant racist remarks. As a result of her knowledge of the Women's War and her experience of the militancy of Igbo women, her statement directed to the colonial government reads, 'The Ibo women in particular, by their number, their industry, their ambitions, their independence, are bound to play a leading part in the development of their country. Their co-operation will be as valuable as their enmity would be disastrous' (1939:19–20).

Igbo women were clearly unlike European women. One less prejudiced would have viewed with an open mind differences in gender systems and consequently gender relations. Leith-Ross had, for example, observed that in the concept of reincarnation in one of the villages, a woman might be reincarnated as a man, but not vice versa (1939:101). A middle-aged woman had remarked that it would be foolish for a man to wish to become a woman and some of the women present had declared that they would like to become men. These statements of obvious identification with authority, privilege and power were completely misunderstood by Mrs Leith-Ross, who was socialized in rigid Victorian gender ideology in which gender corresponded to sex. In their system, male attributes and male status referred to the biologically male sex – man – as female attributes and female status referred to the biologically female sex – woman. To break this rigid gender construction carried a stigma. Consequently, it was not usual to separate sex from gender, as there was no status ambiguity in relation to gender.

The flexibility of Igbo gender construction meant that gender was separate from biological sex. Daughters could become sons and consequently male. Daughters and women in general could be husbands to wives and consequently males in relation to their wives, etc. Leith-Ross was familiar with Igbo women's feminism and ambition for power. That the women she studied did not wish to become *men*, but *males* was beyond Leith-Ross's imagination. As a result, she wrote such ethnocentric remarks as: (misunderstood as bisexually.

I had occasionally caught glimpses of some peculiar conception of sex or of a thread of bisexuality running through everything (yet I think hermaphrodites are 'abomination') – or of a lack of differentiation between the sexes – or of an acceptance of the possibility of the transposition of sex – which it would have been interesting to study.

An insight into this remarkable gender system is crucial to the understanding and appreciation of the political status women had in traditional Igbo societies and the political choices open to them. Green (1947) was also guilty of not distinguishing sex from gender and fell into the trap of confusing sex and gender ideology, and thereby her analysis. Thus, a women's day which showed a remarkable degree of sex-role inversion, Green calls 'feminine'. She actually meant that it was feminine in the sense of the sheer prominence of women and the exclusive nature of their activities (activities which were in fact masculine and which I describe in Chapter 12) as compared to public village activities, where women were present but men were predominant.

The separation of sex and gender in analysis helps to highlight occasions or situations when women can be males and vice versa. Green has omitted the investigation this would entail into gender constructions and the relationship of gender to power. This is surprising, considering that it was as a result of the war the women of this area made against the British colonial agents that Green was sent into the field to study indigenous or traditional Igbo political systems (1947:xiii). Igbo women's aggressiveness and militancy during this war had been regarded by the British as masculine, as a result of the imposition of Western gender norms on Igbo culture.

More recently, however, a number of important publications with a specific focus on Igbo women's political activities have exposed and stressed the dual-sex nature of the traditional political system which gave women power (Okonjo 1976; Van Allen 1976; Mba 1982).

The single-sex composition of these socio-political lineage organizations misled Okonjo (1976) into describing the political system as 'dual-sex':

> A number of West African traditional societies have political systems in which the major interest groups are defined and represented by sex. We can label such systems of organization 'dual-sex' systems, for within them each sex manages its own affairs, and women's interests are represented at all levels. (Okonjo 1976:45)

Okonjo has fallen into the trap of classifying women into a single category, despite her own data (1976:52) which show a contrast between the interests of daughters and of wives. The mere fact of daughters' acting in collaboration with their patrilineage men in the interests of their patrilineage – whether as a police force against the wives or as ritual specialists dealing with confessions of infidelity or adultery by wives, and cleansing the patrilineage of pollutions and abominations – shows that one cannot talk of women's common interests being 'represented at all levels'.

Okonjo further states:

> Dual-sex organization contrasts with the 'single-sex' system that obtains in most of the Western world, where political status-bearing roles are predominantly the preserve of men. In the single-sex system, women can achieve distinction and recognition only by taking on the roles of men in public life and performing them well. (1976:45)

Again, Okonjo's theory fails as a result of the limitations imposed by the use of sex as a tool of analysis in this context. In the Onitsha political system, we see that women as daughters also played male roles in ritual matters or in positions of authority over wives. Yet Okonjo does not define Onitsha's political system as a single-sex one.

I believe that Okonjo is dealing with the socio-cultural dynamism of gender. From a gender perspective, instead of Okonjo's term 'single-sex', it would be more appropriate to describe the systems of the West as characterized by a rigid gender ideology, since gender does not mediate sexual dualism. Hence the tendency for women wielding power in such systems to be thought of, or reclassified as, or to present themselves as 'manly' or 'man-like'.

In contrast, I would modify Okonjo's theory by adding that the traditional Igbo dual-sex social systems were mediated by the flexibility of gender constructions in the Igbo language and culture. The conceptualization of daughters as males in ritual matters, and politically in relation to wives, is a good example of this gender flexibility and did not imply that daughters should be seen as 'man-like'. Another example of the looseness of gender association is the fact that in Igbo grammatical construction of gender, a neuter particle is used in Igbo subject or object pronouns, so that no gender distinction is made in reference to males and females in writing or in speech. There is, therefore, no language or mental adjustment or confusion in references to a woman performing a typical male role.

What is still missing is a detailed study of women in a particular Igbo society, the aim being to examine the structure of the traditional society and how it worked. What structures allowed women to achieve the power that it is generally agreed that they had? What were the effects of colonial institutions on the old structures of the traditional society and on women's choices and situations? Finally, what is happening to women in contemporary local politics and consequently national politics? Are these findings at all relevant to Igbo studies, and to women and politics generally? It is hoped that this study, which has a gender perspective, seeing gender construct as distinct from biological sex, will fill some of these gaps.

Area and Background

This study was conducted in Nnobi, a town in the only Igbo area which has not been studied in detail by any social scientist or anthropologist, or written about from a lay point of view. This area includes the towns in the Idemili local government area in the Anambra State of Nigeria (see Map 1).[3] The 1963 census gives the population as 109,094, with a projection of 150,388 for 1976, for the whole Idemili local government area of 278 square kilometres (see Map 2).

The Umueri clan are an ancient Igbo people who claim common descent with the neighbouring, equally ancient, Igala people. Tradition has it that they all descended from the mythical ancestor, Eri. The ancient Igbo state of Nri belonged to the Umueri clan (see Isichei 1976:4). It is to Nri that the Idemili communities are supposed to owe cultural and political influence. They fall under Forde and Jones's (1950) group of northern Igbo. This area of Igbo settlement has also been described ecologically by Onwuejeogwu (1981:11) as the scarplands of south-eastern Nigeria, where the population density ranges from 450 to 1,000 persons per square mile. The constant theme of famine in their oral tradition reflects centuries of natural disasters caused by soil erosion and leaching.[4] The cultural features of this area include well-developed title systems, *mmuo* ('spirits of the incarnate ancestors') societies, well-remembered genealogies ranging back over eight to ten generations, ancestral shrines and shrines to other supernatural spirits known as *Alusi*. As Onwuejeogwu put it (1981:11), 'It is this ecological area that nurtured the cultures that "produced" and used the Igbo-Ukwu and the Ezira bronze objects.'

Onwuejeogwu (1981) goes on to postulate that Nri hegemony may have arisen as a result of the development of a highly ritualized and symbolic culture in response

MAP 2
POPULATION MAP OF ANAMBRA STATE

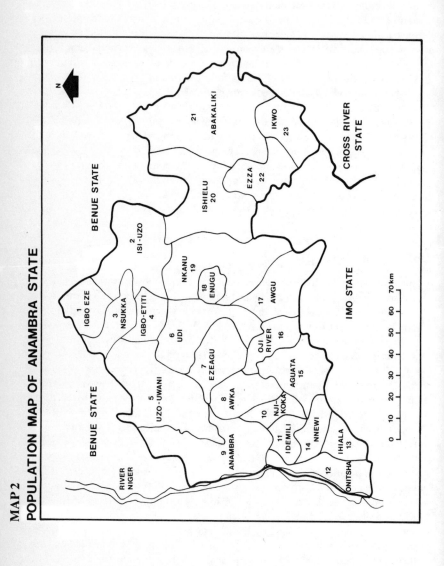

'to the disaster of soil erosion and the resultant low productivity of the soil'. Nri people thus became experts in ritual, and were also traders. Awka and Agbaja people became smiths, and Umudioka people specialized in crafts (Onwuejeogwu 1981), and while Nri town was the spiritual metropolis of the Nri theocratic empire, Awka was the commercial centre (Okoye 1975:73).

It is in the ritualization of the political system and domestic economy that the Nri hegemony and state system were based. As Onwuejeogwu (1981) observed, Nri political élites, that is, the *ozo* titled men,

> travelled generally unmolested from one Igbo settlement to another as agents of Eze Nri to perform political and ritual functions associated with the removing of abomination, the dissolving of the codes of abomination and the enacting of new codes, the ordaining of ritual and political officials, the crowning of chiefs, the making of peace and the creating of markets and shrines.
>
> In the performance of these activities Nri people spread into different parts of Igbo land and Eze Nri held some degree of control over the external and internal politics of the older Igbo settlements.

According to Okoye (1975:73), Nwabara (1977:17) and Isichei (1976:10), Nri civilization flourished in about the 10th century AD and reached its zenith in about the 13th century, when most of Igboland east and west of the Niger came under Nri hegemony in a culture based on divine kingship. By the 18th century, when the transatlantic trade was at its height, the Nri empire had declined, with the emergence of the Aro trade organization.

Of all Igbo settlements, however, only Nnobi people claim that they do not pay ritual homage, *ibu ihu*, to Nri (see Chapter 6). They also claim that they are the only people, other than the Nri, who perform the *ikwu ahu*, or *odinke*, festival (Obiefuna 1976). In Nnobi, this is a festival where a cow is slaughtered by rich men and women for the goddess Idemili (see Chapter 6). If anything, Nnobi themselves claim a ritual dependency of Nri kings. This is implied in the Nnobi saying: *Nshi wukaa, oja ejelili Nnobi* – 'No matter what his fame, an Nri must make a spiritual trip to Nnobi.' In support of this, Henderson (1972:64) names Nnobi as one of the towns through which candidates for kingship travelled on their ritual journey to the throne. The king would end the ritual journey with a sacrifice to the River Niger in Onitsha. Nnobi oral traditions and recent history claim that Nri kings worshipped at the Idemili shrine before proceeding to the Niger.[5]

There are, therefore, strong indications that Nnobi was an independent ritual centre and the seat of the Idemili religion. This was based on the worship of the goddess Idemili which was superior to the cult of ancestors and common to all the towns along the Idemili River. There is strong evidence, too, that Nnobi was a matriarchal settlement later encroached upon by patriarchal Nri people. The contradictions and coexistence of gender notions derived from these principles can be seen in Nnobi social organizations and cultural ideologies.

The Town of Nnobi

Fieldwork was conducted in Nnobi (see Map 1) between 1980 and 1982. As a result of the 1976 local government reform, which divided Nigeria into 19 states and 299 local governments, Nnobi became one of the towns in the Idemili local government area of Anambra State of Nigeria. Most of the Igbo people were also separated between two States: the southern Igbo people in Imo State and the northern Igbo in Anambra State. The 1963 population census had put the total number of Igbo people then in the East-Central State of Nigeria at 7,209,716. There has been no subsequent population count but estimates assume a compound rate of growth of 2.5 per cent per annum.[6]

Nnobi can be said to be a town only in terms of the size of its population. The 1953 figure of 6,978 was thought to have been grossly underestimated, since more than half the population (who lived abroad) were not counted. However, by 1963 the population of Nnobi had doubled to 13,445 within the same area of 19 square kilometres. In 1982, Nnobi people estimated their population at well over 20,000; Igbo families, lineages and towns keep membership registers and therefore know their numbers. In September 1976 the number of taxable adult males in Nnobi was put at 6,000 (*Abalukwu*, Vol. 6, September 1977:29).

In every other sense, Nnobi remains a rural area. The administrative reforms of 1976, which, in the rural areas, instituted a local government separate from the State and Federal governments, finally brought government to the inhabitants of the rural areas. The 'principle of participatory democracy' was put into practice, when citizens aged 18 years and over were allowed to vote in local government elections (see Adamolekun and Rowland 1979). Nnobi was, therefore, also guaranteed full participation in modern politics through local and federal elections. There are no large industries, but Nnobi participates in the modern economy through trade and commerce, and the activities of its urban-based wage earners. Its major commercial centre, Afo Nnobi, the central market-place, is basically controlled by marketing women and is thought to occupy an area of about 5.4 hectares (Ezeani 1980). Apart from the exclusively female central section of the market, the peripheral areas, especially the major roads, are marked by open stalls and lock-up shops run by both men and women. In 1980, the daily sales of the market were estimated at 6,000 Naira.[7]

As agricultural production has not proved profitable in these areas, the people have a highly developed sense of commerce and trade, including monopoly over certain commercial items. Thus Nnewi, a town genealogically and culturally related to Nnobi, has a trade monopoly on certain items, including motor parts. Awka-Etiti, a migrant settlement from Nnobi, monopolizes trade in bicycle parts, tyres, Vono beds, etc. At one time, in the 1960s, wealthy traders and business men and women in these areas formed an association known as Okaa Social Club, members of which took on titles or nicknames derived from the commodities they controlled or traded in. These commodity-based names were prefixed by the word *okaa*, those who sold Vono beds or bicycles, for example, calling themselves Okaa-Vono or Okaa-Bicycle, etc. The Igbo word *ika* means 'to surpass'; hence the meaning is one who surpasses or declares a surplus in the commodity prefixed with the word *okaa*.

Nnobi, the mother town, remains the most conservative of all its related offshoots, comparatively resistant to change and perhaps monopolizing *ome-na-ani*, 'that which is traditionally done in the land', or, in brief, 'the custom of the land'.

As a result of the low productivity of the soil, population pressure and the scarcity of land, an economic system whereby women did most of the farm work and men became ritual specialists, *dibia*, evolved. Traditionally, even though the supposed patrilineal system of inheritance and succession prescribed that males allocate and own land, women controlled the subsistence economy. They were, and still are, involved in both local and external trade, as the farm does not meet all their subsistence needs. There was, therefore, a clear sexual division of labour, and an associated gender division of crops.

Similar sexual and gender divisions are reproduced at other cultural levels. In religion, for example, there was an all-embracing goddess religion above the cult of ancestors. Female-orientated and matrifocal notions associated with the goddess were part of social and cultural practices. In the social organization, matricentric units were to some degree autonomous. Nnobi myths of origin associated hard work with the female gender, and praise of women depended and still depends on their industriousness and economic achievements. Thus, culturally, female industriousness was highly valued, and rewarded in the form of a unique female title. Similarly, in the political institutions, there is a sexual and gender division of interest groups. Roles, rights and interests were maintained and safeguarded by men and women in culturally constructed categories, which sometimes meant that sex did not correspond to gender.

Nnobi thus affords ample material for the examination of variables relating to the socio-cultural dynamism of the ideology of gender, showing how women were guaranteed, achieved, or were cheated out of power.

Time Span and Method

This study is divided into three periods: pre-colonial, when the traditional systems operated; colonial, when the British ruled Nigeria; and post-colonial, when Nigeria became an independent nation.

The pre-colonial period, pre-1900, is considered by present-day Igbo as the 'olden days', when traditional customs were 'pure and unspoilt'. In contrast, after 1900, including both colonial and post-colonial times, is considered as the modern period. This division does not imply that in the 'olden days' there was no external contact or change. Change would have been gradual and negotiated, and neither sudden nor immediately apparent. British colonial rule followed a violent invasion: change was imposed and supervised, and many indigenous practices and values became punishable under imposed British law. The question of legitimacy was therefore at issue, but those who had the might claimed legal power.

The colonial invasion was a milestone in the history of the Igbo people, when hitherto autonomous groups came to be grouped together as Igbo. Their history now became a common one, whether in their participation in national Nigerian politics, or the experience of the Nigeria–Biafra war (1967–70), when the Igbo-dominated Eastern Nigeria attempted to secede from the rest of Nigeria. The modern period is marked by the coexistence of indigenous and European-borrowed cultures. The post-colonial period, especially in more recent years, is characterized by an ever-increasing and intensive cultural renaissance.

My account of the traditional system is largely a reconstruction of what took place in the past, based on Nnobi people's own accounts. This is substantiated with corroborative evidence drawn from written and published materials, and from still existing evidence of cultural continuity witnessed during fieldwork. In the absence of written accounts, the relevance and reliability of oral accounts and traditions in Igbo studies have been pointed out and used by established academics, whether historians, such as Afigbo (1972), Nwabara (1977) and Isichei (1976), or anthropologists, such as Onwuejeogwu (1981) or Henderson who discusses these problems in detail (1972:29–35).

Notes

1. These can be found in *Odinani* (a journal of Odinani Museum, Nri); see also Onwuejeogwu 1981.

2. See 'Nigeria's Political Women' in *West Africa*, 10 September 1984, for my assessment of Mba's book.

3. The towns in the Idemili local government area, with the populations for some of them in 1953, are: Abatete (6,631), Abacha, Eziowelle, Ogidi (11,231), Umudioka, Umunachi, Akwu-Ukwu, Oba (9,128), Obosi (7,624), Ojoto (5,112), Nkpor, Uke, Umuoji (8,357), Alor (6,552), Awka-Etiti, Ideani, Nnobi (6,978), Nnokwa and Oraukwa (5,596) (Ofomata 1975:141).

4. In Ofomata's maps, Nnobi appears only on a map showing types of erosion, and is shown to be in the areas of both active and advanced gully erosion (1975:44).

5. See Appendix 1. This is a transcript from a tape-recorded interview with the traditional ruler, *Igwe* Eze Okoli II of Nnobi, which took place in August 1980. In response to my question, 'What is Nnobi?', the *Igwe* read me a document left by an anthropologist in the care of his late father, Chief Solomon Eze Okoli Igwe I. The anthropologist may have been C. K. Meek, who is said to have visited Nnobi on 17 February 1931, as a government anthropological officer (see *Abalukwu*, Vol. 2, December 1975:31). G. T. Basden also collected material in most of the northern Igbo communities. The first *Igwe* himself was a keen scholar (see Chapter 8), as is attested by the number of wide-ranging documents he left. As the present *Igwe* jealously guards all the important documents in his care, and will not even lend them to researchers but reads them out himself, I was unable to establish who wrote what; I may even have incorrectly transcribed some names, such as Dr Achukoson, which sounds neither Igbo nor European. The relevance of this document, however, is in its concern with the origin of Nnobi, its ritual and political status in relation to Nri and other neighbouring towns, as this topic is constantly discussed by Nnobi intellectuals and other citizens. Doubtless this is fertile ground for future research, especially in view of an increasing focus on Nri in Igbo studies.

6. *Statistical Digest*, 1973, East-Central State of Nigeria, Edition 4, p. 2.

7. Nigeria used pounds until 1973, when it changed to the decimal currency unit of the Naira. In June 1980, the official exchange rate was £1 = 1.27 Naira.

Part One:
The 19th Century[1]

1. Gender and the Economy

The upland Ibo traditionally raised a variety of root crops and livestock, but those occupying the leached white lands of the Awka-Orlu area have long suffered chronic food shortages. The soil has in many places undergone such extensive deterioration that it cannot support the dense population, and in these areas textile weaving, oil palm tending and processing of palm produce, blacksmithing, and other specialized economic activities such as slave trading traditionally supplemented farming. In contrast, the lowland-dwelling Ibo have always been able to produce a surplus of yams and to collect enough fish and other river animals for an abundance of protein, but they lack iron, cotton, palm produce, and proper surroundings for livestock raising. Out of such ecological and economic differences developed a trade between these two populations in prehistoric times, and Onitsha has long been a prominent site of exchange in this trade. (Henderson 1972:36)

The Igbo in general and Nnobi people in particular trace the gender ideologies behind their sexual division of labour, and those governing the relations of production, to their myths of origin. This chapter deals with Nri and Nnobi myths of origin, and shows the relationship between ecological factors, sexual division of labour and gender ideology. As a result of ecological factors, agricultural production was not profitable in Nnobi, hence the development of a sexual division of labour and gender ideology which gave women a central place in the subsistence economy, while men sought authority through ritual specialization and ritual control.

The gender ideology governing economic production was that of female industriousness. *Idi uchu*, perseverance and industriousness, and *ite uba*, the pot of prosperity, were gifts women were said to have inherited from the goddess Idemili. Associated with this were strong matrifocality[2] and female orientation[3] in this supposedly 'patrilineal' society. The culture prescribing industriousness is derived from the goddess Idemili – the central religious deity. The name of the town itself reflects matrifocality in Nnobi culture or a matricentric principle in household organization; mothers and children formed distinct, economically self-sufficient sub-compound units classified as female in relation to the male front section of the compound.

There was, therefore, a dual-sex organizational principle behind the structure of the economy, which was supported by various gender ideologies. These principles and ideologies governed the economic activities of men and women. They also governed access to wealth, and prescribed achievement-based statuses and roles, such as titles and the accumulation of wives, which, in the indigenous society, brought power, prestige and more wealth. However, a flexible gender system mediated the dual-sex organizational principle.

Myths of Origin and Gender

Nri

According to Nri myth of origin (Henderson 1972:58–65), Eri, the man sent down from the sky by Chukwu, the Great God, finding himself surrounded by the Anambra River, called to the Great God, who sent down a blacksmith to produce fire and dry the ground. This blacksmith became the ancestor of the Awka Igbo and from him they inherited the secret of smithying, in which they specialized.

Eri is said to have had two wives, by one of whom he had five sons, Nri, Agulu, Amanuke, Onogu and Ududu, who became founders of neighbouring settlements. Nri had come to settle among Igbo people, who were hunting and gathering communities, lacking kingship systems and the knowledge of farming. Nri became very hungry, and appealed to the Great God, who ordered him to cut off and plant the heads of his son and daughter (Henderson 1972:60). From the daughter's head sprang cocoyam, a subsidiary crop managed by women.

Nri had been ordered to mark the foreheads of his children with marks of ritual purification, *ichi*,[4] before planting them. From the scarification of his children, Nri gained certain ritual prerogatives: he held the secret of *ogwu ji*, yam medicine, so that Igbo communities went to Nri to obtain this medicine, and paid annual tribute for it. Yam, which sprang from the head of the son, was the Igbo staple, and is still the most valued crop in rituals and ceremonials; the penalty for stealing yam could be death (see Nwabara 1977:29–32). Men came to monopolize the planting and distribution of this highly prized crop. From Nri's scarification of his children, Nri, the town, became a ritual centre which conferred emblems of ritual purification and ritual experts bestowed the ritual requirements of the *ozo* title. From Nri's ritual relationship with the land, Nri ritual specialists gained the right to travel to other Igbo communities, in order to cleanse their towns of sins committed against the land (Henderson 1972:60–61).

Nnobi

There are two versions of Nnobi myths of origin. According to one account, the first man at Nnobi was Aho or Aro; the first at Abatete was Omaliko; the first at Nnewi was Ezemewi; and the first at Ichida was Otoo-Ogwe; they were all hunters. The one at Nnobi, known as Aho-bi-na-agu – Aho who lives in the wild (nature) – met a miraculous woman called Idemili (supernatural) near the Oji Iyi stream in Nnobi. They married and had a daughter called Edo. As she was very beautiful and highly industrious (culture), other hunters began to compete to marry her. Ezemewi was the most handsome, and he won her love and married her.

The influence of Idemili, a woman, was stronger than that of her husband Aho, and so she spread her idols everywhere. When her daughter set off to Nnewi to join her husband, Idemili took her idol, gave it to her and blessed her. As she loved this daughter very much, she also gave her *ite uba*, the pot of prosperity, and told her that she had taken back the pot of medicine, *ite ogwu*, which she had given to her earlier. So when Edo got to Nnewi, her popularity and influence, like her mother's, rapidly spread. While Idemili established her shrines and influence all over the land of Idemili, her daughter Edo established hers all over the land of Edo, called Nnewi. It is thus that Nnewi inherited hard work from Nnobi, and both these neighbouring towns share their history and culture (*Abalukwu*, Vol. 1, September 1975).

As we have seen, the female gender had the more prominent place in myth and indigenous religious and cultural concepts – the supernatural, a goddess, is female. The stream, Iyi Idemili, is the source of divinity. The cultural result of the mediation of the natural (Aho, the hunter from the wild) and the supernatural[5] (the goddess Idemili from the sacred stream) is a hard-working woman, Edo. Thus, both Nnobi and Nnewi inherit industriousness from females; the most highly praised person in Nnobi is a hard-working woman.

Nnobi traces its matrifocal concepts to another myth of origin. In Obiefuna (1976), Aho's wife is called Agbala, an Igbo word for female deity. Their first son was called Obi, so Agbala was referred to as Nne Obi, mother of Obi, after the Igbo custom of calling mothers by reference to their first child. In Igbo, when going to visit someone, people say they are going to the place of that person. The Igbo expression for going to visit Obi's mother would be going to the place of the mother, *nne*, of Obi, hence the origin of reference to the geographical location; the place of Nne Obi came to be known as Nnobi. The name of the town, Nnobi was, therefore, derived from the mother.

Ecology, Production and Gender Ideology

Both Nnobi and Nri men have manipulated certain gender ideologies implicit in their myths of origin in an effort to deal with the constraints imposed upon them by ecological factors. Nri communities also live in the Igbo areas of poor soil, land erosion and heavy population density, and hunger features in the Nri myth. Soil is poor, and therefore it is necessary to enforce fertility: hence the control of ritual knowledge, derived from the supernatural. In the explanation of the invention of agriculture and the sexual division of labour, yam, the prestige crop which requires expert knowledge for its production, both in the ritual and technical senses, sprang from the male head, and, as we have noted, was grown and distributed by men. Only ritual heads and male heads of families distributed yam medicine and performed the ritual which permitted the eating of yam. Yet, in reality, the role played by men in yam production in the Igbo areas where less food was produced was minimal.

Cocoyam, according to the Nri myth, grew out of the female head. This crop, grown by women, required less specialized knowledge than did the yam. To ensure a good yield of sizeable yam tubers a lot of work was necessary, first to thoroughly dig the soil with a large hoe. Then the soil dug out had to be heaped into huge mounds, both to survive erosion by the rains and to hold the growing tubers, some of which have been known to grow as large as a human being. Cocoyam is grown in small mounds or ridges which can easily be worked by women, and no special ritual secrets were associated with them.

Similarly, cassava, when introduced into Igboland, was regarded as an inferior crop, grown by women. Although it demanded a lot of time and hard labour to harvest and process into food, the actual cultivation required little specialized knowledge, as it can grow wild. In areas of poor soil and low yam yield, cassava became the main staple, while men monopolized the small yam harvest for ritual payments and other ceremonial exchanges.

There is, then, a clear interrelationship between ecological factors, economic production and gender ideas. Nri, for example, relies heavily on trade and craft production; the skill and secret of blacksmithing (a male prerogative), derived from the supernatural (male), and was jealously guarded by men in these areas. The cultural emphasis was, therefore, on male monopoly of ritual knowledge, craft specialization and external relations. This could explain the ritual link between the *Omu*, queen of Onitsha women and head of the Association of Women Traders, and Nri; Nri dwarfs crowned Onitsha 'queens' (see Henderson 1972:314).

In Nnobi myth of origin, Edo inherits industriousness from her mother, the goddess Idemili. Here, female crops such as cocoyam, plaintain and cassava compensated for the shortage of yam for staple food. Nnobi, therefore, depended very heavily on female labour in agriculture.

One begins to see a system of prescribed achievements and rewards. From it women in Nnobi might be expected to derive prestige and power from their control and successful management of, and effective organization around, this subsistence economy.

Wealth and Gender

What were the traditional scarce resources, the control and management of which the politics was about? How did men and women have access to them?

Economic resources include material and non-material things considered scarce in society, and therefore involve the principles of control, ownership and sometimes exchange. In Nnobi, immovable property included land and food trees; movable property consisted of domestic animals and food, agricultural produce, textiles, household goods and utensils, and human labour, especially women's productive and reproductive powers including their sexual services. Ritual knowledge and titles were also bought.

Material wealth was converted into prestige and power through title-taking, the acquisition of more wives and more labour power, and more material wealth. Social wealth was redistributed through commensality and exchange associated with life-cycle ceremonies such as child-naming, marriage and funeral ceremonies. Inter-lineage exchanges were based on relationships traced through women as daughters, wives or mothers. Religious festivals and title-taking ceremonies were also occasions for the redistribution of goods.

Wealth for men consisted of the possession of houses, many wives and daughters (who would bring in-laws), livestock, voluntary and involuntary titles, yam and cocoyam farms and a huge *oba ji*, yam store, an extensive *ani obi*, ancestral compound, with surrounding lands, and *osisi uzo*, food and cash-crop trees.

Wealth for women included livestock, fowls, dogs, rich yields in farm and garden crops, lots of daughters, who would bring in-laws and presents, and many wealthy and influential sons. It included the *ogbuefi* title, the only voluntary title shared by men and women who have killed a cow for the goddess Idemili, and other involuntary titles taken only by women, and possession of wives by 'male daughters', first daughters, barren women, rich widows, wives of rich men and successful female farmers and traders, that is, the kind of women to whom I shall refer as 'female husband'.

One might therefore ask to what extent there was evidence of 'class' differentiations on the basis of wealth in the indigenous society. Capital comprised land, wives and children; possession of these immediately put the owner ahead of others. Igbo say, *inwe nmadu ka inwe ego*, 'to have people is better than to have money'. Numerous people was the greatest advantage large ancestral compounds had over smaller ones, which as a result of lack of wealth tended to be monogamous. It was therefore a question of a large workforce versus a small workforce. The wealthy had more agricultural produce, a larger number of livestock and people who would carry on the trading and marketing of surplus; material wealth would be converted into titles. Poorer people merely subsisted; diet demonstrated wealth difference, as the poor could not afford fish and meat.

The titled formed exclusive clubs, danced exclusive dances; they sat on exclusive chairs in exclusive places during ceremonies, and had bigger funerals. They dressed exclusively, wearing distinguishing symbols on their hats, hair, wrists and ankles. Principles of social inequality were therefore present in the indigenous society. But the degree to which people were differentiated and disadvantaged on the basis of 'class' was minimal – some would argue non-existent – as variations were possible in the economic and social position of members of the same family or patrilineage, in the same generation or between generations. There was nothing approaching the rigid traditional Western feudal system or later class system.

Male and female symbols of wealth were apparently similar, even though in principle men and women did not own the same things. A very important economic resource which women did not own was land. Were we to go by strict patrilineal rules of ownership, succession and inheritance as did formalist anthropology, the dynamism of gender would seem irrelevant, women would be marginalized and their role in the economic structure invisible. Land will therefore be considered in terms of gender politics. Firstly, what was the effect of a flexible gender system on rules governing the inheritance of land? Secondly, how did the ideology which sees women as hard-working providers place them in relation to land?

Land and 'Male Daughters'

Nnobi people were, traditionally, subsistence farmers and traders. Land was therefore a major economic resource; ownership of land was both communal and individual. Mythological and genealogical charters were used both for land acquisition and structural distribution. As a clan, Nnobi considered itself a territorial unit occupying the original lands of its founding ancestors. Each subdivision, down to the minor patrilineage, was a sub-territorial unit in collective ownership of the space occupied. Minor patrilineage land was then distributed to component ancestral compounds, *obi*(s) (see Chapter 3).

Following in this way the principle of unilineal descent in inheritance and succession, land dwindled, until virgin forest land collectively owned by patrilineages was shared out to sub-lineages and their component ancestral compounds which, as their subdivisions multiplied further, shared out land to its extended families, which redistributed land, where available, to its family units. The principle of individual ownership of land applied in the family as long as the owner was alive and had male descendants or 'male daughters' to inherit the land. Where there was no one to inherit land, right of ownership returned to the extended family, the deceased man's brothers.

As a result of Nnobi's flexible gender system, the institution of 'male daughters' was manipulated in the conflicts which arose as a result of the coexistence of principles of individual and collective ownership of land. I shall illustrate this point by the case of Nwajiuba Ojukwu, the 70-year-old 'male daughter' who is the present head of the first *obi* in Nnobi, which is in the minor patrilineage of Umu Okpala in Umuona ward. (See Appendix 2, Figure 1.)

Nwajiuba's father was Ojukwu Isi Ana, priest of the Land Spirit, who occupied the 'first son' position in the whole of Nnobi. He, therefore, held a very important office, which was more ritual than political. Although Ojukwu was a very wealthy man, as he was also a *dibia*[6] and a successful farmer who cultivated the very large type of yam, he was poor in people, as he had no sons, and his only brother died without issue. According to Nwajiuba, because of this absence of close relatives, when her father became ill, he decided to recall her from her marital home and allow her to remain in his house as a male. She would then have the status of a son, and be able to inherit her father's property. This practice was known as *nhayikwa* or *nhanye*, a kind of replacement, in Nnobi custom. Nwajiuba said that she had married as a child, did not like her marital home and wished to return to her father's house; when her father recalled her, he returned the marriage payment to her husband. According to Nwajiuba, her father had said that he and another man named Aghaji had decided to put girls in their *obi*, as they believed that one's *obi* should not be lost because one did not have a son.

One day, after Nwajiuba's father had died, his first daughter went to cut a bunch of plantains from her father's compound. Patrilineage men saw her, and asked her why she was doing so; as they did not recognize females as having any rights to their father's property, this became a court case. Nwajiuba recounted what took place in court:

On the day of the court hearing, the *igwe*[7] asked them if they were aware of the fact that his father's mother and my father's mother were sisters. He asked them whether they did not see that Ojukwu's wife was pregnant and whether they were able to see what was in her womb before going to usurp what was in Ojukwu's compound. He then ruled that I should remain in my father's house. He told them that they should only look after the place, since a woman does not become a shrine priest.[8] He ruled that as soon as a man was found in Ojukwu's house, he should take over. That was how that case was settled.

I asked Nwajiuba if her father had invited members of his patrilineage to announce his decision officially, after he had stated to her sister's husband his intention to make her 'male'. Nwajiuba said that he had been unable to do so before he died. Had he called members of his patrilineage and given them palm wine, the matter would have been settled. Aghaji, in his case, approached his lineage members, but died before he could finish the required ceremony. His pregnant widow then bore a son, and so the girl who was to be left at home married instead.

The case of Nwajiuba set a precedent, as she was the first female to be left in an *obi* following a court ruling rather than the traditional ceremony. But, according to Nwajiuba, most of her father's property had already been shared out by members of his patrilineage and, after the case, only the immovable property, such as land and trees, was returned.

As the position Nwajiuba's father had occupied was very important, men who held that office were usually fortified with powerful medicines and were *dibia* in their own right. Most powerful men in those days were called names descriptive of their deeds and achievements. Nwajiuba's father, for example, was called Ogbunikpo, meaning, perhaps, 'one who kills his enemies in masses or by the score'. It is in this context that one can understand Nwajiuba's account of 'strange' activities against her sons, her mother and herself.

Her story not only contains material on the traditional interpretation of misfortune or cause and effect, but also shows the unease and anxiety of women occupying very much sought after positions normally filled by men.

Nwajiuba and her mother remained in the *obi*. She lost two male children, each dying after the outing ceremony. No outing ceremony was done for the third child and he survived. It was on the advice of a *dibia* whom her sister had consulted that she went to have the baby at her sister's house, returning after seven market weeks. There is a clear insinuation of foul play by lineage men. The same suspicion was also associated with her mother's death and her own illness. According to Nwajiuba,

It was all because of that case. They had prepared something and left it here. When I described my symptoms, out of ignorance it was not realized that it was as a result of somebody's doing. My whole body was swollen like an overripened fruit, and squashed when pressed or squeezed. I am now suffering from all that they did at that time. We did not know then that we should have gone to a *dibia*. We did not know of a *dibia* to go to. Had it been now that our eyes are open, we would have known what to do.

Wicked people know how to set about things. They made my mother not to know what to do, they blinded her. My father was such a great *dibia* that any ailment he could not deal with was considered hopeless. Imagine a man who could tell *ideyi* [flowing wet sand, like a river] to stop for him to cross and then order the sand to flow again!

As any other male who owned property, Nwajiuba paid tax when it was introduced although other women did not pay.

Land and Wives

The formalist approach in anthropology to the patrilineal system of inheritance is that sons inherit their father's land and daughters do not; therefore women do not own land. As we have seen in the case of Nnobi, the institution of 'male daughters' disproves this theory. In social process, gaining access to land, or the right of use of land, may prove more important than actual ownership. This was the case with Nnobi wives.

In Nnobi, land, the most scarce visible resource for subsistence farmers, was owned by men but worked by women, who also managed most of the produce. Women ideally did not inherit or own land, having access to land only as wives or sometimes as daughters especially favoured by a father or brother, as, for example, Ochom, the female founding ancestress of the minor lineage of Umu Ochom in Amadunu ward, represented in the structural genealogical chart (see Appendix 2, Figure 3). In rare cases, women owned land as 'male daughters' when they had been accorded full male status in the absence of a son in order to safeguard their father's *obi*, line of descent and the property associated with it, as, for example, in the case of Nwajiuba.

Following the unilineal descent principle of succession and inheritance, the first son replaced his father in the *obi*. The section of immovable property associated with the *obi*, called 'obi land', and the house in it should never be subdivided. It was automatically inherited by the first son, and became the ancestral home to all those who traced descent to that *obi*. The rest of the land and trees were usually divided among the sons through their mothers, with the first son also getting a share, which meant that the first son inherited twice. Normally, the father would have distributed land as he married wives, since access to farmland was essential to women's role as wives.

Women had access to two types of land: garden land, which was usually at the back of each matricentric compound section, and farmland, which might be near the compound, or at the outskirts of lineage or village territory. On the death of a husband, a wife's continued access to farmland depended on her having a son, or a 'male daughter'. On the death of a woman as wife and mother, the continuation of her matricentric household depended on the woman's son, or a 'male daughter', or respected *ada*, first daughter, marrying a woman to take the place of the dead wife. In this way, the wife of a son took over farmland from the wife of the son's father. Thus one wife replaced another as women continued to manage the land.

There were two ways in which family land might be shared out. Land was either divided equally among the wives, regardless of how many sons each wife had, or shared equally between the sons, so that a wife with more sons would have more land. In the former case, wives with more sons would later be pressed for land, as the sons acquired wives and redistributed the land. In cases where land was plentiful, wives could be given their own portion of farmland, and as sons reached maturity, they too would be apportioned land on which to build their own homes. If any died childless, the land would revert back to the original *obi*. This was also the case with monogamous households, where the sons might decide to stay in one *obi*, and receive portions of land as they married. Either way, land was forever a cause for dispute, murder, treachery and intrigue in Nnobi. There was a chronic shortage of land for younger sons, who were therefore encouraged to move out and acquire land elsewhere and found their own *obi*, but they remained ritually and politically subordinate to the original *obi*, even when they had changed their family name.* In the ranking order, they would be junior to the original *obi*. In many cases where there was no available land for subdivision, as the sons matured, they built their houses in their mother's sub-compound units in the original compound; their wives would, therefore, help their mother-in-law on the farm.

Men owned both types of land: compound land for building houses and gardens, and farmland. Gardens, where the subsidiary crops were grown, were exclusively a female domain: wives worked them and controlled the produce. Farmland, where major crops were grown, was worked by both men and women. Men were involved mostly during the initial planting and later harvesting, but the daily job of tending was done by wives. The produce from this farm was shared by husband and wife, with men controlling the distribution of yam.

Redistribution of Other Family Wealth

The principle of equality did not exist in the sharing of wealth, whether among brothers or among brothers and sisters. Consequently, first sons started life more advantaged than their younger brothers, and brothers started life more advantaged than sisters. Embodied in the principle of sexual division of labour was the gender division of economic and social wealth. Sons and 'male daughters' inherited property, such as land, and trees such as kola-nut and palm trees. Daughters inherited woven cloth, certain trees, and their mother's household utensils.

The mourning period following the death of a father lasted for one year, after which his wealth was shared among his children. Male members of his minor patrilineage were usually present and acted as witnesses. The first son, as *onye isi*, head, received what was called *ihe isi*, headship share, before the division of wealth. Four things were usually put aside for him, for example, one kola-nut tree and three palm trees, or two palm trees and two kola-nut trees. In addition to these, he would select other food trees, such as Igbo pear, coconut, orange and breadfruit, and money, since, as first son, he would have spent more money than the others on the funeral. In fact, a first son's share depended upon how greedy and powerful he was, and it was not uncommon for first sons to claim all their father's wealth. The rest of the food trees and livestock were shared among the younger sons. Most often, the principle of picking and sharing, *aghota eke*, was applied, as food trees were immovable property. Each son usually took whatever share he received back to his mother. Married daughters would take the cloth presented by their husbands at the funeral, while unmarried daughters inherited their father's cloth.

Individual ownership of property was associated with the principle of *ilu aka*,

* A son could choose either to keep the family name, or to drop it and instead use one of his own names.

pointing at a thing. This suggests that it was recognized that any head of a family had the right to dispose of family land to members of the family. The usual method for the distribution or the giving away of land was to go to the spot and point at the land involved. For this reason, any tree planted by a son was never divided at the death of his father, for his father would have pointed out the spot on which he planted the tree. The same principle of individual ownership applied to land pointed out to a son or daughter, or to food trees so pointed out, especially *nkwu ana*, palm tree, pointed out to a daughter by a father as a wedding present. Some maintained that only first daughters got palm trees as a wedding present, while others maintained that any daughter could get them. The idea behind the gift was said to be the need and desire for daughters to visit their father's *obi* regularly after they had left it to settle in their marital homes. This indicates that the ritual and political role of daughters was not severed after marriage, as the patrilineal theory would have us believe.

Women's Economic Activities

The sexual inequality entailed in the patrilineal principle of inheritance with regard to access to economic resources for daughters was quickly offset by women at marriage. This was usually achieved through their economic resourcefulness, supported by Nnobi matrifocal principles in domestic organization and encouraged by the ideology of female industriousness.

In the household, a wife's domain was a matricentric unit, consisting of herself and her children; it was a farming unit, with a specific farm. It was also an eating unit; all the children of one woman ate out of their mother's pot – from one *ekwu*. This was the unit bound by the closest and strongest sentimental sibling tie, *nwanne*. The survival of this unit depended on the mother's resourcefulness, and she expected loyalty and gratitude from her children in return.

At marriage, a girl's father would take yam and cocoyam seedlings from the stacks, arrange them on sticks, as was customary, and give them to his daughter; this was her farming capital. If she was an *ada* (first daughter), or a favourite daughter, he would point out her marriage present palm tree. The girl's livestock capital – a she-goat and hens – would be given to her by her mother, as would spices and vegetable seeds for her garden, a basket of seasoning ingredients for cooking (*ngigo*), a soup ladle and a few pots and pans. The she-goat was her ritual goat, *eghu chi*, and would multiply and produce her first cash capital, and when it died, it could be eaten only by the woman to whom it was given.

Male and female roles were given ritual expression at birth. Eight days after birth the child's head was completely shaved. A baby boy's hair was buried in the roots of a kola-nut tree, and that of a girl under a palm tree. One of the principal objects an adult male heading a household hoped to inherit or otherwise possess was a kola-nut tree, as kola was very important to his role. The rules governing the breaking and sharing of kola symbolized authority, status and gender differentiation in Nnobi (see Chapter 6).

The palm tree under which the hair of a baby girl was buried was called *nkwu ana*, and was the tree a father would point out to his first, or a favourite daughter, at her marriage. She would then periodically visit her father's compound to collect the palm fruit from the tree. As long as that palm tree stood, and there was someone alive to recognize it as her palm tree, marriage might not take place between descendants of that woman and those from her father's *obi*.

Palm Tree

One of the most valuable household resources for a woman was a palm tree. Every part of it served an important economic function. The sap of the tree, palm-wine, was controlled and distributed by men, except, of course, 'male daughters' controlled the circulation of that from their father's compound. Women fed the palm-fronds to goats. They made brooms from the side branches; the trunks were used as building material, or to support climbing plants, especially yam, or to make cooking fires. The sale of palm-oil, which women extracted from the fruits, was a major source of cash for both sexes; proceeds from the sale of the kernel were, however, exclusively owned by women. The shells of the fruit were used for fuel, and the fibre or chaff extracted during oil processing was used to make medicinal soap. The women used parts, or extracts from the tree to make light. For example, they made torches from pieces of *izuke* (a bunch of leaves produced by the palm tree) which were broken off one by one and soaked in heated palm-oil. They extracted rope from the skin or bark of the palm tree trunks, which they used for weaving various items such as sieves, long baskets to hold foodstuffs drying in the sun, carrying and storage baskets, etc. They also wove floor and sleeping mats from them.

Staples

The same versatility can be seen in women's production and management of staples. The processing, sale, storage and preserving of all foodstuffs was done exclusively by women. It was, however, through the control of the circulation of yam that men asserted their authority over women.

According to an Nnobi saying, 'a woman answers her husband's call sharply or rudely when she knows there is no yam left in the yam store.'[9]

Although both men and women farmed yam, those cultivated by women did not compare in size and quantity with those produced by men, for a husband also enlisted his wives' labour to cultivate his yam, and the greater part of his farm was devoted to yam.

For the whole town, the call for the annual Eating of New Yam Festival, *ikpo ji*, was the prerogative of the man who held the title of *Ezeani Nnobi*, priest of the Land or Earth Spirit of Nnobi, for he held the yam medicine without which people could not begin digging out new yam from their farms and eat.[10]

Following the signal for *ili ji*, the male head of the family would buy a cockerel and perform the Eating of New Yam ritual for his family. He and his sons would kill the cockerel and pound the yam medicine. He would then put the medicine into a little gourd and give some to his wife and daughters to lick before eating their own yam. The chicken was eaten by the male head of the family and his sons and not shared with the women. After this ritual yam could be eaten from the store or dug up from the farms to eat.

Within households yam medicine was held by the head of the household. After harvesting, yam and cocoyam were stored in the *obi*, the male section of the compound, which held the huge family yam stores. Successful women farmers and other wealthy women also had yam stores in the female section of the compound at the back of their units, but could not eat yam from them until their husband had performed the ritual for eating new yam. Men, therefore, supervised and controlled the use of yam from the family store.

The man's contribution to household subsistence was mainly the daily supply of yam, referred to as *itu ji abani*, which he would hand to his children to take to their mothers. When husbands were away, wives were expected to use yam from their own stores.

The smaller species of yam require up to six months in the ground to mature, the larger species up to ten months. Poor output owing to poor soil, overcropping and poor storage meant that yam served as a staple for a very short period of the year, after which everyone turned to the women's crops: cassava, cocoyam, plantain, maize and melons. These were therefore secondary staples only in terms of prestige and in so far as they were female crops.

During discussions with the present traditional ruler, describing the indigenous economy, he said,

In the olden days, men cultivated yam, and women also cultivated yam. But it was the job of the women to tend the yam plants, *ilu ji*. It was the job of the women to plant maize, bitterleaf and various other plants in the yam plot. Women cultivated cocoyam. It was also their job to dig out the cocoyam. Marketing – buying and selling, selling and buying – was a women's job. Women played a vital part in the production of foodstuff. As for men, once they'd cleared the bush and planted the yam, the rest of the job was left to their wives. It was the job of the women to go to the market, produce food and feed their husbands. Women played the lion's part in the economy of the town even up till the present century. The cultivation of cassava is completely done by women. Men don't cultivate cassava. They only grow yam.

During my fieldwork in Nnobi in 1980 and 1982, the general accounts of the traditional economic activities of women had not changed, as the traditional ruler himself observed. The most important difference is probably the introduction of food processing machinery, but from my observation, most women thought it too expensive, and still used traditional implements, such as mortars and grinding stones. Another difference is in diet. General accounts of the economy and diet of the olden days showed that owing to the scarcity of meat the food was mainly vegetarian. The very poor could barely afford even fish.

Apparently people became rich in earlier times by raising and selling livestock, such as goats, poultry and dogs. Those who could went to Onitsha and bought fish to sell. Some took palm kernels to sell in Onitsha and bought fish, yam, oil-bean seed (from which *ogili*, the fermented seed for flavouring sauce was made) to sell.

Women, Marketing and Cash

Cowrie shell, referred to as *ego*, money, was the most common currency used. Most transactions involved money; marriage payments for daughters, sale of livestock, fruit trees, tubers, grains, vegetables and spices, all involved money. Palm fruit was the main cash crop, with palm-wine and palm-oil both being sold for money. Except for palm-wine and yam, which were sold by men, most marketing was done by women, so that most of the cash passed through female hands from the sale of either their own or their husband's goods. Following the principle of the sexual division of labour and gender division of crops, women kept their own profit and what was considered theirs; nothing considered as female and nothing belonging to women was sold by men. But women marketed most of what was considered to be male and as belonging to men, and kept some of the profit. The control of goods and cash by women was as a result of their monopoly of market space. This accorded with the Nnobi ideology of female industriousness, economic self-help, and self-sufficiency of the matricentric unit and also was supported and reinforced by the gender ideology which demarcated male and female space.

The sale of livestock and poultry was the quickest way of raising capital. Women tended and helped sell their husbands' livestock. When handing over the proceeds to their husband, they would say for how much they had sold a goat or hen; or they might increase the agreed sale price and keep the profit. This was also the case with the sale of palm-oil, yam, plantain, banana and other fruits, as most immovable property belonged to husbands, but was cared for and the produce marketed by their wives. Money derived from any food trees planted by a wife, however, belonged to her, as did money from the fruits of the palm tree pointed out to a daughter by her father, or to a wife by her husband.

The surplus of all food items, processed or raw, was sold by women in the markets. A woman's garden was a regular source of petty foodstuffs, vegetables and spices used in the household or sold in the markets. Women's involvement in agricultural production and their control of the subsistence economy gave them easy access to markets and cash. Whereas most of the cash turnover from women's marketing was put back into the subsistence economy, men's profits were mainly for their personal use, such as marrying additional wives, or taking titles for themselves or their sons. Their main means of getting large sums quickly was through marriage payments received for their daughters, or the sale of livestock such as a male goat, castrated and fattened to fetch a large sum of money.

As a result of the redirection of money back to subsistence and household needs, a woman had to be extremely successful economically, and have a large labour force, to save enough money to be able to participate in the achievement-based title-taking open to women as well as men, such as the *ogbuefi*. The incidence of women's title-taking was, therefore, lower than that of men. The tendency was for women to take the *Ekwe* title, which was involuntary, and granted through divination. Though based on the idea of social recognition of hard work, candidature was controlled through ritual, and thus only a limited number of women were chosen. The *Ekwe* phenomenon, which I see as an essential part of a system which sets a high premium on female economic success, is described in the next chapter.

This chapter has traced the possible origins of the central position which Nnobi women held in the traditional economy, and a sexual division of labour directly related to ecological factors has been described. As women took control of the subsistence economy, men sought authority through the control of ritual specialization. Even though women were economically self-sufficient, men monopolized the right to tell them when, for example, they could begin to eat yam every year. Various patriarchal and matriarchal ideologies embedded in myths of origin were used to justify this sexual division of labour. At the same time, the presence of strong matrifocality and female orientation in the culture gave women in general a favourable position in both the domestic and public sectors of the traditional society. Female industriousness was, for example, rewarded with both prestigious and political titles *ogbuefi* and *Ekwe*. But, more importantly, we find that a flexible gender system encouraged the institutions of 'female husband' and 'male daughter'. This meant that certain women could occupy roles and positions usually monopolized by men, and thereby exercise considerable power and authority over both men and women.

Notes

1. Most of the data in this part of the book were collected in 1980. My first approach involved visiting the oldest people in Nnobi, asking them about indigenous customs and traditions. But I discovered that age did not necessarily guarantee knowledge, or the ability to communicate information, and that some middle-aged and even younger people were more articulate and knowledgeable than their elders. Some, as boys, had carried the bags of certain elderly male relatives, which meant that they were constantly in the company of elders and had listened to and become familiar with their discussions. The data reported in Part One are the result of a joint effort by all Nnobi people, which I then translated, interpreted and arranged. It is important to point out that although I am an Nnobi daughter, I was not born or brought up in Nnobi, but in Hausaland in northern Nigeria; I have, however, been familiar with and close to Nnobi traditions and culture from childhood, through my father and his relatives, and I have a good command of the Igbo language and Nnobi dialect. Having studied in Britain for over ten years, and taken an honours degree in social anthropology and the Hausa language, I had some measure of distance from which to view Nnobi society and culture.
2. Matrifocal/mother-focused: a household arrangement around the mother and her children, the focal or reference point being the mother. Similarly, the matricentric unit is the mother and her children (see Tanner 1974).
3. Female orientation: culture or principle derived from the female gender.
4. Recent archaeological excavations at Igbo-Ukwu, only nine miles from Nri, have revealed the burial chamber of an ancient Nri king and objects of material culture dating from the 9th century. The findings include a roped bronze vase, which tradition associates with the migration of a section of Nri to Oreri, where a rival ritual centre was set up (Isichei 1976:10). The portrait of a human face discovered in the Igbo-Ukwu excavation and dating from the 9th century bears *ichi*, ritual facial markings of purification. It is reproduced in Isichei (1976: 112). *Ozo* titled men in some Igbo areas still have to have the same markings today.

5. This contradicts earlier anthropological theories which equated woman with nature and the wild and man with culture (see Mathieu 1973; Ortner 1974; MacCormack and Strathern 1980).

6. *Dibia*: the terms 'ritual specialists', 'ritual experts' or 'native doctors' do not give full insight into the nature of this profession. The diversity of their practices and involvements is such that they are best described as men of knowledge, who became extremely important and powerful in social systems where knowledge was a very scarce commodity, shrouded in secrecy and jealously guarded by powerful elders. Oral rather than written traditions and an open literary system make this monopoly most effective. Thus, the *dibia* as a herbalist, *dibia mgbologwu na mkpa akwukwo*, is a scientist involved in experimental, curative and destructive medicine and chemistry. They often act as midwives, too.

The *dibia* as a diviner, *dibia afa*, helps analyse misfortunes and social abnormalities. Basden mentions some of the titles by which a *dibia* is saluted, as, for example, *Agbaso aka* (able adviser), or *Okwuka-Ojelu* (one who is able to explain by divination) (1938:51).

Possession by the spirit *Agwu* is followed by misfortunes which indicate that a person is being claimed by *Agwu* to become a *dibia*. It is believed that failure to heed *Agwu*'s call results in insanity. The *dibia* profession is a strongly guarded 'closed shop', shrouded in mystery and secrecy. The office is hereditary, but it is believed that a boy who picks the divining seed, *mkpulu afa*, is also invited to be a *dibia*. In precolonial times, these *dibia* practitioners, being great travellers, were also conversant with other branches of knowledge which, in modern terms, would include history, geography, astronomy, biology, zoology, etc. Perhaps their area of greatest specialization is in psychology and mysticism. The terms 'ritual specialists' or 'experts' are not really adequate translations, and can be used only for convenience. It is preferable, therefore, to retain the Igbo term *dibia*.

7. The traditional ruler then was Chief Solomon Eze Okoli (see Chapter 8).

8. This is my rendering of the Igbo expression used by Nwajiuba – *Nwanyi aha ebu isi nmuo*.

9. The Igbo saying is *nwanyi n'aza oku n'ike na omalu na ji agwu n'oba*.

10. He was always the head of the first and most senior *obi* in Nnobi. The last man to hold this title was the father of Nwajiuba, the 'male daughter' mentioned earlier.

2. Women, Wealth, Titles and Power

In indigenous Nnobi society, there was a direct link between the accumulation of wives, the acquisition of wealth and the exercise of power and authority. The ultimate indication of wealth and power, the title system, was open to men and women, as was the means of becoming rich through control over the labour of others by way of polygamy, whether man-to-woman marriage or woman-to-woman marriage. The Nnobi flexible gender system made either possible.

Ekwe[1] Title

This title was taken only by women, and was associated with the goddess Idemili. From all descriptions of the title, it was believed to be based on involuntary possession (beyond one's wish or control), but, in reality, it had a strong association with a woman's economic abilities and charismatic attributes, real or potential. Thus taking the title might mark the climax of economic success, but the Nnobi people would generally claim that it was the goddess herself, through her possession of the woman, who would give her the money or wealth with which to take the title. Nwajiuba, for example, said, 'If *Ekwe* is coming to you, it shows you the sign and throws in money for you.' She made this sound as though someone threw in baskets of money from outside the compound wall.

There were two ways in which the potential title-taker controlled the services of others. People went to work for her voluntarily or she practised what was called *igba ohu*, woman-to-woman marriage. Such wives, it seems, came from other towns. The 'female husband' might give the wife a (male) husband somewhere else and adopt the role of mother to her but claim her services. The wives might also stay with her, bearing children in her name. Potential *Ekwe* women were, therefore, wealthy women, who through control of others' services were able to create more wealth.

The signs of possession for the *Ekwe* title were well known. It was like possessing green fingers, or hands of gold. Whatever such a woman touched yielded multiple profits: all her crops increased, her domestic animals reproduced prolifically and were not killed by diseases, her chicks were not carried off by hawks. These signs were reported to the messenger of the goddess Idemili, who would then, through divination, tell the woman that the goddess Idemili was knocking at her door. This meant that she had been favoured and chosen by the goddess to take her title of *Ekwe*.

Descriptions of the *Ekwe* phenomenon show its economic base. People were quick to notice thrift, industriousness, a money-making ability and leadership qualities in a woman. They would begin to point out such a woman as a potential candidate for the *Ekwe* title. Even a young girl could be identified as a candidate and thenceforth she would be encouraged in her economic ventures. As Eze Enyinwa's account shows, a potential *Ekwe* candidate had to have the material or practical support of her co-wives at all levels of social organization, from the extended family to the major patrilineage.

The taking of the *Ekwe* title *na awa awa* (is involuntary). One who is being called to take the title, if she goes to the market and buys ten chicks, all of them will survive. If she plants things, they'll stand out from those of other people. Her goats will bear triplets. Such a woman would have been notified by a diviner, so she would start trying her hand to find out whether it is true. For the actual taking of the title, she would invite her *inyom di* (her co-lineage wives) and tell them that she wished to take the *Ekwe* title. They agree on a day when they will come and work for her weekly. They usually work for her for about six months before she announces to her quarter or village her intention to take the title.

After the announcement, it took another nine months before the whole of Nnobi was informed. As soon as such news reached the whole town, everyone went to the woman's house for a feast.

Payment (by the woman taking the title) for this ceremony was said to be as much as one cow, seven goats and seven hens, which were given to those who could sanctify and validate the title, that is, the messenger of Idemili and the existing *Ekwe* titled women. Describing the abundance of food during this ceremony, Eze Enyinwa said, '*Ogili* is heaped like a huge anthill. One woman's share is enough to fill a mortar. She will in turn take it home to share with her co-wives. The same is true of pounded cocoyam.' (Pounded cocoyam was called *nni ocha*, white pounded food.) Members of the woman's minor patrilineage and her patrilineage co-wives would go to her home on the eve of the ceremony to cook till dawn.

For the ceremony, a very tall pole called *agba*, was stuck into the pounded food. Strong, young men would then pile layers and layers of pounded food round the pole, from the base to the tip, until it looked like a small, white hill. Titled *Ekwe* women would then take portions of the food from this food tree and distribute them to the guests. When all the food had been removed, the messenger of Idemili would give the woman a long pointed stick, known as *mgba Ekwe*, the *Ekwe* staff of authority. The messenger of the goddess then named her whatever name or epithet she might have chosen to be known by. The names chosen testify to the sense of achievement associated with this title, for example, *Ome Nyili*, the undaunted one; *Agba Ekwe*, the chief *Ekwe* woman; *Ekwe Nyili*, she who has vanquished, that is, achieved, the *Ekwe* title; *Chinyelu Ekwe*, one to whom her god has given the *Ekwe* title, etc.

After taking the title, the woman would wear a string anklet, *njada ukwu*, like all titled men. As Eze Agba, priest of Idemili, said, 'That woman who has taken the

Ekwe title will not lift things on her head. She will comb out her hair, just like this woman's.' (He showed me his wife's hairstyle, which was not plaited, but combed out into a neat 'afro'.)

The newly titled woman was expected to buy a towel, in which she would stick a small knife called *nma eneke*; she would then sling this towel on her shoulder. With her hair combed out and carrying the long pointed staff, she was expected to walk in a dignified manner.

Six months after the ceremony, the co-wives in the *Ekwe* titled woman's lineage were each expected to take a tin containing about four gallons of palm-oil, and present it to her in order to show their respect and give her prestige and honour, *iko ugwu*. Through the ceremony of crawling, one after another, between her legs, while she sat with legs astride, the co-wives accepted her superiority and authority. Without this acknowledgement by her co-wives in the lineage, her title was said to be a failure. This ceremony, entailing the donation of palm-oil, a very important cash crop, was repeated periodically.

All the *Ekwe* titled women formed an exclusive club, and shared the money, livestock and food donated by the new initiates each time the title was taken. Their leader, who was also the leader of all Nnobi women, was always the longest-standing *Ekwe* title holder. She was the one known as *Agba Ekwe*, chief *Ekwe* woman. (The ritual and political significance of the *Ekwe* title will be discussed in the next chapter.)

Involuntary Male Titles

There were a few involuntary male titles which, like the *Ekwe*, were associated with a strong economic base; the signs of their possession were also similar. While candidature to the *Ekwe* title was open to all the women of Nnobi, the involuntary male titles were specific to certain lineages, and only one man held each title at a time. These male titles were referred to as *oke ozo* high *ozo* titles, as they were superior to the voluntary (bought, normal, contractual) *ozo* titles. In Nnobi, *ozo* is synonymous with *eze*, kingly, a prefix which *ozo* titled men attach to their names or epithets. This ambition, and the possibility of its achievement by every Igbo man who becomes wealthy, led to R. N. Henderson (1972) calling his book *The King in Every Man*. The Nnobi high *ozo* titles were *ozo Aho* (which will be described and discussed in detail in Chapter 6), *dunu*, *dim*, and *eze ana*, usually held by the priest of the Land Spirit, and *dunu n'ebo*.

The structural significance of these titles in relation to the female *Ekwe* title will also be examined in the next chapter.

Two Prominent *Obi*(s) in 19th-Century Nnobi Society

In the two case studies which follow, the economic activities of individuals in two prominent ancestral compounds in Nnobi society of the last century are described, and also the degree of affluence, the aristocratic lifestyle in the traditional society, and the means whereby men and women accumulated wealth. As will be seen from the practice of 'female husbands' women benefited from the accumulation of wives in the same way as did men. Rivalry existed between wealthy women and their husbands; extremely powerful and assertive women were able to dominate their husbands and not be stigmatized for it.

The 'Big Man', Eze Okigbo

Eze Okigbo was the 'big man' in Nnobi at the time of the British military expeditions into the Igbo hinterland between 1901 and 1919. Nnobi falls into the area of the Onitsha–Awka axis, which came under attack between 1904 and 1905.[2] Eze Okigbo probably died in 1905, as a result of humiliations suffered at the hands of British military officers (see Chapter 8). He was said to have been in his declining years at this time, which suggests that his period of influence was during the second half of the 19th century.

Eze Okigbo was the seventh in a succession of generations of *ozo* titled men to have wielded power in this particular *obi*. The most influential and powerful of all, the 'big man' during the first half of the 19th century, still remembered and respected in Nnobi today, was Ezike – Eze Okigbo's biological father. The early 19th century was a period of inter-village wars, slave raids and slave trading. As Igbo names throw light on the history of the bearers, the name Eze Ike (Ezike) indicates strength and power. Similarly, the name of his father indicates the affluence of this *obi* long before the 19th century. He was called Eze Eziafuluaku, which means a titled man from a compound where there is wealth.

Vivid accounts, from oral traditions and eyewitnesses, of daily life in the *obi* of Eze Okigbo reveal the extent of aristocratic life in this hitherto assumed egalitarian society. John Eze Okigbo, born in 1928, who himself holds a chieftaincy title, is the great-grandson of Eze Okigbo and the present head and occupant of this *obi*. His claims and stories were verified by a much older man, Johnson Ume, whom I interviewed independently. Johnson was born in 1909, and his mother, Egoeme, was the favourite daughter of Eze Okigbo. She was an *ogbuefi* titled woman, as she had killed a cow. She wore an ivory anklet and bracelet, ornaments described by Basden as very costly and highly prized: 'They are worn by few women and are associated with the aristocracy' (Basden 1938:207). Egoeme died in 1948. Johnson, in his position as a *nwadiana*, child of a daughter (see Chapter 3), in the *obi* of Eze Okigbo, was always a privileged and welcome visitor there.

Eze Okigbo is said to have had about 13 wives, a few of whom were inherited from his father, Ezike. As was the custom with 'big men' who collected many wives, only his favourite wife cooked the food he ate, and no one else was allowed to touch his drinking cup. Basden attributes this general practice among Igbo men, especially those with several wives, to fear of poisoning (1938:157). According to John Okigbo, when Eze Okigbo's favourite wife did not cook his food, his favourite daughter did so instead. Only one particular man tapped the palm-wine he drank. Although each of his wives had her own piece of land, and he himself had a great deal of land, he did not eat food grown on his land, as this was how rich and powerful men were poisoned and removed in those days. Similar precautionary measures were observed by rulers of other Igbo societies which had a divine kingship system. For example, it was said of Eze Nri that 'No one may see the king eat and no boy above the age of puberty may cook for the king, nor any woman' (Nwabara 1977:25). In fact, according to Johnson Ume, Eze Okigbo did not eat food cooked by his wives, but only that cooked by his daughter. His special plate was made from an elephant's skull.

In keeping with the protocol observed by Igbo aristocrats, Eze Okigbo did not emerge from his private chambers in the afternoons. In the mornings he sat in his inner *obi* and his wives came and called him by his titles and praise names, and brought food to distribute to his servants and workers. Typical of 'big men' at that time, Eze Okigbo had two *obi*(s): one in the compound where he went when he emerged from his bed-chamber, and another outside the compound walls where he received outside visitors and all Nnobi.[3]

How Eze Okigbo Became Very Wealthy

Eze Okigbo did not become wealthy simply because his father was wealthy and, as a first son, he would have inherited a substantial portion of his father's wealth. The position of heir had its dangers and disadvantages. The jealousies between co-wives, the dangers surrounding an heir, and the harassment of one man by 'a horde of children all claiming paternal benefits' is well described by Basden in his comparisons between polygamous and monogamous households (1938:236–9).

The wealth of Eze Okigbo seems to have derived from funeral gifts from his maternal relatives. Eze Okigbo was apparently the only child that his mother bore to Ezike. When Ezike died, all his sons decided that each person should keep whatever funeral gifts he received for himself. In this way, they hoped to incapacitate Eze Okigbo, who was the first son. Through these gifts, he would have obtained liquid capital sufficient to enable him to establish himself firmly in the place of his father, with all the costly titles his father had. When Okigbo learned of this plot, he immediately travelled to Nnewi Ichi, to his mother's patrilineage, to report what he had heard. The members of his mother's patrilineage in turn called a meeting of members of their *obi* to discuss how to come to the rescue of their daughter's child. Consequently, as the story goes, when they came to mourn the dead, they brought Okigbo many cows, innumerable cowries and goats, etc. As John Okigbo told me, 'That was how Eze Okigbo became rich and repeated his father's fame.' He went on to say, 'We are not going to hide anything. Slave trade was a normal practice of the time. Human beings were bought in the same way as goats and fowls were bought. He also bought people who worked for him.'

How Eze Okigbo's Wives Became Wealthy

As men increased their labour force, wealth and prestige through the accumulation of wives, so also did women through the institution of 'female husbands'. When a man paid money to acquire a woman, she was called his wife. When a woman paid money to acquire another woman, this was referred to as buying a slave, *igba ohu*, but the woman who was bought had the status and customary rights of a wife, with respect to the woman who bought her, who was referred to as her husband, and the 'female husband' had the same rights as a man over his wife. I therefore translate *ohu*, in the context of woman-to-woman marriage, as wife. It was through this practice of marrying other women that the richest of Eze Okigbo's wives obtained their wealth.

Among the wives of Eze Okigbo was Nwambata Aku, who was said to have been his favourite. He had inherited her from his father, Ezike, so that economically she had a head start over the other women, having been the wife of a 'big man'. She is said to have had about 24 wives. Among the qualities attributed to her were hard work and perseverance. She was described as a clever woman, who knew how to utilize her money. As well as having her wives trade for her, she herself sold kola-nuts, and would buy pots of palm-oil during times of plenty and sell them at a high price when oil was scarce. She lent money and her husband's influence ensured that it was always repaid. She also had livestock which were tended by other people who shared the profit with her. Some of her wives are said to have been involved in hairdressing[4] too, and would hand over money received to Nwambata, their sponsor. As well as making money for their husband, Nwambata's wives also made money for themselves through the palm-kernel trade, buying kernels in bulk from neighbouring towns and retailing them.

When Nwambata died, she is said to have left her wealth to her daughter, Nnuaka, whose name means countless wealth, and, like most Igbo names, gives an insight into her history and background. While the bulk of Eze Okigbo's capital had come from funeral gifts, Nwambata's trading capital came from her marriage gifts.

In those days, it seems it was not enough for a woman to be merely wealthy. She had to be known for something else as well, such as the number of sons she bore, or the number of wives she married. Hence the comment of an Nnobi elder about one of Eze Okigbo's very wealthy wives, Nwaoye Ojeka: 'It is said that she was very rich, and that she did not bear any children at her husband's home, yet she was talked about a great deal.' According to the elderly Johnson Ume,

Nwaoye Ojeka was mentioned in the sense that she got wealthy, but I did not hear that she gave birth to anyone. Nwambata, for example, was also wealthy, but she married wives and was therefore known for that. As for Nwaoye Ojeka, I do not know why she should have been popular, as she has no children: perhaps others know why.

Another well-remembered wife was Iheuwa. In her case, she had no children, but married a woman called Onudiulu, who bore three sons. Another wife, Ochiekwe, was the reincarnation[5] of a very famous and wealthy *Ekwe* titled woman of the same name. She had children and wealth. Her name was sufficient incentive to become wealthy.

As well as being remembered for economic and social achievements, a number of the wives were remembered for their beauty and their roles as symbols of prestige and wealth, as their names indicate. The names, when translated, range from descriptions of facial and physical beauty, to a reflection of a father's or a husband's wealth. Nwambata Aku, for example, suggests a child born into wealth. Onu Aku indicates beauty of the neck, and the presence of wealth or fortune. Ihuaku Enyo

Nma, on the other hand, indicates fortune and a face in which beauty is mirrored. Okwuaku means fortune, or the prediction of it. Mgboli means a very beautiful girl, and Odikanekwu means beauty that compels remarks. Kwelie Aku Na Obi is, in fact, an appeal to enjoy the wealth in the *obi*. Those young women known for their beauty were referred to as *agbogho ofe*, maidens of the bed-chamber, and they are said to have paraded mostly in the bed-chamber compound. It is therefore possible to postulate that, with accumulation of wealth and increased social stratification, while certain women shared in the glory of wealth and power, other less glorious roles as objects of prestige and pleasure were found for females.

A popular story, about the counting of property between Eze Okigbo and his favourite wife, Nwambata, told in the *obi* of Eze Okigbo, attests to the economic mobility of women in the 19th century, as well as rivalry between wealthy women and their husbands. Apparently Nwambata had become so wealthy she was beginning to overshadow her husband, and wished either to show off her wealth or reduce it. According to the story, however, she said that she wished to share her wealth with Eze Okigbo, so he invited the whole of Nnobi to divide the wealth between them, and they divided the property in half. Then Eze Okigbo, being a man, was asked to take the first share, so he picked Nwambata herself, and consequently told the people of Nnobi to stop calling him Eze Okigbo Nwambata, as he now owned Nwambata and, therefore, all her property.[6]

His objection seems to have been to the object relationship in terms of reference. My impression during fieldwork was that this appears to have been a common practice in the past. Very wealthy women soon overshadowed their husbands to the extent that the men were no longer known by their own names, but by reference to their role as husband. Ideally in this culture, wives should be in object relationship to their husbands, not husbands to wives. This mode of address would cause embarrassment in English gender relations. A wife is addressed as Mrs, and her husband's name, and a man is addressed as Mr and his own name – not in terms of his role as husband.

Eze Okigbo could object to this reversed term of reference because he himself was a very wealthy and powerful man. Were he just an ordinary citizen, the reversal would have gone uncorrected. This seems to have happened, to some extent, in the case of the dominant wife to be described next.

The Dominant Wife, Ifeyinwa 'Olinke'

Ifeyinwa Olinke, a very wealthy woman who died in the first decade of this century, is an example of a wife who became so rich and popular that she completely overshadowed her husband. Her epithet referred to the fact that she was a woman who had nine wives. Ifeyinwa was Johnson Ume's paternal grandmother (his father's mother). Ifeyinwa was supposed to have died an old woman, carrying Johnson in her arms, and since Johnson was born in 1909, she presumably died around that time.

As Ifeyinwa's praise name was Ifeyinwa Olinke di ya, Ifeyinwa who enjoys her husband's wealth, I asked Johnson whether she became rich through her husband, or whether her husband was wealthy. His reply indicates that Ifeyinwa had so much overshadowed her husband that little is remembered about him. Johnson said, 'It was not really said of her husband whether he was rich or not. What I do know is that she was wealthier than her husband.' When asked why she was called 'one who enjoys her husband's wealth' if she was richer than her husband, Johnson's reply was still that she was wealthier than her husband. In this case, it might be more accurate to translate her praise name as 'one who has full control over her husband's property'.

Ifeyinwa also overshadowed her co-wife, Akueshiudu, who was a senior wife to Ifeyinwa and should, therefore, have been senior in status. The story of Akueshiudu shows that in those days, being the wife of a rich man, or the co-wife of a wealthy woman, was no guarantee of wealth for oneself. It was important for a woman herself to be industrious and self-sufficient.

According to Johnson Ume's account of Akueshiudu, Anozie had two wives, Akueshiudu and Ifeyinwa, and a brother, Ezeana. One day, Ezeana was supposed to have been visiting his brother Anozie. As they were sitting in the *obi*, Akueshiudu passed by to pick vegetables from her garden for the evening meal. She filled the basket with vegetables, and went back inside. As Akueshiudu was known as a lazy woman, Ezeana asked Anozie if Akueshiudu kept anything at home to cook with the vegetables. Anozie replied that he usually gave her what she was to cook, that is, meat, fish or yam. Ezeana asked his brother not to give her anything, so that they might see what she would do. One who is not hard-working, especially a woman, used to be called *oha agho ohu* (a slow mover).[7] As her husband gave her nothing, Akueshiudu cooked the vegetables and ate them, without giving him a meal. The following morning Anozie asked her what was the cause of their quarrel, and why she had not given him any supper. Her reply was to ask how she was supposed to know that he would eat *akwukwo ukpum* (steamed vegetables with plaintain or banana). Though very tasty, it was a supplementary dish and regarded as a diet of the poor, as it contained no meat or fish. (*Ofe ukpum* was similar, but thickened with cocoyam and cooked without salt.) Anozie then asked her, 'Did you give it to me and I refuse?' Johnson, who himself has had four wives, went on to comment that Akueshiudu was a lazy woman. Here, he used another expression, *aha acho ndu*, literally, one who does not try to survive, which in fact means one who is not industrious, or *idi uchu* (persevering and hard-working). The judgement passed by this elder on Akueshiudu was that there is nothing as bad as one who never has her own.

These cases demonstrate the social enforcement of the ideologies governing the sexual division of labour and gender relations. A non-industrious woman was despised and her senior status could be taken over by a junior but enterprising and wealthy co-wife. This also applies to the relationship between husband and wife. But more importantly, in the traditional title system there were both social and political rewards for economically successful women.

Notes

1. *Ekwe* was a wooden drum used in traditional Igbo societies for public summonses or announcements. As will be seen, the women so titled had rights of veto in village constitutional assemblies, and can be said to have been the mouthpiece of the villages and town.

2. The expeditions in this area are described in Nwabara 1977:132–3.

3. A plan of the *obi* of Eze Okigbo is given in Appendix 3. When I visited the place in January 1982, some of the old walls were still standing, but most of it had been knocked down. The foundations were still visible.

4. Indigenous Igbo hairdressing is described in Basden 1938:210–11, 224.

5. Igbo people believe that people are the reincarnation of those who have lived before and have both the qualities and attributes of those whose reincarnation they are.

6. Nwambata may have been much older than Eze Okigbo, as he had inherited her from his father, Ezike. She may therefore have dominated him as a much older woman.

7. This refers to the movement of the bottom, *ohu*, but it means one who did not move fast; in short, a woman who is not smart or quick at her work.

3. Gender and Political Organization

In Chapter 1 we saw how a flexible gender system affected women's access to economic resources and positions of authority and power through the institutions of 'male daughters' and 'female husbands'. This flexible gender system resulted not only in role ambiguity, but also in status ambiguity. In the political system there was a flexibility in gender classification which allowed the incorporation of certain categories of woman into the male category, giving them positions of authority in the power structure. Daughters were, for example, regarded as males in relation to wives. Consequently, sex, in this context, did not correspond to gender. In this chapter, the different social categories in Nnobi, their political groupings, roles and statuses in relation to one another are examined. What issues were they organized around? What politics did they make of them?

Descent Structure

Nnobi presents itself as a clan with a charter of descent based on the genealogical structure of founding ancestors. The Nnobi genealogical tree also provides a geographical map of the town, as descent coincides with settlement, which was patrilocal (see Appendix 2, Figure 1). All Nnobi shared a common ancestry. The people themselves said that three hands, *aka n'ato*, usually referred to as villages, make up Nnobi. These three villages shared the same structure. The subdivisions into territorial units followed a system of ranking based on the principle of social and ritual seniority of first sons. The taking of shares and the right to initiate or terminate rituals and ceremonies followed the ranking order.

Ebenesi was the largest village[1] and the most senior, since it was founded by the first son. Second in seniority was Ngo, which was founded by the second son, and the last was Awuda, founded by the third son.[2] Following the ranking order, Ebenesi would always take first share, followed by Ngo, then Awuda. By the same rules, the most senior male in the most senior patrilineage had the right to initiate or terminate ceremonies involving the whole of Nnobi. In each patrilineage, the most senior of the component *obi*(s) had this right. In each *obi*, the right belonged to the most senior male.

Each village was divided into village wards bearing the names of founding ancestors, following the principle of succession of father by first son. Thus, Ebenesi was divided into six wards which, according to their order of seniority, were: Umuona, Umuhu, Ubaha, Ifite, Amadunu and Umuafo (the most junior since it was founded by the last son. See Appendix 2, Figures 1 and 3).[3] Umuona was, therefore, the first ward in all Nnobi and its most senior minor patrilineage would contain the most senior *obi* in all Nnobi. This *obi* always produced the priest of the Land Spirit, who could hold the title *Ezeana*, the last of whom was the father of Nwajiuba, the 'male daughter' mentioned in Chapter 1. As Nwajiuba is now the most senior 'male' in this *obi*, she is the highest ranking person in all Nnobi (see Appendix 2, Figure 2).

The wards were made up of corporate patrilineages, each defined and integrated by patrilineage ancestral cults and spirits. A patrilineage group was said to constitute a town of its own, thus emphasizing its autonomy. The patrilineage ancestral cults were ranked in a hierarchical order which coincided with the hierarchical order of the descent structure. In the same way, social representation and political administration were embedded in the descent system, forming a hierarchy of descent- and kinship-based political organizations, with men dealing with male affairs and women with female affairs. *Ofo*, the symbol of authority, was held by *di-okpala*, first son, and *ada*, first daughter, who were considered male and female heads in the family and patrilineages, in the same hierarchical order of the descent structure.

Amadunu ward is taken as an example, since I have a more detailed genealogy of their group. Amadunu[4] was divided into seven minor patrilineages in order of seniority. These were Umu-Dunnebo, Umu-Nshim, Umu-Oshuga, Umu-Nnamelighi, Umu-Uhunyaluagu, Umu-Ezeobi and, lastly, Umu-Ochom, founded by an ancestress (see Appendix 2, Figure 2). Amadunu, as a major patrilineage group made up of these seven minor patrilineages, would have its original ancestral home and shrine in the oldest *obi* of Umu-Dunnebo.

Following the Nnobi principle of unilineal succession, founding ancestors were usually male, including 'male daughters', but Umu-Ochom, the most junior minor lineage in Amadunu, was founded by a woman, who was Oshuga's sister.[5] This is an example of a daughter who was allowed to remain at home and have children by informal lovers. Each minor patrilineage in turn had its own original ancestral home and shrine, but Umu-Ochom, which was founded by a female, would not have an ancestral shrine, as Ochom was not officially declared male. Her descendants would pay ritual homage to the ancestral shrine of Umu-Oshuga, the brother of Ochom.

In Ochom, we have an example of a founding ancestress of a patrilineage, while in Nwajiuba we have an example of a woman in a first son position. Both women owned land.

Political Administration

As political administration was embedded in the religious structure, we find both patriarchal and matriarchal ideologies juxtaposed in the indigenous political structure of Nnobi.

At the descent level, where the defining and integrating force was the cult of ancestral spirits, we find that the ritual élites, who constituted the ultimate political groups in the patrilineages, were guided by rules derived from a patriarchal ideology. These ritual élites were first sons and first daughters, following the hierarchy of the descent structure right up to the patrilineage head priest and head daughter. These held symbols of authority by which they derived sanction and authority from ancestral spirits.

The maleness of patrilineage ancestral spirits and the patriarchal ideology surrounding their worship meant that head daughters, being women, had to undergo a ritual of purification before handling ancestral symbols of authority, as menstrual blood was feared and tabooed. Ordinary men who took the *ozo* title also had to go through a ritual of purification which would bring them closer in identification to the ancestral spirits, just as patrilineage priests were. For this reason, *ozo* titled men were regarded as holy and just. They therefore acted in a judicial capacity in their patrilineages and, when necessary, in the wider society.

Authority and ritual sanction at the descent level was an integral part of the status of maleness, embedded in patriarchal notions. This was not so at the extra-descent level of political administration, where the religion of the goddess Idemili was the all-binding force.

At the extra-descent level of political administration, again, ritual élites such as members of title societies, priests and messengers constituted the ultimate political organization deriving sanction and authority from the goddess Idemili and the hierarchy of lesser deities. The religion of the goddess provided an integrated administrative and judicial system, which extended from Nnobi to all the communities along the Oji Iyi Idemili stream, which flows from Nnobi to Idemili Obosi. *Ukozala* titled men acted as the police in charge of the maintenance of law and order. As in other Igbo societies, the crime of theft was punished very severely. Those guilty of theft were paraded round the town before being taken to the central market-place, where they were executed.

As the goddess was a water spirit, her shrine was located by the stream and was considered holy; hence not everyone had the right to enter it or to consult her directly. Only Idemili's shrine priest, called her messenger, a hereditary office, and the senior *Ekwe* titled woman, *Agba Ekwe*, who was considered second in rank to the goddess, could consult her directly. The shrine priest carried out the act of divination in consultation with the *Agba Ekwe* titled woman. They would then relay the wishes of the goddess to the *Ukozala*, who acted as executives. Not even an *Agba Ekwe* woman could enter the forbidden ground called *Ogunzu Idemili*. According to myth, Idemili was supposed to have grown so important and influential that no longer did anyone dare to enter her shrine, apart from her shrine priest – a 'female man' in the sense that he had to tie his wrapper like women and not wear it loincloth fashion, like men.

The shrine of the goddess became a sanctuary for such social offenders as thieves, adulterers, debtors and those sent there as gifts to the goddess. Anyone else who entered, except the priest, became an *osu*, a social outcast or cult-slave dedicated to the shrine and the goddess. As the stream was considered sacred, all creatures in it were considered sacred and taboo by the community. The python was personally associated with the goddess and was taboo among the communities settled along the holy stream. It was a totemic symbol and was referred to as mother just as the maternal role of the goddess was stressed. Anyone who killed a python, if they were lucky enough to escape death, was expected to mourn its death for a year.

As well as the maternal role of the goddess being stressed, peaceful qualities were also attributed to her. She was said to believe in peace and to forbid bloodshed, human sacrifice, witchcraft and conquest. Those in the community who violated any of these taboos were ostracized. Internal wars were fought only with stones, clubs and sorcery, and not with knives or other instruments that could draw blood. Her shrine was demarcated by the *ogilisi* tree, the holy tree, sacred to the Igbo and always used to mark their important shrines. This notion of holiness was extended to her shrine priest and the *Agba Ekwe* titled woman. In the ritual greeting of the goddess through the throwing of *nzu*, white clay, before entering any of her shrines, three things were stressed: peace, love and justice.

As the goddess owned all Nnobi, the markets belonged to her. She therefore had a shrine in the market, called *Chi Idemili*; this was the market spirit in the main or central market. The markets were organized round a four-day cycle,* *eke*, *oye*, *nkwo* and *afo* serving as the main market days and *afo* the central market day. The *eke* market day was divided into *eke ukpolo* (ordinary *eke* day), and *eke okwu* (holy *eke*), which occurred every eight days and served as a Sunday – Idemili's day, when there should be no fighting, no oath-taking, no life-cycle ceremonies and no sexual intercourse. There was a ritual of cleanliness required of those caught having sexual relations on the holy *eke* day.

The Idemili religion was an integrating force which bound all Nnobi under one law. The various village Idemili shrines, the *Chi Idemili* shrine in the central market-place, and their priests were subordinate to the central shrine occupied by *Oke Nwanyi*, the Great Woman, whose epithets included 'one who seals her roof with zinc', in contrast to everyone else who lived under thatched roofs.

In the power structure, therefore, in the household and patrilineage, *di-okpala*, the first son, had hereditary rights in the *obi* and held the symbol of authority, the *ofo*. *Ada*, the first daughter, had special rights, including mediatory and vetoing rights in all matters of wrongdoing. Lineage priests too, who might or might not also be lineage heads, held *ofo* of the particular spirit they tended. At the descent and extra-descent levels, other people who held *ofo* and exercised considerable power and influence were achievement-based title holders, such as *ozo* men and *ogbuefi* men and women. Others who held symbols of authority were holders of involuntary titles linked to religion and ritual cults, such as *Ukozala* titled men, shrine priests of Idemili, *Ekwe* titled women, the high priest of Aho, and *aho* titled men (see Chapter 6), the priest of the Land Spirit *Isi ana*, and *dibia* professionals.

But by far the most honoured of title holders was the *Agba Ekwe* woman, who symbolized Nnobi concepts of womanhood derived from the worship of the goddess. Structural or formal power was, therefore, allowed to women. Idemili's

---

*Traditionally the Igbo have a four-day (*eke*, *oye*, *nkwe*, *afo*) week, hence the name of the market days. Each rural community has a main or central market day and for the Nnobi this is on *afo*, and the location of this market happens also to be called Afo.

shrine was worshipped by all Nnobi, and not that of 'her husband', Aho.[6] Idemili's daughter, Edo, was worshipped in Nnewi, and not her husband, Ezemewi. In the names of these goddesses, oaths were taken and offenders sentenced to death. The influence of the goddess thus elevated *ichi Ekwe*, the taking of the *Ekwe* title, after which the most senior *Ekwe* woman became something like a queen. The *Agba Ekwe* titled woman had the most central political position in all Nnobi – she held the vetoing right in the village and general town assemblies. Other, male, titles, voluntary or involuntary, were either hereditary or lineage specific and were associated with ritual prerogatives. Only the *ozo* titled men and their kingly prefixed names can, to some extent, be compared with the *Ekwe* titled women, as they sometimes wielded considerable power at the extra-descent level. While the extent of their power could be challenged, the position of the *Agba Ekwe* titled woman was never disputed.

'Big Men' and *Ekwe* Women Compared

Nnobi did not have kings in the sense of a centralized system under a monarch. It had *Ekwe* titled women at each wider level of political organization who ruled over women, while *ozo* titled men with *eze*, kingly, prefixed names, played the role of 'big men'. Sometimes these men wielded power only in their own villages, at others, depending on the needs of the time, their power was felt in the whole of the town. Sometimes a succession of powerful men would appear in an *obi*, bringing that *obi* to prominence, and then the *obi* would decline after the death of a particular powerful man. In some other cases, certain *obi*(s) seem to have produced successive generations of 'big men' in their histories, right up to the colonial conquest and after. An example of such an *obi* that came into focus during my research in Nnobi was that from which Eze Okigbo originated.[7]

Both John Eze Okigbo and Johnson Ume gave me a genealogy of this *obi*, which had a depth of ten generations of titled men. According to John Okigbo, the first person who lived in the *obi* was Eze Umeagha Ukwu, a name which suggests an association with a great war. He sired Eze Ochiagha, another war-associated name, who in turn sired Eze Dimopuna II. He then sired Eze Eziafuluaku (a name associated with great wealth), who sired Ezike (this name suggests strength and power). He sired Eke Okigbo who sired Okanume who sired Anadi, who sired John Okigbo, my informant. Johnson Ume's list differed in the first three names. According to his version, the first man in the *obi* was Abadaba, who sired Onyedule, who sired Akaonu, who then sired Eziafuluaku; from there on his list corresponds with that given by John Okigbo.

Such powerful men in the uncentralized Igbo communities during the indigenous period have been described by Meek (1937:III, 335) and Stevenson (1968:199). Both used the term 'big men' to describe them. Isichei (1976), however, refers to such men as the 'New Men', as she places their emergence in the 19th century. About these men she writes,

Outside the inherited structures of Igbo political life, they seize eminence and authority, either in consequence of their wealth, or sometimes in consequence of their military exploits and bravado. It is difficult to know to what extent this is truly a nineteenth-century phenomenon – the result of circumstances such as the insecurity bred by the slave trade, and the increasing circulation of wealth in the society – and to what extent it had existed earlier in the past. (1976:104)

The history of the *obi* of Eze Okigbo indicates that 'big men' had existed in Nnobi at least as early as the 16th century.

Nnobi, in fact, appears to have been centralized during the period of Ezike (roughly during the first half of the 19th century) as Nnobi was said to have been called Nnobi-Ezike during that period. According to oral history, this was the period when the neighbouring town of Nnewi was harassing Nnobi by stealing their livestock. Then Ezike, who was the richest and most powerful man in Nnobi at that time, bought a gun. He gave the gun to the young men so that when Nnewi people came to raid they were shot at, and consequently they ran away. Nnobi people were so amazed that they went to Ezike and told him that he owned them, and as a result they began to call themselves Nnobi-Ezike. This description of Ezike and the history given to me of this *obi* is very similar to the description of an Igbo 'big man' reported in Stevenson (1968). Stevenson, following Meek, writes,

Such a person obtained his position for 'obvious reasons'. As he was able to purchase firearms and powder, he was not only able to protect his own lineage segment but others as well. He had the power to decide whether to go to war or not, for only he could provide the necessary means for waging war successfully. This placed the younger age sets under his control. By supplying financial aid he constantly added to his freeborn followers, and by effectively claiming a major portion of the captives (in compensation for his outlay on arms) he constantly added to the number of his slaves. Such men tended to become principal judges and centres of authority in their localities; and their families tended to become hereditary rulers, unless their wealth subsequently diminished to the point where they could no longer act effectively in this role. (1968:199)

Ozo titled men came to prominence in the history of Nnobi as a result of might, prowess, wealth and power. This was not so with the guaranteed, honoured and respected central political position of the chief *Ekwe* titled woman. The revelation that there had always existed powerful and very politically ambitious men in indigenous Nnobi society, and the fact that they had never attempted to usurp or ban the position of the chief *Ekwe* titled woman, shows even more clearly the reverence in which that position was held, as it was embedded in the religion of the people.

Traditional Political Organizations: Gender Status, Interests and Rights

These organizations existed not only in pre-19th century Nnobi society, but still function today. Their interest and rights in the life-cycle ceremonies of their members remain the same. The only difference is that many of their indigenous rituals have been replaced by Christian ceremonies. Many of their judicial roles have also been taken over by law courts. But the ranking order of seniority governing inter-lineage relations and relations within the patrilineage remains the same. This is also true of the gender status of these political groupings which is associated with their status of authority *vis-à-vis* other groups. Here, again, we see the mediating role of a flexible gender system in the face of sexual polarization.

The traditional political organization, at the descent level, was the *umunna*, the organization of patrilineage members, sons and daughters alike. But, following the rule of sexual dualism, patrilineage daughters formed a separate organization known as *umu okpu*, while their brothers and fathers held their separate meeting, *umunna*, even though, in principle, daughters were also understood to belong to their meeting. Patrilineage wives, on the other hand, formed a separate organization known as *inyom di*. But the oneness of blood of daughters, brothers and fathers meant that daughters were conceived of as 'males' in relation to wives, and therefore superior to them in authority. Separate from, and above the descent-based organization of patrilineage wives, was the organization which controlled all Nnobi women. This was the Women's Council, *Inyom Nnobi*, headed and controlled by titled women and elderly matrons.

In these separate organizations the daily affairs of Nnobi society were conducted, with men – which sometimes included certain categories of women, for example daughters – taking care of male affairs, while women took care of female affairs. This way, interests were negotiated, defined and safeguarded.

Organization of Patrilineage Men

Umunna means children descended from one father. Both men and women born in a patrilineage were regarded as sharing the same blood and were equally subject to the rules and taboos associated with patrilineage spirits, even though men and women held separate meetings. Together, they were the 'we' social group to 'other' similar patrilineage groups. Only women crossed these lineage boundaries, as daughter from a 'we' group to wife in an 'other' group. Wives were, therefore, outsiders in a 'we' group and held separate meetings. Social functions and roles in the patrilineage were shared out to members in their different official organizations as lineage men, lineage daughters and lineage wives.

There were two levels of patrilineage organizations, the major and the minor level. All everyday life-cycle ceremonies and rituals involving birth, marriage and death were performed at the minor lineage level. Other yearly ceremonies and festivals, for example, the Eating of New Yam Festival, were organized at the major patrilineage level. The eldest was always the recognized head of a lineage group, and was called 'our father', *nna anyi*, since he was regarded as the father of all the members of the group; meetings were held at his place. But the first son in the most senior *obi* in the patrilineage tended the patrilineage ancestral shrine which contained several figurines representing both the goddess Idemili and other lineage spirits, including the spirits of the ancestors.

The most important function the patrilineage group performed was judging land cases. Other duties involved the life-cycle ceremonies. The lineage group named each child born into the patrilineage, and performed the naming ceremony. Any member who failed to perform the naming ceremony for his child was fined. If a man went to get a wife and was not accompanied by his patrilineage group, the marriage was not recognized. Similarly, if a man married off his daughter without performing the 'carrying of palm-wine', *ibu nkwu*, ceremony for his lineage group, the man would be struck out of the group. It was the duty of lineage men to erect shades under which people would sit during ceremonies. They helped by contributing wine and kola-nuts. If a woman came to her husband's house and became troublesome, it was the duty of the lineage men to return her to her father's house, or to say what was to be done to her. If husband and wife were caught fighting, they were fined by the organization of lineage men. They would bury their dead together and stay with the bereaved. If a man died while his son was absent from home and unable to return quickly to bury him, the lineage group took over the responsibility.

As the organization of lineage men was duty bound to help members, so also were members individually bound by certain codes of conduct in order to remain members of the group. The minor patrilineage, as a kindred group, was bound by the taboo of incest. As a kindred group, they were expected to be guided by *umunne* principles, the spirit of common motherhood, which compelled love and trust. No one should take another's wife, at least not while he was still alive.[8] There should be no scandal-mongering, no theft, no treachery and no lies against one another. Murder should not be committed within the patrilineage. In short, they should not wrong one another.

If any member was in need, he turned to his patrilineage members, who would contribute money to help him. Everyone was expected to participate in the activities of the others. Any one of them who suffered a mental breakdown would be assisted by the others through the contribution of money towards medical care. They also contributed money to help very poor members build a house. Those unable to afford marriage expenses were also assisted by their patrilineage group. A patrilineage was said to be a little town of its own, governed by its own rules. They kept peace in the lineage, and built footpaths in their locality. Such prestige-conferring ceremonies and rituals as the taking of *ozo* titles and the *ogbuefi* title for those who had killed a cow were undertaken only with the support of the lineage group. During any social disorder, the lineage group collectively consulted a diviner. It was also their duty to visit rainmakers, to suspend rain before any ceremony in the lineage.

They punished anyone who defied his lineage group by levying fines; those who refused punishment were ostracized. This was supposed to be the greatest misfortune a man could bring upon himself, for it was said that if a man had neither power nor a say in his lineage group, he could not have it in the town; he was said to be better dead than alive. That person's crime was called 'crime against the land', *nso ani*. When such a man died, no one bothered about him – he died like a dog – this was a term of abuse and a curse in Nnobi.[9] To have an honourable burial was a strong incentive binding members to the rules of their groups. As we shall see, patrilineage daughters derived much power from their control of the funerals of patrilineage members.

Organization of Patrilineage Daughters

The original ancestral home of a minor patrilineage was called *ani okpu* or *obi okpu*. Daughters born into the original *obi* were called *umu okpu*, children originating from *okpu*; *okpu* can be interpreted to mean core or nucleus. The organization of lineage daughters was formal, and consisted of both married and unmarried daughters of the patrilineage group. Like the organization of patrilineage men, leadership in the organization of patrilineage daughters was based on seniority in age. The oldest daughter, married or unmarried, was usually the leader and meetings where strategies were planned and fines levied were held in her home. She always presented kola-nuts and food to the others, but in return for this, she was exempt from contributions, and was highly respected by the others.

Lineage daughters had strong powers in the place where they were born. Townsfolk gave them special prestige and respect, because no matter how difficult a case was, they were believed to be able to solve it, whether in the lineage at home or abroad. It was their duty to ensure that their father's household was strong and at peace. If there was a quarrel in the lineage, they were called in to settle it. If the quarrel was among lineage wives, they were called in and, after settling the dispute, the married daughters would return to their respective marital homes. If one of their wives had maltreated her husband, lineage daughters as a group would sanction her and lay down laws for her. If the woman became stubborn, it was up to patrilineage daughters to decide how to deal with her;[10] their options included physical violence. But if their brother was in the wrong, they would scold him. The men had the highest respect for them. If the quarrel was among lineage men, lineage daughters were usually able to persuade the men to resolve their differences by threatening to boycott their funerals; no funeral took place if lineage daughters were not present.

Although lineage daughters had specific duties in the patrilineage, their most important role was during funerals, when they were called sisters of the corpse, *umunne ozu*. They washed the corpse of a lineage member, decorated it and guarded it through the night until it was buried. They then slept with the bereaved for a number of nights. If a lineage daughter died or suffered bereavement, they slept there for four days, but if another male lineage member died they slept there for three days. Throughout the day and night, lineage daughters would sing and dance. In return, they would be given fish, wine, yam, cocoyam and various foodstuffs. As they sang, those people who arrived for the funeral usually gave them salt, pepper, fish, yam, money and so on. The rump of any cow or goat killed during the funeral belonged to them alone. To those who gave them nothing they sang songs intended to annoy.

It was said of lineage daughters that they ran errands only where profit could be obtained. It was believed that this was the reason behind the rule made by daughters that they must always be given a very important position at the funeral ceremony of very elderly or titled people. Such funerals involved feasting and the giving of gifts.

Lineage daughters would spend several nights at such funerals, singing various songs, especially ridiculous ones at night. For this, they would again receive presents, including food, meat and wine. They were noted for their greed, and never considered anything given to them to be enough, and were said to be never satisfied or grateful, hence the saying, 'as greedy as lineage daughters'. If they were not treated well at a funeral, they could refuse the presents given to them and thus bring disgrace to the funeral; those who gave them money during a funeral, however, were blessed by the head daughter with her *ofo*.

When a lineage daughter died as a wife elsewhere, the others went to bring back her body or her *ngiga* to her natal home, where she would be buried. Their song, as they returned with the body of a sister, was authoritative and demanded that everyone should get out of their way as they were on a mission. Lineage daughters were also responsible for carrying out investigations into the cause of the woman's death. If she had been maltreated in her husband's home, they would refuse to take her body back, and her husband and his lineage would be left with a decomposing corpse in a tropical climate, since they had no right to bury it. This situation usually led to war. It was lineage daughters who usually brought back the goat given by in-laws as the returning soul of the deceased woman to her lineage (see Chapter 4).

All members of the organization of lineage daughters were bound by the same rules. Any lineage daughter who did not attend a funeral was fined, as were those who fought, gossiped, were caught stealing or arrived late for meetings or ceremonies. If the treasurer embezzled money she was ostracized. The younger ones were required to respect the older ones; no member should be ill-treated; all lineage daughters had to return home when a lineage member died; they must provide music when a lineage member died; and all money collected or whatever was bought with the money should be shared out between them.

From all accounts, it was believed that when patrilineage daughters made up their minds to be troublesome, no one could deal with them. They were as capable of causing havoc as they were of making peace. Their power and importance in their patrilineage was so secure that a woman's husband could not tell her not to participate in her lineage activities. In relation to lineage men, their role was mediatory. Their relationship with lineage wives was one of authority. In Nnobi classificatory kinship terms, they were also husbands to lineage wives, and were addressed as such, and could overrule any decision made by lineage wives. When a daughter and a wife were together, the daughter, not the wife, should break kola, but she might touch the kola and hand it over to a wife, thereby giving her authority to break it.

To the question, 'Why are patrilineage daughters given so much power?' the answer given to me by an Nnobi elder, Eze Enyinwa, was,

Because, had they been men, they would have had the same power as lineage men. This is the reason they are given more power than patrilineage wives. For this reason, lineage wives will bow down their heads to lineage daughters. If the daughters tell them to leave, they'll pack their things and go. Was Ochom not left at home by her father? She did not get married, so her father gave her the right to remain at home. She then left her father's compound and founded a home. It was thus that she founded the lineage of Umu Ochom.

To show how little the rules governing traditional roles and statuses in the lineage have changed since the indigenous pre-colonial society of the 19th century, the following is an account of my first-hand experience of the power conflict between patrilineage daughters and their wives during my fieldwork in Nnobi in 1980. This occurred at the funeral of a male member of a patrilineage.

At funerals, wives in the patrilineage where the death had occurred usually cooked, while lineage daughters of the deceased supplied entertainment, singing and dancing. But this division of roles did not prevent lineage daughters from watching carefully to see what food was being cooked and distributed, and who was getting what. In the household adults usually distributed such sweet things as biscuits, cakes, coconuts or groundnuts to the children. During ceremonies, lineage daughters usually applied this principle to claim most of the snacks supplied, since wives were also their mothers!

At this particular funeral, lineage daughters had been singing and dancing continuously for two days, taking turns to snatch some sleep at night. By the third day, they had become tired, restless and bad-tempered. They had started to accuse lineage wives of cooking and eating the best part of the food and feeding lineage daughters rubbish. This was not correct, since I personally kept watch over the additional food brought for lineage daughters every day by wives of the deceased's closer relatives in turn.

A plate of coconut was given to the lineage wives, whereupon the oldest lineage daughter, who was also the oldest member of the minor patrilineage of the deceased, a woman of over 80, a little bent with age, but still very dignified, feared and highly respected, quickly got up and ordered the lineage wives not to share it out among themselves. She told them that if they did, they would be fined. The lineage wives only laughed at her and thought she was not in earnest, but simply being difficult and seeking attention as usual. So they went ahead and ate the coconut. This head daughter quickly called everyone's attention to this[11] and ordered the lineage wives to pay a fine of one kola-nut each. Those who did not have any kola had to put money in the plate. The lineage wives dared not disobey her and the plate was soon full of kola and money. She then asked one of the older daughters to count the money. When this was done, she gave some of the kola to the men and some to the daughters, and then took a very little of the money and actually threw the rest back at the wives. Immediately, the place was in uproar, everyone clapped, laughed and praised her. Even lineage wives called her praise names, such as Great Daughter, *Oke Ada*. Thus this ancient woman reminded everyone of the superiority of daughters to wives.

Soon after this incident, one of the wives, who was from a neighbouring village, got drunk and decided to harass and embarrass lineage daughters. She had been a child-bride, married to another woman. This woman's praise name carried the meaning implied in the expression, *oli aku*, which was applied to a man's wife, one who enjoyed wealth. This particular woman was said to enjoy the wealth of the woman who was her husband. Later she was inherited by her 'female husband's' first son, who had died a few years before; she was, therefore, a widow, and had not been inherited by anyone.

At this funeral, the lineage daughters were her husbands. She was one of the wives who had cooked privately and brought food to the lineage daughters. Having got drunk she accused lineage daughters of failing in their conjugal and sexual responsibilities to her as a wife. She became extremely 'vulgar', and claimed that she had not had sexual intercourse for years; her vagina was therefore getting rusty, and she was hungry for sex! The unmarried daughters hid their faces for shame and disappeared from the scene, because they were expected to be virgins and therefore ignorant of sexual matters.

The woman's dead husband's sister, also a widow in her late 60s, took up the challenge and confronted her. Looking very concerned, but all in jest, she patted her on the shoulder and asked her to be patient, saying that she was going to visit her that night. This brought uproar among the women, and they all laughed and joked about it. Embarrassed, the younger girls accused the older women of vulgarity. Thus in matters of sexuality or fertility wives proved their superiority over daughters.

Kinship Morality and Gender

Nnobi kinship morality is expressed in the notions of *umunne*, *imenne* and *ibenne*. The smallest and closest kinship group are siblings in the matricentric unit, *umunne otu afo*, children of one womb. Their closeness and solidarity can best be understood in the context of polygyny, in the alliances and intrigues embodied in that system. This primary group, to whom the term *umunne* is applied, should be distinguished from the kindred group to whom the same term is applied. In the case of the kindred group, the term is qualificatory and applies to the expected relationship between members of the minor patrilineage which is the kindred group said to belong to one *imenne*, inner-mother circle, and are therefore *umunne* to one another, that is, bound in the spirit of common motherhood. Both the primary *umunne* unit and the kindred *umunne* unit are bound by the taboo of incest.

Ibenne is the supernatural sanction applied to the relationship among siblings and other blood relations right up to the whole *imenne* group in the minor lineage, to ensure continued intimacy and relations of trust among members. *Ibenne* is referred to as a deity; it has no shrine but nevertheless is said to be very powerful. When brothers or close blood relatives betray, steal from, or kill one another to usurp land or commit incest, it is said to strike, to kill outright and to be deaf to pleas for mercy: *ibenne ada anu biko ghaluba* – *ibenne* does not listen to 'please forgive'.

Umunne, *imenne* and *ibenne* are all suffixed by the Igbo word for mother – *nne*. The sentiments expressed in them fit in with other female gender ideologies and notions of motherhood in this culture. In contrast to this, dealings among *umunna* – suffixed by the word for father, *nna* – are associated with distrust, suspicion, greed, jealousy, envy, witch-hunting and sorcery; it is in the *umunna* group that status is reckoned. In contrast also to the relationship with one's father's group, the *umunna* group, is the relationship associated with one's matrilineage, *ikwunne*. This is the daughter's child and members of the mother's patrilineage categories bound by the relationship of indulgence and respect.

Daughter's Child, *Nwadiana* Category

The honour, respect and indulgence shown to the daughter by her patrilineage extended to her children. This attitude was symbolized in the very important social category in Nnobi known as the *nwadiana*. This term cannot easily be translated into English, I shall therefore explain to whom it refers, and retain the Igbo term, but when convenient use the expression 'child of a daughter'.

All children of daughters of a minor patrilineage born into other patrilineages were each a *nwadiana* to all the members of their mother's patrilineage. They were collectively referred to by the plural *umudiana*. Male members of the mother's patrilineage, in turn, collectively formed a category referred to as *ndi nna ochie*, ancient- or grand-fathers to the children of daughters, while the female members were referred to as *ndi nne ochie*, ancient- or grand-mothers to the same children. As 'grandparents' may be misleading, 'ancient-parents' will be the term used to refer to these classificatory terms. Certain rules and regulations guided relationships between these two categories. They were also bound by the taboo of incest.

Umudiana (plural) were given certain powers in their mother's lineage. Their role, like that of lineage daughters, was mediatory; they arbitrated during quarrels. Through them, inter-town or inter-lineage quarrels were settled. They were the most indulged people in Nnobi, and of them it was said, *agha aha eli nwadiana*, 'they were never lost in war', for they were never killed, taken captive or sold; it was forbidden to draw the blood of a *nwadiana*. They should never be wronged, because they were said to be holy. When they visited their mother's patrilineage, whatever they requested was given to them. They received such trifles as fried cakes (*akara*), fruits and coconuts, and were free to drink any wine they might find in gourds on the palm trees. If they happened to be around when an animal was being killed, they would be given meat bones, such as the tail or the head.

Umudiana, for their part, were expected to respect their classificatory ancient-parents, members of their mother's patrilineage. The behaviour expected of them by their ancient-parents was stated in the expression *ikpa nku*, picking wood. Each time they visited their ancient-parents they should carry firewood to them, on their heads. They should show respect and sing the praises of their ancient-parents, kneel down to greet them, bow their heads when addressing them and carry palm-wine to them during ceremonies. They were expected to work on their ancient-parents' farms during planting and harvesting, after which they would be given fruit. When praising their ancient-parents by saying their titles or praise names, they would say, '*ochie*, ancient one, I kneel down.' Then *ochie* would reply, 'I acknowledge it. Rise my child. Good boy or good girl.' The idea was to be as patronizing as possible to a *nwadiana* who should be modest and humble to their ancient-parents. Adult *umudiana* were expected to buy tobacco for their ancient-parents when they met in the street or market-place, and ancient-parents were expected to buy them biscuits, cakes, and so on.

Anyone who was on the run would go to their *ikwunne*, where he or she was sure to find help and shelter. There should never be a quarrel between these two categories.

Organization of Patrilineage Wives

Inyom di, married women, was the traditional organization of patrilineage wives. Leadership was not based on age, but on seniority as wife in the patrilineage; that is, the woman who was first married into the patrilineage was considered the leader of the organization, and this usually proved to be an elderly woman. Meetings were held periodically at her place to discuss lineage problems. Since most of the work during ceremonies was done by them, they also discussed and planned their duties at the meetings. Like other lineage organizations, specific duties were assigned to wives, and members were bound by strict rules and regulations. As a body, too, the organization of lineage wives claimed certain rights.

During any ceremony, it was lineage wives' task to sweep the compound, make seating arrangements for the visitors, fetch water and cook food. It was their duty to carry pots of palm-wine and gifts to be presented by the patrilineage. The method of carrying was by head-loading, organized according to how long a woman had been a wife in the lineage. The new arrivals head-loaded first, and only when they were carrying as much as they could did the older wives lift things on to their heads. Titled women should never carry things on their heads. Older wives dominated the younger ones and it was their duty to ensure the smooth outcome of the ceremonies. They were, therefore, usually vigilant and firm, giving strict advice and orders to the younger wives.

Lineage wives were most important during marriages and child-naming ceremonies. As initiates and custodians of the fertility cult, payments were made to them during ceremonies concerning marriage and childbirth. Only they had the right to remove the young bride from the state of sexual taboo by untying her waist charm and initiating her into the fertility cult (see Chapter 4). Later, through the fertility ritual, *upiti* dance, they introduced the bride and groom to the act of sexual intercourse and wished them procreation from it. For this they received payment in the form of yam, palm-oil, salt, pepper and palm-wine. During the naming ceremony, when a child was formally introduced to the rest of the patrilineage members, lineage wives also received yam and palm-oil. These items were not distributed according to age, but according to the seniority of the *obi*(s) into which the women were married. Thus, wives of older *obi*(s) got shares before those married into more recent ones. It was also this organization which levied a fine on any groom who made his bride pregnant before the marriage ceremonies had been completed.

It was the duty of lineage wives to bring back a new bride and explain to her the rules and regulations guiding the conduct of wives. When a husband wished to take an additional wife, he sought the support of his wives, who would then carry pots of wine to him as their contribution to the marriage requirements; it was their task to enliven the marriage ceremony. To show their approval of a marriage, co-wives had to go personally to bring back the bride who would be their co-wife. Marital quarrels were dealt with by lineage wives. If the wife was guilty, she was advised to buy kola, a cock, or even a goat, depending on the gravity of her offence and the status of the man, and to beg her husband's forgiveness; the penalty for offending a titled man was more severe. If the husband was found guilty, they sanctioned him through the lineage head or reported him to his sisters. If all else failed they would take the matter to the Women's Council.

If a death occurred in the patrilineage, lineage wives would immediately go to the bereaved compound, sweep it, arrange seats and share out the responsibility of providing food and water. None of them could go to the market to sell, or to work on the farm that day. If any member lost her husband, they had to stay by her, comfort her and try to make her eat some food.

Patrilineage wives were also responsible for the general cleanliness of the areas occupied by the patrilineage. It was their duty to see that footpaths, areas surrounding their compounds, shrines and village squares were kept clean. If lineage men wished to build a meeting place, they asked lineage wives to carry sand and fetch water. Each organization of lineage wives was responsible for ensuring that their section of the market-place was kept clean. Women sat in the market according to their marital lineages, and market space was divided on the basis of patrilineage.

As with any formal organization, there were penalties, usually fines, for breaking the rules. Those who refused to carry chairs, sweep or cook at funerals were fined, as were those who fought or exchanged abusive words in public. Anyone who refused to pay a fine was ostracized. Laws set down by this organization and accepted by the whole of Nnobi demanded that a bride's mother should buy yam and palm-oil for lineage wives in order for them to initiate her daughter into the fertility cult. Also, when one of their members had a child, lineage wives were invited to pray for and bless the child in order to show their joy.

Since most of their duties involved work – cleaning, cooking or head-loading – wives emphasized the importance of co-operation and solidarity among women. They had loan schemes whereby money was lent to members in rotation, according to how their names were entered in the register as they arrived at the lineage and became members; a little interest was payable on these loans. Most of the money lent was used as trade capital, or to purchase items for the farm.

As the women co-operated to carry out their duties, so also were they able to co-operate to make their demands heard by their menfolk. Such demands usually included the repair of dangerous roads, sanctions on those who maltreated their wives, and on youths who harassed young girls on village paths or roads. At the worst, if lineage men proved stubborn, wives went on strike, in which case they would refuse to cook for or have sexual intercourse with their husbands. In this culture, men did not cook: control of food was therefore a political asset for the women. In sexuality, too, gender realities were such that it was believed that females provided sexual services; hence the political use of the threat of collective withdrawal of sexual services by women.

Organization of Nnobi Women

Inyom Nnobi, Women of Nnobi, was the Women's Council which represented all Nnobi women. Its representatives were drawn at ward level, that is, at major patrilineage level. For example, each ward provided about five representatives drawn from the component minor patrilineages; these representatives were not necessarily the most senior wives in the patrilineage. They were women of strong character and charisma, articulate women who could speak without fear on behalf of those they represented. Thus leadership was based on achievement and personality. A Women's Council was said to be more like a magistrate's court than an ordinary meeting. Above all the rest of the women were those who took the title of *Ekwe*. This institution, with its own rules and regulations, dealt exclusively with matters concerning women, and the policing of Nnobi markets. Representatives to the Council acted as policewomen in their wards, watching for offenders; when a Council was called, they judged the cases and took the decisions of the meetings back to the lineage level organizations.

Inyom Nnobi was responsible for the general welfare of Nnobi women. No decisions about women could be made without its knowledge and consent. It was its duty to review the amount demanded for bride-price from time to time. If the men demanded too much money for their daughters, the Women's Council said so and lowered the amount. To ensure the good behaviour of women in general, they fined those who fought in public, or stole, gossiped, spread scandal, were treacherous or indulged in bad sorcery (*igwo ajo ogwu*), or in any undesirable characteristics demeaning to women and which gave them a bad name. It was also their duty to see that rules to safeguard or protect women against physical abuse were obeyed, for example, the ban on sexual intercourse with a nursing mother, and the two-year spacing of children.

Not only did the women monopolize market space, they also monopolized its cleaning and policing. Their representatives at the lineage level were responsible for their own sections of the market. It was therefore their duty to select women to sweep it. Those who fought in the market were fined. For example, a woman who hit another woman with a chair, or bit her, paid a double fine. Those who urinated in the market were fined. Anyone who left her goat to wander into and damage another woman's garden paid a double fine. Those who fought by the spring were fined.

Women were also concerned with the welfare of the town. Decisions to contribute money for public works and repairs or for other services were taken at their meetings. In times of epidemics or great unrest, women consulted diviners for the well-being of Nnobi. If the dry season became too dry, hot and unbearable, the Women's Council met and contributed money for visiting the rainmakers. Decisions on contributions of money by Nnobi women were usually passed on to the Women's Council, where representatives from the various wards ensured that the money was collected. Even if contributions of money were demanded from the whole town, it was the Women's Council which would be informed. Representatives would, in turn, take the word round, for they had fully representative authority.

The women were aware of their strong communications network and took full advantage of it, and were consequently feared and respected by the menfolk. Traditional leaders dared not meet to discuss matters concerning women without women representatives being present. But the Women's Council was held in private; great secrecy surrounded the meetings. Any representative who revealed what transpired there would be ostracized by the women. The men were said to be uneasy every time a Women's Council was called, since they were unaware of what would be discussed, or what the women might decide to do. Indeed, the rest of the women were said to search their conscience and worry in case they were going to be judged at the Council. What the men feared most was the Council's power of strike action.

The strongest weapon the Council had and used against the men was the right to order mass strikes and demonstrations by all women. When ordered to strike, women refused to perform their expected duties and roles, including all domestic, sexual and maternal services. They would leave the town *en masse*, carrying only suckling babies. If angry enough, they were known to attack any men they met. Nothing short of the fulfilment of their demands would bring them back; but, by all indications, their demands were never unreasonable. They attacked viciously any decision or law which denied them, or interfered with, their means of livelihood, or the means by which they supported their children. Inter-town or inter-village wars might, for example, necessitate a temporary closure of some or all markets, or might render all market routes unsafe. Sexual harassment of young girls by young men might also make bush paths to markets unsafe. Disrespect by the men, such as making laws binding to women, or deciding levies for the whole town without the knowledge and consent of the women, were all matters dealt with by the Women's Council.

The Women's Council appears to have been answerable to no one, for at the head was the *Agba Ekwe*, who held the most honoured title in Nnobi. She carried her staff of authority and had the final word in public gatherings and assemblies. She was the favoured one of the goddess Idemili and her earthly manifestation. If a quarrel arose in the town and a deadlock was reached which could not be settled even by *ozo* titled men, the Women's Council was invited to settle it. The chief *Ekwe* woman had the last word when she stuck her long pointed staff in the ground. But the women were called in by men to settle disputes only as a last resort. It was generally claimed that *ozo* titled men, or high *ozo* titled men, were usually able to settle quarrels. They were thought perhaps to be the only people who might have been able to check any excesses of the Women's Council, since it was an autonomous organization.

The fact still remains that even though there was a unifying organization which safeguarded women's interests, female solidarity was neutralized, to some extent, through the division of women on the basis of gender; daughters were seen as males in relation to wives and superior in authority to wives; in this context, sex did not correspond to gender. Daughters, in alliance with their fathers and brothers, identified themselves with male interests. Nevertheless, this flexibility of gender allowed women to take on typical male roles, which gave them authority. Favourable matriarchal ideologies, on the other hand, guaranteed an important position for women in the central political structure. In addition, other shared strong female beliefs and practices united all women in a sense of sisterhood, as we shall see in the next chapter.

Notes

1. In 1980, Ebenesi was thought to contain about 10,000 people. This would be about half the population of Nnobi.

2. Ngo and Awuda together had a population of 10,000.

3. However, people from Umuona put Ifite last in order of seniority. This does not alter my thesis regarding the position of Ifite discussed in Chapter 6, as it is still in the position of junior lineages.

4. In 1980 its population was about 10,000.

5. Some said that Ochom was Oshuga's sister, others believed that Oshuga was the father of Ochom. Either way, she was in the same classificatory kinship category with either father or brother, since they all belonged to the same patrilineage in the sense of oneness of blood.

6. Discussed in detail in Chapter 6.

7. See case study in Chapter 2.

8. Widow inheritance was practised.

9. Dead dogs were not buried but left to be devoured by vultures or to rot.

10. The expression used with regard to the consequences for a wife who proved stubborn to patrilineage daughters was, 'the woman would see with her naked eyes how the python basked in the sun': *iji anya fu ka eke si anya anwu*. This implies being exposed to the danger from a python out in the sun. The python is known to loathe the sun, consequently it usually lies in the shade of bushes, under trees or in caves. Only as a result of acute hunger does it appear in the sun. When it does, it appears full of rage, becomes entangled and suffocates and swallows anything within sight, human or animal. It then returns to the shade and lies there for months, digesting its victim. During this period it is the most harmless creature in the world! The implication, therefore, is that a wife who proved stubborn risked seeing patrilineage daughters in full rage!

11. In Nnobi, even today, these traditional groups sit apart from each other. Patrilineage wives sit together, patrilineage daughters sit together, patrilineage men sit together, with elders, titled men and those whose ceremonies were being attended sitting at the head table. Other visitors sit with their contingents, men sitting separately from women. They all face a central space where gifts are displayed and received.

4. The Politics of Motherhood: Women and the Ideology-Making Process

Although this section deals with the indigenous period, many cultural beliefs and practices surrounding women and their role in life-cycle ceremonies have survived unchanged in modern Nnobi society. Even though people went to the church for baptism, marriage and funeral services, traditional ceremonies were also performed in their homes. In order to illustrate the extent of cultural continuity, traditional songs still used during life-cycle ceremonies are included here. Since these express orally transmitted beliefs and customs of a community, the people's own traditional gender ideas should be apparent in them.

The women have always monopolized singing and dancing during most ceremonies. Sometimes, their songs contained statements from dominant Nnobi models which they shared with the men. At others they contained ideas generated by the women as commentaries on dominant ideas or as statements of facts from the women's point of view. Nnobi women were not, and are still not, tongue-tied. According to a popular Nnobi saying, *Onu umu nwanyi n'agba ka ukpaka*, 'The mouth of women opens at random or pops like the pod of the oil-bean tree.'

In Nnobi society, whether in the past or today, women are essentially seen as producers, be it in the management of subsistence production or in biological production. In this culture, as we have noted in Chapter 1, women were thought to have inherited the gift of hard work and the pot of prosperity from their goddess Idemili. In Nnobi, when a woman has a miscarriage, it is said, *Nmili rufulu mana ite awaro*, 'The water spilled but the pot was not broken.' When a woman, as wife, had served her period of productivity and reproductivity in her marital home, at her death she became a daughter again and her body was returned to her natal home for burial.

Since women were basically seen as producers, the principles of control and protection applied to them throughout their productive period, whether as daughters, wives or mothers. It is said that when a woman outgrows the question, 'whose daughter is she?' people then ask, 'whose wife is she?' Only as matrons were women no longer valued in their sexual and reproductive capacity; matrons were, therefore, beyond control. A woman could then begin to reap the profits of the years of labour. An Nnobi saying describing an old woman goes like this: *Onabu ekilibe onu agadi nwanyi, odi k'obu na osoro nu ala*, 'Looking at the lips of an old woman, it is as if she too did not suck the breast.' Thus, the sexual unattractiveness of the old woman was stressed by focusing on her wrinkled, toothless mouth, probably stained with tobacco. This mouth usually produced uncompromising statements, commanded, and insisted upon respect. A woman at this stage of her life no longer sought to be sexually attractive to men, and was no longer in sexual competition with other women. Matrons, in order to succeed economically and wield power, had to free themselves of 'messy' and 'demeaning' female domestic services, which included sexual services (Rosaldo 1974; Chodorow 1974). Woman-to-woman marriage was one of the ways of achieving this. The younger wife would then take over the domestic duties.

Chapter 3 revealed major Nnobi classifications of women, namely: daughters, wives/mothers and matrons which correspond to stages in the life of a woman – maidenhood/virginity, wifehood/maternity and matronhood/post-menopause. The socio-cultural significance of these stages will be examined, and related to the formal and informal power structure.

In order to present women as social subjects and actors, the political use of culture by Nnobi women in their formal organizations based on their social roles as daughters, wives and mothers is also examined. In Chapter 3, we saw that daughters organized themselves around the control of funeral ceremonies, while wives and mothers organized themselves around fertility – birth and marriage. Through the involvement of these women and their prominence in public rituals and ceremonies, they had access to the medium of communication and were, therefore, involved in the ideology-making processes and the management of meaning.

Marriage

Nnobi choice of marriage settlement was the patrilocal system, whereby patrilineage men remained on the patrilineage land and guarded patrilineage property. They then sent their daughters off to serve as wives elsewhere, while they brought in non-lineage women for the purposes of procreation and domestic and economic labour. Thus, lineages were not economically or socially isolated. Women linked lineages in in-law relationships forged through them. During marriage and funeral ceremonies goods were circulated through relationships traced through women. Daughters, as virgins, were under the control and protection of their lineage men in relation to non-lineage men with whom the rules of incest did not forbid sexual intercourse. Through marriage exchange, daughters stepped into wifehood and motherhood and control over them passed from their natal to their marital lineage men. The significance accorded to maidenhood centred on guarding the virginity and fertility of the young daughters and preparing them for their future roles as wives and mothers.

Nnobi had a strong preference for village endogamy; the closer the marriage in terms of geographical space the better. People did not like to send their daughters to distant places because they retained important ritual and political roles in their natal homes and patrilineages after marriage. The minor lineage, as a kindred group, was the only exogamous unit. Marriage was allowed between minor lineages which belonged to the same major lineage. Apart from the minor lineage, the other category under the taboo of incest was the *nwadiana*, who might not marry anyone from his/her mother's minor patrilineage. Before such a marriage could take place, a ritual called *igba udu oma* had to be performed to separate blood ties and ward off the incest taboo.[1] This idea was expressed in the saying, 'After three generations, from the fourth one, one may go ahead with marriage, but when desired at the third generation, one must perform the ritual to separate blood relationship.'[2]

In Nnobi, to have the support of one's lineage was to have power. For women, it was the support of their brothers which was important. At marriage, a woman's husband's lineage acquired rights over her sexual services and her reproductive and labour powers. Even though control over her passed from her lineage men to both men and women of her husband's lineage, her own patrilineage did not give up the right to protect her. This can be seen in the aggressive attitude of her brothers during marriage negotiations and the ceremonies.

During the carrying of palm-wine ceremony, for example, young men of the bride's patrilineage were given one jar of palm-wine by wife-takers. The name of this gift means that whether or not they drank the wine, if they had to, they would still fight those who gave it to them. This drink, as the name suggests, was regarded as a bribe to make the youths consent to part with their sisters, for they were regarded as the girls' protectors, and would fight on their behalf if ordered to. They therefore usually behaved in a very aggressive manner in the presence of wife-takers, generally causing trouble and making their presence and strength felt. By so doing, they showed reluctance to part with their sister, and also dissociated themselves from the 'old men', lineage elders, who had accepted money for her.

The money given to lineage men was usually taken out of the marriage payment made by the wife-takers. The money for yam and palm-oil to be shared among lineage wives was also taken out of the marriage payment, as was the money for the food cooked for the carrying of wine ceremony. In a sense, therefore, it can be said that the marriage payment was used to meet the costs of a marriage, and did not mean the woman was bought. If the girl given to wife-takers was already pregnant (called *ima upo*) everything given during this occasion was doubled.

The term commonly used for marriage was *ibu-nkwu* – carrying palm-wine. Patrilineage men recognized patrilineage daughters as married when they (men) had drunk their (lineage daughters') palm-wine. Marriage payment, commonly known as brideprice or bridewealth, gave a man legal right only over a child born to the woman on whom he had deposited money; she was recognized as his wife only when he had carried her palm-wine. For a divorce to be total the woman's family must return the marriage payment to the husband; any child the woman might subsequently have would then no longer be claimed by her husband. For this reason this marriage payment has sometimes been referred to as childwealth – that is, the child belongs to whoever has made that payment; otherwise it belongs to the child's mother's patrilineage.

The minor lineage was the group concerned with marriage of lineage members. It was through the exchange of daughters that lineages were linked together in in-law relationships. Client/patron relationships were also formed through marriage. A man who owned a lot of land needed a large labour force, and he was able to recruit more labour through the practice of polygyny and by marrying off his daughters to potential workers, who would remain grateful and loyal to him. For wife-givers were superior to wife-takers, in the sense that one should be grateful to one who gave him his daughter.

Rich or powerful women were also able to form client/patron relationships or master/servant relationships by undertaking to pay bridewealth for a man's marriage. In such cases, the man and his potential family would remain obliged to the woman patron. This way, women were able to recruit a large labour force and strong clientage. A barren woman was also able to gain her husband's favour through woman-to-woman marriage. Rich and powerful women, too, were able to free themselves from domestic responsibilities through woman-to-woman marriages First daughters especially had this privilege of woman-to-woman marriage, especially when there were no males in their natal homes. Men and women were therefore involved in the practice of marriage exchange.

Marriage Songs and Gender Roles

At no other time were wifehood and motherhood more stressed than during marriage ceremonies, especially during the carrying of palm-wine ceremony, after which a husband gained full rights over his wife. During this ceremony, wives as initiates and custodians of the fertility cult reigned supreme. Two payments were made to the lineage wives of the girl who was getting married. First, they were paid to remove the girl's waist charm which signified that she was sexually taboo. Then they were paid again to initiate her into the fertility cult, the climax of which was the ritual dance performed by the new bride and her husband to the song of the women. The women voiced the dominant ideology which gave women honour in wifehood. They sang:

> Be you as beautiful as a mermaid, the beauty
> of a woman is to have a husband.
>
> Be you one who has been to the land of white
> people, the beauty of a woman is to have a
> husband.
>
> If a woman does not marry, her beauty declines.
> One who is beautiful is best to be in her
> husband's house.
>
> When you get to your husband's house, have
> a baby.
>
> After you look after the child, the child will
> look after you.

The end of the marriage ceremony was symbolized by the *upiti*, fertility 'mud dance', when women poured palm-wine on the ground and sang to the newly married couple who danced on the mud. This was an exclusively female affair, performed behind the bride's mother's house. Some maintained that although a lot of youths join in this dance today, traditionally the only male present was the groom. During this occasion, wives as seasoned women and non-virgins sang lewd songs reproducing the sound and rhythm of copulation. Dancing on the mud made it even stickier, while the women sang,

> *Ana nwa-oo* [twice]
> *Udegwurude-e-e*
> *Biam biam ka m n'ebe-e-e* [twice]
> *Biam biam kanma n'ute*
> *Abiachaa ya, ka – a bialu nwa-o-o*
> *Biam biam ka nma n'ute* [twice]

The cry was for a child, and *biam biam* being in imitation of the act of copulation, the women sang that they cry *biam biam*. The verb *ibia* means 'stuffing up' or 'pressing down'. So the women sang that, after pressing down, or copulation, may a child result. They sang that *biam biam* was better done on the mat!

While producing sticky mud with their feet in rhythmic dancing, they sang,

> *Upiti upiti upiti nwa-o-o* [twice]
> *Onye muta ibe ya muta-o-o*
> *Upiti upiti upiti nwa-o-o*
> *Ka anyi zolu nwa n'okpa*
> *Zolu, zolu, nzolu nwa n'okpa.*

They sang about the mud associated with the desire for a baby, the idea of having a baby and the hope that others have babies, too. Again they sang about the mud,

> Oh mud, oh mud, baby mud.
> May we catch a baby in our feet.
> Catch, catch, catch a baby in my feet.
> Let me not be denied a child in this world and the next.
> Catch, catch, catch a baby in my feet.

Thus the marriage between a man and a woman was sealed by the women when they gave the couple licence to copulate and wished them conception through the act.

Two groups of women exercised power during marriage ceremonies: one, the wives of the bride's patrilineage, the other, the wives of the husband's patrilineage. After the fertility dance, the girl's patrilineage wives would hand her over to the wives of her husband's patrilineage, her new co-wives, who, after lifting an empty palm-oil pot on to her head, led her home. As they did so, the songs changed, and these other women reassured her of a better home. They sang that beauty was off to a better town, that she was going home, to her husband's home, and that her husband's town was a better town. As she approached her new home, the women would sing,

> She has arrived.
> If you look in the street you'll behold a beautiful one.

The women then declared their goodwill and support, welcoming the new member as they sang,

> *Umu nwanyi anyi ji obi ocha,*
> *Obi salasala obi sam*
> *Umu nwanyi anyi jikwanu obi ocha,*
> *Obi salasala obi sam.*

As the lead woman declared that the hearts of their women were clean, the others replied that their hearts were as clean as clean could be. Thus they accepted one more member into their own group of patrilineage wives.

Nnobi men called wives *oli aku* (one who enjoys wealth). Lots of women were known to grumble or retort sharply when addressed by this term, for their material situation or experience of strife denied such a claim. The term was perhaps true of the first few months of marriage in traditional times, when a young bride went through elaborate fertility rituals, after which she untied her elaborate, high-pointing hairstyle. She was then considered *nne nwanyi*, a fully fledged woman, with a household to cater for, and was expected to begin the business of selling and buying, buying and selling, *itu mgbele*, like other wives. She also received her own portion of land from her husband, which she was expected to farm for subsistence.

Birth

From the day of the carrying of palm-wine ceremony to the birth of a woman's first child, she went through various fertility rituals associated with sexuality and childbirth. The sequence of some of these rituals is no longer clear in the minds of Nnobi people who know about them, since most of them are no longer practised, the 'mud dance' being an exception. However, most of the rituals appear to have centred on a custom referred to as *ima ogodo*, in literal translation 'tying wrapper', which could indicate the process of becoming a woman or a mother.[3]

From Nwajiuba's and other women's accounts, most of the rituals involved in this ceremony were performed at a new bride's mother's home as soon as the first signs of pregnancy began to show. Uzuagu, however, reports that these rituals took place before pregnancy.

Two main people performed these initiations into motherhood. They were a female *dibia* and a woman referred to as *onyo ekete*, 'one who would tie a black string round the waist of the bride'. The ritual of tying the string was called *iwoyi ekete* or *itunye ashi*. It was accompanied by prayers and the pouring of libation and was attended by relatives and friends. The importance of the woman who conducted this ritual was signified by the fact that she received a jar of palm-wine during the carrying of palm-wine ceremony. This same woman, who appears to have had the status of 'mother of maternity', would also be given the 'gift to the mother of maternity', *ibu nne amu*, when the first child of the bride was born. This gift comprised yam, cocoyam, banana, plantain and a hen. It was not clear who exactly performed this role, but obviously she was a maternal relative of the bride. Those suggested were the eldest sister of the bride's mother, or the oldest woman in the bride's matrilineage. If there was no one to receive the gift, it was said to have been offered to the sun.

When the newly married girl became pregnant and her belly swelled with child, the preparation for the *ima ogodo* ceremony began with an elaborate plaiting of her hair. Then her body was beautified with fanciful tattoos, *egbugbu*, from her throat to her waist.[4] In Uzuagu's account, this was done at the husband's home, but according to the women, it was done at the young bride's mother's. During the tattooing, the girl's husband would meet all the expenses for a goat and the delicious dishes which the girl would feed on to help her endure the pain from the cuts, until the scars healed.

Then *ima nsi*, the ritual which symbolized both nodality of a man and a woman in procreation, and training in motherhood, was performed. One double-seeded palm-nut, *aku nkpi*, and a fish were provided. A female *dibia* would then ask the couple to interlock their fingers while the kernel of the palm-nut and the fish were broken in two and shared between them. This symbolized their unity, regardless of what the future might hold for them. The female *dibia* would then pray for good health, long life and prosperous children.

Next, the female *dibia* would either make or buy a wooden doll and paint it with red paint, *ushe*. This doll was put in a straw basket and given to the bride to care for as if it were her child. A token payment of eight yams and eight cowries, *ego n'asato*, was made to the *dibia*.

Next was the ritual for warding off evil spirits, referred to as *aja uke*. On the eve of this ritual, a bride was not supposed to sleep with her husband, or in her father's home, but stay with a bachelor relative of her husband. On the day of this ritual, a *dibia* would wake the girl before first cock crow, and take her to the evil forest, *ajo ofia*. There, he would prepare a concoction which the bride would throw into the evil forest, and then walk to her husband's home without looking back. She was expected to wash her hands with potash, *ngu*, before entering her marital home.

From the ceremonial return to her marital home, the young bride would be treated as a full adult woman and dressed as such. This was symbolized by tying the wrapper.* She was expected to hang the little bag containing the painted doll on her wrist, and carry it wherever she went, even to the market. On her way to the market, other women seeing the bag would ask to see her baby; she would then bring out the doll and give it to them. The women would take the doll and rub off some of the red paint on to their own bellies, while they told the young wife how pretty her baby was; then they would give the doll back to her with some money for the baby, *ego nwa*.

This went on until the young wife had a real baby and could pet it rather than the doll; she would then take the doll off her wrist. Some women were believed to have kept their doll till they had had three or four children; it was thought that the doll then disappeared by itself.

The *ima ogodo* ceremony was said to end when the child was presented in the central market. During this ceremony, relatives and friends made merry and gave gifts to the child. The husband would buy his wife a nice piece of cloth for a wrapper. On the day of the outing, the woman was dressed up by her mother's relatives and given an umbrella to shield her from the sun. Relatives from both sides would then lead the young wife and her husband to the market, accompanied by a young boy and girl carrying the chairs on which they would sit. They would stop at each stall, sit on the chairs and receive presents, including money and palm-wine, from well-wishers.

*Prior to this she had worn only waistbeads, now her body is covered. Tying the wrapper in Igbo society is a symbol of female social maturity; the passage from girlhood to womanhood.

The Post-Natal Confinement: *Ino Ngwuo*

It was generally claimed that traditionally, when a woman gave birth, a hole in which she could urinate was dug at the back of her house. It was also in this hole that the afterbirth, *akpa nwa*, was buried. For the first child, they would take a banana leaf and put it on the ground in front of the woman's house and place her child on it. Even if the woman went to a midwife to have the baby, the child was still washed and placed on a banana leaf. Then the wooden door was removed and taken indoors and the child was placed on it. A pestle was then hit on the wood four times, to accustom the child to shock and prevent it from starting at unexpected sounds. Palm-nut or coconut was chewed and rubbed on the breasts of the woman for four days to help them ripen. The child would then begin to drink its mother's milk. It was said that a nursing mother in the neighbourhood used to feed the baby till its mother's breasts were ripe enough for the baby to suck.

Only a woman's husband was allowed in on the first day after the birth of a child. While a woman was giving birth, men were not allowed in, although there were male *dibia*(s) who acted as midwives. Immediately after the birth, if the woman's mother lived close by, she would visit her daughter daily to help her. After 12 days, the mother was expected to move into her daughter's home to fulfil the post-natal services required for her, as it was taboo for a new mother to work; she was supposed to stay in bed, and be washed there.

The mother's visit, *ino ngwuo*, was institutionalized and followed prescribed rules. As she was going to take over duties normally performed by her daughter, especially cooking, she would take with her sauce, seasoning ingredients and dried fish. She would also bring herbs and spices specially used in preparing soup for a woman who had just given birth and was lactating. A man had to treat his wife's mother with respect. He was expected to provide his wife with enough yam and meat for the period of her mother's visit, which lasted for seven market weeks, 28 days, at the minimum. At the end of the visit, the wife's mother would be given presents by her son-in-law and her daughter. A clever daughter usually assessed her mother's material needs and used this opportunity to procure them for her; they normally included pieces of cloth for wrappers, jewellery and cooking utensils. Her husband provided or contributed money for their purchase, and also gave his mother-in-law food items, such as yam and palm-oil.

The post-natal confinement in bed was also called *inu nmili oku*, 'drinking hot water', because of the very peppery thin soup prepared with smoked fish and medicinal herbs. It was believed to help clean out the womb, enrich the blood and restore energy quickly. The mother at the same time pressed her daughter's womb and vagina morning and evening with very hot water, to ease aches and bruises. The stomach was tied very tightly with dry bark from the banana stem to help contraction of the womb. Some believed that it was the girl's mother who breastfed the baby for the first few days before milk began to flow from her daughter's breasts. The drinking of palm-wine was also supposed to help the milk flow.

During the period of post-natal confinement a woman was in a state of sexual taboo.[5] She was restricted to the female section of the compound while her mother took over both her household duties and farm work. A popular Nnobi saying especially used by women was that one did not visit a new-born baby empty handed, and women visitors would invoke blessings on the baby with presents. Women also made white chalk marks on their faces to indicate that they had been to see a new-born baby; this was supposed to bring good luck. Generally, contact with a new baby was greatly desired and cherished. Women said that it brought good luck when a baby urinated or excreted on someone; infertile women pressed a new baby to their wombs and silently prayed for a child.

Circumcision took place after eight days, and the baby's hair was also shaved. A girl's first hair was buried in the roots of a palm tree, a boy's in the roots of a kola-nut tree. In Nnobi both sexes[6] were circumcised and after circumcision, it was believed that a baby should be nursed and touched only by its mother. If someone else were to touch it, the wound would not heal. The ceremony called *ime mputa*, coming out, was performed after 28 days. The child was brought out to the *obi* to be introduced to its lineage group and named. After this ceremony, the woman's mother could go home, but if her daughter was still weak or ill, she might postpone her departure.

An effective sanction used by mothers against their daughters was the refusal to make the post-natal visit. If that happened, the woman would be left at the mercy of co-wives, who were not to be trusted, or her mother-in-law or husband's sisters, who might dislike her and wish to get rid of her. They were not really duty bound to help her, but might do so out of goodwill. In this culture, with its strong belief in sorcery, only an immediate sibling or a mother was to be trusted, not even a husband and father, who might prefer one wife and her children to another. One Nnobi saying, used mainly by women, is, 'a man's hatred for a wife affects her children'. Scapegoating in Nnobi was through the accusation of sorcery, not witchcraft.

After a few months, the new mother and her baby would be dressed in their best clothes and accompanied to the market, where they would be given presents, and the women would sing songs of the joys, pains and rewards of motherhood. The woman would then go back to her farming, selling and buying routine, carrying her baby fastened on her back, with a piece of her wrapper.

Maternity Songs and Gender Roles

When a child was born, statements about its future sex role were made through songs. In modern versions of some of these songs Western commodities feature. Thus in one song a male child was referred to as a taxi.[7] The Nnobi say that first parents look after children, later children look after parents. Males were regarded as those who would remain in the natal home and later inherit the responsibilities of their parents. For male children, the women sang that having a boy was very good, because it was men who owned profit, or fortune, *obu nwoke nwe ulu*. They added that their sons would build storeyed houses and buy cars.

When a female child was born, she was referred to as a bag of money. The song is as follows:

> One has given birth to a bag of money.
> Thanks be to God.
> This cloth I wear is money.
> This meat I eat is money.
> This fish I eat is money.
> This child I have is money.

Thus the importance of women in terms of exchange was stressed. Women also sang that they had given birth to a daughter who would cook for them and marry a good husband.

They also sang about the reality of their situation. Both power and security for women as wives were linked to their ability to give birth and to their role as mothers. For this reason, at the birth of a first child, the women sang that a child had been born, one may enjoy wealth and fortune and the mind was now at rest. They sang,

> If not for the power of giving birth, who will give me?
> Buy white fowl, who will give me?
> Bring white palm-white, who will give me?
> If not for the power of giving birth, who will give me?
>
> *O bughi ma nwa-o-o, onye ga enye m*
> *Gota okuko ocha-a-a, onye ga enye m*
> *Bute nkwu ocha-a-a, onye ga enye m*
> *O bughi ma nwa-a-a, onye ga enye m.*

Usually the atmosphere was highly charged emotionally when women sang and danced to such songs. Barren women might weep, women maltreated by their husbands in spite of having had many children could become uncontrollably violent. The happy ones became radiant and some, with tears in their eyes, sang to their fellow women to remain in their marital homes for the benefits of childbirth. The song went like this,

> We have come here because of the birth of
> a child.
>
> Spectators, it is for the sake of a child that
> we have come here showing our happiness.
>
> The mother who has given birth to this child,
> stay in your husband's house and look upon what
> is good.
>
> Chika's mum, remain in your husband's house
> and behold what is good.

They did not fail to offer some advice to the baby and also make a statement about the sleepless nights mothers have for the sake of crying babies! And so they sang to the baby,

> Listen to what your mother tells you,
> Listen to what your father tells you,
> Keep awake during the day
> But sleep during the night.

As the culture stressed and glorified maternity, so did the women stress their power and importance as the bearers of children. They claimed that they were principal, for without them children would not be born. They sang,

> *Nwanyi bu isi okwu . . . bu isi okwu,*
> *Ogbughi nwanyi kedu ka aga esi muta nwa*
> *Kedu ka aga esi muta nwa.*

'Woman is principal . . . is principal,
Without a woman, how can a child be born?
How can a child be born?'

Death

At funerals, as in marriage, the circulation of goods and the involvement of non-lineage members were traced through women. At marriage, a daughter's mother would give her a goat, which at her death, owing to her status as a mother, was returned to her patrilineage.

A first son was duty bound to provide a goat for the funeral ceremony of his mother. For the funeral of either father or mother, the first daughter's husband was also expected to provide a goat. A goat was always returned to where a movement had taken place, that is, to those who gave away a woman to another lineage where she produced a child. A goat was therefore always given to the dead person's mother's patrilineage, who would be the classificatory ancient-parents of the deceased.

When a father died, one movement was traced: that made by his mother. His mother's patrilineage would therefore be given a goat. But when a mother died, two movements were traced. One movement was that made by the dead woman. Her patrilineage would get a goat, which would cancel out the original goat given to her at marriage. The second movement was that made by the mother of the dead woman. A goat would also be given to the patrilineage from which the mother originated. A goat was always returned to the owners of, or the lineage of, *isi nmili*, the source of the spring – the mother. This was compulsory, regardless of whether the parents of the deceased were alive or not. The ancient-parents category was usually considerate and would accept whatever was available, but they could not be deceived or cheated. If they were offered something below the status of their daughter, they could refuse it and nothing could then be done about it. Their quick eyes would assess what was generally available, and accept what was best. In most cases they would get a goat. But with high-status funerals they would be given no less than a cow. Whatever animal was given to them, it symbolized the returned soul of their daughter. When given this animal, they would go home pretending they were going back with their daughter.

The ancient-parent category, though very lenient towards their daughters' offspring, could be difficult to please during funerals. The gift exchange involving these categories was always the most dramatic part of a funeral. This can be seen from the account of the funeral of a 79-year-old man I attended in 1980. It is also further evidence of how little customary procedures involving life-cycle ceremonies have changed since the 19th century. At this funeral, the deceased man's mother's patrilineage had refused the goat offered to them and almost brought the funeral ceremony to a halt. The husband of the deceased man's first daughter had presented a cow, which was displayed in front of the compound; the dead man's sons, who were mostly traders, had provided four goats. As with most ceremonies in Nnobi, display was an essential part of the event. Each group of people bringing presents moved in procession, displaying what they had brought for all to see, so that everyone knew what had been presented. In fact, a man was usually assigned to announce the groups as they arrived and shout out what presents they brought. During this funeral, the dead man's classificatory ancient-parents had seen the cow displayed outside the compound, and had assumed it would be offered to them. But the sons had planned to sell the cow to offset some of the funeral expenses, and therefore offered a goat instead.

The goat they offered was the smallest of the four, and this enraged the deceased's ancient-parents, who were squatting on the ground in anticipation, man and woman. Their response was to treat the dead man's sons with contempt by pretending not to notice them, and continuing to chat to each other. The sons quickly assessed the situation and called their father's brother to plead with his ancient-parents, as they expected them to be more lenient towards him. As the dead man's brother approached, he was told to kneel down, take off his hat and bow his head while he spoke. This was the uncompromising customary way in which he was expected to address his ancient-parents. He relayed to them the excuse given by the deceased man's sons, that they were short of money and that their father had not left them enough cash for his funeral. The goat was still refused, and a huge crowd was beginning to gather: the rumour would soon spread that the ancient-parents had refused their present. This would bring shame on the dead man's sons.

The sons quickly sent their uncle back to offer two goats, which were still refused. Their uncle was now on his knees, pleading. Then a question was put to the sons. They were asked to say whether their daughter (the dead man's mother) had not produced a child worth a cow. That is, was their father not worth a cow? To this question, there was no reply. The cow was there before the eyes of the ancient-parents, yet the sons had dared to offer them the skinniest of the goats. Throughout, people standing by made such comments as, 'They've seen the cow, they'll not accept anything less.' Others said that the sons were insolent by daring to offer a small goat to their father's *ikwunne*, when in-laws had presented no less than a cow. People were commenting that there should have been two cows. They said that the sons should be ashamed of themselves, since they would have buried their father, a man of such high status, without a cow. Had he not lived to old age? Did he not have two wives who had produced many sons? Had in-laws not provided a cow? In the end, the classificatory ancient-parents of the deceased took the cow home in jubilation.

The more married daughters one had, the grander one's funeral in terms of the number of goats, pieces of cloth and presents to be offered. The married daughters whose husbands brought cloth, took it back when they left after the funeral. Money, wine, white cloth and live animals presented at the funeral were for disposal by the sons; in-laws who brought presents took presents home. Classificatory ancient-parents, as well as receiving presents, also brought presents, such as pound notes, stuck on long sticks for all to see, wine and kola-nuts. The white cloth they brought was buried with the dead.

As presents and people were mobilized for funerals through married daughters, so were they mobilized through marrying many wives. Each wife's patrilineage was an in-law group and classificatory ancient-parents to her children, and took presents to support these children at any funerals affecting them. They alone shared presents brought by their ancient-parents. Any of the sons who was married would take what was brought by his in-laws. Daughters or their siblings would take what their husbands brought and share it with them. Any of the sons in an organization would take whatever that organization brought. Those who took what was brought by any specific group were the only ones who would buy presents required to support the specific group when they in turn suffered a bereavement. Their family or lineage members would only accompany them. What was left after each group had gone off with its return presents was sold to meet the cost of the funeral. The sons shared the money according to how much they each contributed to the cost of the funeral.

All those who were meant to bring things to a funeral were involved in relationships traced through the female sex. They were in-laws of the deceased; the dead person's mother's patrilineage; in the case of a woman, her own patrilineage, too; the lineages of the mothers of the dead person's children; and the children of the deceased person's daughters. All these categories received presents in return. The all-important category of patrilineage daughters of the deceased brought no presents, but took presents home.

The display of presents and the wrangling over who got what took the grief out of a funeral. While lineage daughters sat around watching carefully to see when an animal was going to be killed so that they could claim its rump, the dead person's mother's lineage waited to claim the best animal available. Usually only wives of a deceased man were expected to look miserable and forlorn.

Mourning

In the traditional society, as in the present day, hardly any taboos surrounded a man's mourning of his wife. He was said only to have feared possible accusations of maltreatment or murder, founded or unfounded, by his deceased wife's group of patrilineage daughters and her patrilineage as a whole. They owned the body, they had lost a member, therefore they were expected to arrive at the funeral suspicious and angry. If they discovered that their daughter had died as a result of maltreatment, they could refuse to take the body back until compensation was paid. As a wife's marital lineage did not have the right to bury her, the patrilineage's refusal to bury her usually led to war.

A man was said to be free to remarry soon after he had buried his wife. Thirty-six days after the burial, he would shave his hair and go about his business. This was not the case with a woman mourning the death of her husband. Women who recounted the indigenous mourning rituals said that women in mourning for their husbands went through hell-fire, *oku nmuo*. When they cried and feared the death of a husband, it was not so much out of loss, but through dread of the punishment in store for them.

Traditionally, on the day a woman's husband died, she would undo and spread her hair and begin to look sorrowful as she entered a state of ritual taboo, which lasted for a period of one year, *ino na ijita*. During this period, she was expected always to hold a kitchen knife; she would not socialize with other people; titled men would not eat food cooked by her or speak to her or respond to her greetings.

If she had not been living in peace with her husband, she would begin to 'buy', that is, bribe the *ukozala* titled men who acted as the police (see Chapter 3) to permit her to shave her hair. If in any way she broke the rule of mourning, it would be revealed to these same titled men, and she would then have to negotiate with them. For two consecutive nights before talking of cutting her hair, she would perform the ceremony known as *ibo ihe nze*, paying the titled men their due. This involved giving them two she-goats. She was then allowed to shave her hair completely.

Then a small hut would be built for her, and she had to wear a wrapper of black bark-cloth (*aji*) which she could discard only after a one year mourning period. She remained isolated in the little hut, and should never wash her hands before eating food; whoever cooked her food would only pass it to her from a safe distance. After the ritual of shaving her hair, she was not allowed to wash her hands with water for three market weeks, 12 days; then the hand-washing ritual was performed, *ikwo aka ito*. At the same time, the ceremony called *ikpo ntu ito*, clearing the ash of three market weeks, 12 days, was performed. All the rubbish was swept and put in the bad bush. The woman was then allowed to wash her hands before and after eating her meal. It was *onye nke ya*, her own person – her child or her sister – who would feed her. After seven market weeks, 28 days, she performed another cleansing ritual known as *ikpo ntu isa*, clearing the ash of seven market weeks. She would then come out of the little hut. While she was still in the little hut, those who were not present during the ceremony when her head was shaved had to rub money over their eyes and then throw it to her when they came to visit her.

On the day of coming out of the little hut, she would invite lineage daughters of her marital lineage and present food to them, *itukwu ha ashi*, in the same manner in which her husband used to give foodstuff to her. She would take a small, flat basket in which she arranged yam, cocoyam and plantain; the lineage daughters would then cook the yam for breakfast, mix the cocoyam and plantain with palm-oil and spice, and eat. A female *dibia* would then shave the widowed woman's hair and release her from the little hut. On the same day she would put on a black neckband. For this ritual, the female *dibia* was given pounded food and wine, and additional pounded food to take home. All the clothes used by the woman while she was in the little hut were disposed of in the bad bush.

After three market weeks, 12 days, she performed the ceremony known as *izu afia uchichi*, selling in the market at night. She would take her trading basket and, accompanied by another woman, would trade by night. After this, she performed yet another trading ceremony – *izu ahia mbu ego* – by which she learnt to trade for cash or money again. The widowed woman would go to the market with a female companion to whom she would give some cowrie shells, asking her to go and buy her some snuff. They would then go home. She could then begin to trade again on market days.

I asked the elderly woman, Nwajiuba, what happened to a woman at the death of a husband with whom she was known not to be living in harmony. Nwajiuba, who clearly considered the mourning ritual to be a punishment, replied,

Her punishment was not greater. She went through the same ritual, except that her father's lineage daughters might fine her if they so wished. Witch-hunting after a death has always gone on. Someone may go and tell lineage daughters that a woman died from ill-treatment by her children, quarrels might result from this and fines might be levied. This in fact happened when my mother died. She told my older sister to go and call Egoeme, who belonged to the same organization of patrilineage daughters as herself, and another woman at Ezenabo's, called Ochaekwe. These women were summoned but I did not know why they were sent for. My mother's elder sister did not visit during my mother's illness. My mother therefore told these women that she knew that, when she died, her elder sister might tell them that it was Nwajiuba, her daughter, who ill-treated her. She told them that this would be incorrect.

A widow, *ajadu*, was still legally bound to her husband's patrilineage. After the year's mourning, she was ritually cleansed and accepted back into society. The widow, especially if she was still of childbearing age, was inherited by her husband's brother, a custom known as *nkuchi nwanyi* (widow inheritance).

Since women had access to land only as wives, a husband's death placed a woman in a state of great insecurity. As a Nnobi saying puts it, 'The woman whose husband died was crying, saying that while there was discussion about who should bury her husband, one should also discuss who should inherit her.'[8] Though there was the notion of group marriage, group consummation was not practised. When a woman was inherited by her husband's brother, the marriage ceremony was not repeated, for she was the collective wife of the group. All the man would do was to give her a kitchen knife, *nma ekwu*. Thus he would symbolically welcome her into his particular household.

The legal right on the fertility of a wife was so strong that if a widow produced a child by a man not in her husband's lineage, the child would still belong to her husband's lineage. For this reason, there was a very male saying, 'If a woman refused her husband her vagina, it would not deny him the child from it.'[9] It is no surprise then that, in this culture, if a man with no brothers died his adult son might inherit the widows except, of course, for his own mother (see Chapter 7). This happened most frequently in the case of a son who was to replace his father in the *obi*. A son who would succeed his father in the *obi* need not allow his own mother to be inherited by other lineage men if she did not wish it, for he would be in a powerful position to protect her and *obi* property.

Funeral Songs and Gender Roles

During birth and marriage, women as wives and mothers controlled communication through song and dance. They stressed the importance of wifehood and motherhood. At death, the deceased's daughters transmitted cultural norms through songs and dance. Qualities and roles ascribed to males and females were echoed in their songs. A dead man was, for example, referred to as a leopard, a much feared carnivorous animal. His lineage daughters sang that no one should touch a leopard, *agu*, on its tail, whether it was alive or dead; that no one should poke his finger into the eye of the baby of a leopard, whether it was alive or dead. They thus perpetuated the fearful, punitive and protective image of the male. Those men who lived up to the ideal image of a full male would be expected to leave behind property and family when they died. It was therefore important to warn off would-be usurpers. To perpetuate the forceful and courageous male image, the dead man was also referred to as *ebunu ji isi eje ogu*, 'ram who fights with his head', that is, one who meets danger or takes on a fight head-on.

In this culture, the death or loss of a mother was the most painful experience, since motherhood was glorified. When a woman died, other women, especially those close to the deceased, expressed their grief freely in uncontrolled shrieking, weeping or throwing themselves on the ground, generally in a state of disarray. In this culture, even though it was not a manly thing to weep, people spoke kindly of a man who wept at the death of his mother. Women especially spoke of how impossible it was to exercise self-control on issues affecting one's mother.

At no other funeral did lineage daughters sing their hearts out as during that of a sister who had died as a wife elsewhere. The grief was usually so great that they opened their songs with statements of disbelief such as 'Our sister who came here on marriage journey, we heard she is dead, so we have come to find out if it is true.' Having thus established death as a fact, they would accuse death of theft: 'Death is a thief, yes. Death, I say you are a thief. You carry things and run away with them.'

Another very moving song when a woman died before old age was: 'Do you know that hot pepper has gone into our eyes? Since she died suddenly, we will mourn her or cry her death heatedly with all our emotions.' '*Onwulu n'ike n'ike, anyi ga akwa ya n'ike n'ike.*' In another song, they sang praises of the dead woman as having fulfilled all that was expected of her as a woman – economic resourcefulness and motherhood. But they regretted that she did not stay to enjoy the fruits of her labour.

> This woman has goats,
> She has left food.
> This woman has dogs,
> She has left food.
> This woman has brought up children
> And has not reaped the reward,
> May God accept your soul.

Folk-tales and Gender Roles

Women transmitted cultural ideas and their own comments on them through stories as well as songs. Men also told stories, but as children spent most of their time with women, their stories were the best known. Men told stories about wars, travels, adventures with spirits; these were very male tales told to boys. But what was common to most of the stories, whether told by men or women, was the fact that the heroes and heroines were motherless children, orphans or paupers, who always vanquished the more privileged by miraculous or magical means. Motherhood was glorified by showing the suffering and loneliness of children who had no mother. Usually their mothers reappeared to kill off their foes. The loss of a mother caused greater suffering than the loss of a father. Stepmothers were always villains; favouritism by fathers was common.

As each wife's dwelling was autonomous, that is, demarcated and independent from those of the other wives, when a wife died, if her children were still too young to fend for themselves, they usually moved into the abode of one of their father's other wives. If their mother was an only wife, their father quickly remarried, or the children were sent to live with the wife of one of their relations. They might even be sent to their mother's lineage, to be raised there and returned later. Orphans, in any case, usually found themselves living as servants with relatives or strangers. As folk-tales show, orphans suffered, since they had no one to protect them.

There is a story about a child maltreated by a stepmother: a woman died after giving birth to one child. Her husband remarried and the motherless child was ill-treated by his new wife. She soon had a child of her own and would put food for the motherless child high up out of reach and that of her own child on the ground within reach. The motherless child cried and sang and mourned the death of her own mother, and begged her to appear. Then one day when the child was crying on her mother's grave, spirits appeared and asked what was troubling her. When she told them, they asked her to be patient, her mother was on her way to her. When she appeared, and the child told her of her troubles, her mother said she should go home, that she would look into the matter. Again the stepmother cooked and left the child's food high up and the child began to cry again. Her mother immediately appeared and beat the other woman to death.

The most popular of these stories known by every Nnobi, or every Igbo child for that matter, is the *udala* story. Udala is a fruit tree under which children played. They picked its fruit to eat between meals or while their mothers were away. According to this story, a child's father's wife, her stepmother, bought *udala* from the market and gave only to her own children and none to the motherless child. The other children tantalized the motherless child with their own *udala*, and after they had eaten it and spat out the seeds, the motherless child picked up a seed and planted it, and wet it with her tears while singing to it:

> Oh my *udala* grow,
> Grow, grow, grow,
> My father's wife bought *udala* from the market,
> gave only to her children and did not give to this
> motherless one.
> This world is a visiting place,
> We stay and depart.

As she sang, the seed germinated, grew and produced fruits. The other children, out of greed, quickly climbed the tree; again the motherless child sang and the tree grew very high and the children stayed up there and died.

According to another story, the father gave yam to his wife to cook for all his children. The stepmother cheated and gave the motherless child the tail end, which is always bitter. The child expressed its grief in song:

> King Ndumuche when going to cultivate yam,
> Gave yam to his children, but gave the tail
> end to an orphan.
> When roasted, it is bitter;
> When cooked in a pot, it is bitter;
> If this is wrong, may it rain all day.

Immediately, it started to rain, and went on for countless days and disturbed the farming. Soon someone went to tell the king the cause of it all. From that day onwards, the child got yam like the other children.

Stepmothers were more cruel to male children, especially if the child was the first son, who would inherit his father's position. They might even poison the child's food. They were not so wicked to female children, for Nnobi say that *nwanyi bu aku*, 'woman is wealth'. After a girl had grown up, she was married off, and the stepmother would then have in-laws, with all the benefits that entailed. The state of being motherless, *ogbenye nne*, was considered a terrible thing. *Ogbenye* is, in fact, the word for a poor person.

In the male-oriented stories, orphans and paupers, on account of their modesty, were, in war, usually aided by supernatural powers to show such gallantry that, for example, they rescued their town from enemies; they might then be made king. Sometimes a king showed his gratitude by giving his daughter in marriage to an orphan. In these stories, in common with similar tales in many cultures, the greed and arrogance of the more privileged children were usually punished. A group of children, for example, would be lost in the wild and come to a crossroads where each direction promised something. The privileged, 'spoilt' children usually followed the road which promised the richest reward, only to meet seven-headed devils or some other monsters who would beat them to death. The pauper or motherless child was usually modest, and accepted little, but then met with the greatest reward at the end of the road. In the women's stories, the stepmother's greedy children were usually punished with death.

What I have tried to demonstrate here is that Nnobi women have always been articulate and not mere objects circulated among or acted upon by their men-folk. On the contrary, Nnobi women made political use of their roles as daughters, wives and mothers. While daughters sought and exercised power through the control of the funerals of patrilineage members, wives and mothers also exercised power through the control of fertility ceremonies during marriage and childbirth. Through songs dealing with these life-cycle rituals and ceremonies, women generated favourable gender ideologies and stressed the social importance of their various roles and duties, irrespective of anti-female rules and practices embodied in the patriarchal aspects of the culture.

Notes

1. *Igba udu oma* is not easily rendered into English. *Igba* means to dance, *udu* is a kind of pot used as a musical instrument, *ibi oma* means to embrace. This could therefore be translated as a 'ritual dance of embrace'. As this does not indicate the purpose of the ritual, I have used the expression, 'a ritual to separate blood relationship'. I have sometimes found conveying meaning more useful than literal translations which have no equivalent meaning in the English language.

2. *Ndudugandu si na nke ito pua na ino, si mebe, mana oto na nke ito, a'gba udu oma.* A similar compromise solution by the Onitsha Igbo to allow marriage between certain people in incestuous relationships was recorded by Henderson (1972:197) and already cited in the Introduction.

3. Detailed data on this were given to me by Nwajiuba, who has already been acknowledged several times. See also Uzuagu 1978.

4. An illustration of a tattooed woman is reproduced in Basden 1938, between pp. 336 and 337.

5. A man was forbidden to have sexual intercourse with his wife from the birth of her child to the end of the recommended lactation period of at least two years.

6. Female circumcision in these northern Igbo areas is described in detail by Basden (1938:176–8). During fieldwork in Nnobi, I found no evidence to show that it is still practised. On the contrary, this was one of the old customs which Nnobi women spoke about with bitterness. The last women to have been circumcised must now be over 60 years of age. The ban on circumcision was one of the church regulations which was welcomed by the local people. As Basden writes, 'it is interesting to note that this prohibition was enacted by the native members independently of the Europeans' (1939:178).

In view of the controversy between Third World women and Western feminists surrounding the issue of female circumcision, I do not propose to deal with this problem in detail here; it is, anyway, no longer practised in Nnobi. However, many reasons why it was practised can be suggested. The obvious one, from a feminist perspective, is that it was a means of controlling women, checking their sexuality and ensuring their subordination. It might even be claimed that this custom marked the point of an incursion of patriarchy into a matriarchal community. My own opinion is that originally Igbo society was matriarchal and only later were patriarchal ideologies introduced, either by some other group or groups or influential individuals. However, the women I interviewed claimed that circumcision was done for hygienic purposes: to keep the passage clean and open for safe and easy childbirth. From Basden's account, the operation entailed excision of the clitoris and the labia minora, and the vagina was slit at the base as far as the thick tissue; this would support the claim that it was associated with childbirth. Some also said the purpose was to treat male and female babies in strictly the same way; simply left the clitoris fully exposed, that what was removed was equivalent to a circumcised penis. This would support Seabrook's account (in Basden 1938:177–8).

7. Taxi may have been used in the true meaning of the word, that is, something which carries passengers. If so, the women may have been acknowledging the position of authority of the male as someone who would have dependants, like wife and children.

8. *Nwanyi di ya nwulu n'ebezi akwa si, ana agbakwa izu onye g'eni di ya, si na*

agbakwa izu onye ga ekuchi ya. I am grateful to Professor John Umeh, a keen Nnobi traditionalist, for this information.

9. *Ilopulum otu, oya apum nwa.* This saying was also provided by and explained to me by Professor John Umeh.

5. The Ideology of Gender

The preceding chapters demonstrate a system of social organization in indigenous Nnobi society, based on strict sexual dualism, whereby women's economic and political organizations were separate from those of men. We have also seen how, through the manipulation of gender concepts and flexible gender construction in language, the dual-sex barrier is broken down or mediated. Thus, certain categories of women, for example daughters or wealthy women, defined or classified as 'males', gained access to positions of authority in the power structure. The aim of this chapter is to examine the contradictions and inconsistencies in Nnobi culture that made this gender system possible. To this end, the gender structure of the language and the socialization process will be considered.

Language and Gender

It is my thesis that the Igbo non-distinctive subject pronoun allows a more flexible semantic system, in which it is possible for men and women to share attributes. This system of few linguistic distinctions between male and female gender also makes it possible for men and women to play some social roles which, in other cultures, especially those of the Western world, carry rigid sex and gender association.

There is a biological gender distinction of male and female of any species in Igbo terminology. *Oke* means male, and *nyi* means female. The terms for man and woman are *nwoke* and *nwanyi*. These are contracted forms of two words, *nwa*, child, and the respective gender words, *oke*, male, and *nyi*, female, hence the distinction, male child and female child. But in subject pronouns, no distinction is made between male and female. The third person singular, *O*, stands for both male and female, unlike the English gender construction, which distinguishes male and female as 'he' and 'she'. As a result, many Igbo people, when speaking English, interchange 'he' and 'she', 'his' and 'her'. In Igbo, the third person singular of the possessive pronoun *ya* stands for both his and hers; thus there is no reminder in speech to distinguish between the sexes.

It can, therefore, be claimed that the Igbo language, in comparison with English for example, has not built up rigid associations between certain adjectives or attributes and gender subjects, nor certain objects and gender possessive pronouns. The genderless word *mmadu*, humankind, applies to both sexes. There is no usage, as there is in English, of the word 'man' to represent both sexes, neither is there the cumbersome option of saying 'he or she', 'his or her', 'him or her'. In Igbo, *O* stands for he, she and even it, *a* stands for the impersonal one, and *nya* for the imperative, let him or her.

This linguistic system of few gender distinctions makes it possible to conceptualize certain social roles as separate from sex and gender, hence the possibility for either sex to fill the role. This, of course, does not rule out competition between the sexes, and situations in which a particular sex tends to monopolize roles and positions, and generates and stresses anti-opposite sex gender ideologies in order to maintain its own interests.

The two examples of situations in which women played roles ideally or normally occupied by men – what I have called male roles – in indigenous Nnobi society (see Chapter 1) were as 'male daughters' and 'female husbands'; in either role, women acted as family head. The Igbo word for family head is the genderless expression *di-bu-no*. The genderless *di* is a prefix word which means specialist in, or expert at, or master of something.[1] Therefore, *di-bu-no* means one in a master relationship to a family and household, and a person, woman or man, in this position is simply referred to as *di-bu-no*. In indigenous Nnobi society and culture, there was one head or master of a family at a time, and 'male daughters' and 'female husbands' were called by the same term, which translated into English would be 'master'. Some women were therefore masters to other people, both men and women.

The reverse applied to those in a wife relationship to others. The Igbo word for wife, *onye be*, is a genderless expression meaning a person who belongs to the home of the master of the home. The other words for wife, *nwunye* or *nwanyi*, female or woman, also denote one in a subordinate, service or domestic relationship to one in a master position.[2] It was therefore possible for some men to be addressed by the term 'wife', as they were in service or domestic relationship to a master. An example of this was the hereditary title known as *nwunye nonu*, wife *nonu*, as the holder of this title was in domestic relationship to the man who held the title known as *ozo Aho*.[3] There is a series of contradictions here, for on the one hand, there is a suggestion of gender, not sexual, asymmetry; there were, for example, women in master or husband roles and men in wifely or domestic roles. On the other hand, even though domestic roles embodied a classification into a subordinate female gender, apart from 'male daughters', the master or husband role did not necessitate a male classification. 'Female husbands' were not males in the way that daughters were. In spite of these contradictions in gender statuses and roles, in general men were husbands, women wives.

The term for family, *ndi be*, which means people of one's home, is normally used in relation to the head of the family, who is, ideally, a man. This expression indicates the subordination of all other members of the family to the family head. The same idea is indicated in terms of address and greeting. To a family head, the usual question in greeting is, 'How are the people of your family?' *Kedu maka ndi be gi?* Of a wife, it would be asked, 'How are the children?' *Umuaka kwanu?*

Thus, terms of relationship state the ideal, while in daily speech describing social actions or processes, the ideal is contradicted when language states the factual. For example, people say that they are going to visit sections of the family compound by name. If they are going to the female section, they identify the woman they are going to visit either by her name or by reference to her first child, using the expression 'the place of the mother of so-and-so'. If they are going to the male section, then they use the expression 'the place of so-and-so', using the name of the male head of the family. The female section was most frequently visited, with women and children constantly borrowing things and transmitting messages. Households were therefore best known in the social process by the names of wives and children. Ideally, family compounds were understood to be the *obi* of the male master of the compound, yet the expression for natal home is *ebe nne nolu mua onye*, 'the place where one was borne by one's mother'. But, collectively, everyone was of the male master's compound, *ndi be* so-and-so, the people of such-and-such a man's compound. There was therefore a clear distinction between family and household, household being female-headed, while family was headed by a male.

Terms of subjection were contradicted in social process by facts of female autonomy, whether in the family structure or the relations of production. As the contradiction in gender relations in indigenous Nnobi society was between subjection and autonomy, subordination of the female did not necessarily result in subjugation. As was shown in Chapters 3 and 4, males and females made political use of the roles in which they were defined. According to an Igbo saying, 'When a man begins to ill-treat his wife, his world becomes confusing, and when a woman begins to ill-treat her husband, her vagina becomes dry.' Weapons of war, in this context were food and sex. Men showed grief, hurt and resentment by refusing to eat the food cooked by an offending wife. Similarly, a hurt wife would refuse her husband sexual compliance.

The use of these weapons of war must be understood in the context of polygynous marriage and compound structure. Of course it was possible for a man to turn to another wife when one wife refused to have sexual relations with him. The important point here is that women lived separately. The fact that a wife did not spend the night with her husband made it possible for her to use sexual refusal as a weapon of war without running the risk of marital rape. This is not the case for women in monogamous marriages who cling to the Christian idea of the sanctity and sexual exclusiveness of their matrimonial beds. Western feminists are still finding it difficult to have rape in marriage recognized as a legal offence.

Refusal of sexual compliance by a wife still proved effective even when a man had sexual access to other wives. Such refusal implied defiance and denial of rights, and was ultimately a challenge to a husband's authority over his wife. The customary solution was not for the man to take the law into his own hands; he had the option of calling in other members of the family or appealing to the formal patrilineage organizations described in Chapter 3. Obviously the weapon of sexual denial was most effective when used collectively, either by all the wives of a man, all the wives of a patrilineage, or better still, all the women of Nnobi.

Gender Division of Space

The terms of ideal relations of gender which defined males as being in authority over females, also claimed the superiority of males over females. To ensure this pattern of authority, males and females were physically and ideologically distanced. Familiarity, they say, breeds contempt.

In the indigenous architecture (see Appendix 3), the family compound was always divided into two; women and young children lived at the back section, adult men lived in the front section. There was a wall to mark this physical and ideological division. Little children carried messages between the two sections of the compound. From the entrance gate, the first house at the front of the compound was the *obi*. This was exclusively male. There, the master of the family received his guests and held meetings and discussions. Women and small children entered the *obi* only when sent for. It was at the *obi* that the master's food was served. There too, he would arrange for sexual visits to his bed-chamber, *ofe*, by his wives. Just behind the *obi* was the house that served as the master's bed-chamber. It was very personal to him, and not even adult sons were allowed in there. The first wife's sub-compound was usually closest to the master's bed-chamber house, followed by that of the second wife, etc.

A man, ideally, should never eat in the women's quarters. If he did so, he was ridiculed in public and called unbecoming names, for example he was said to crawl on hands and knees into his wife's house. But this rule was overlooked in situations of crisis, like sickness or death, or when a ritual had to be performed. Adult sons were not so rigidly bound, and could go to their mothers, either to seek advice or to help with the more strenuous household duties, like chopping firewood.

The family compound was conceived of and planned as private from the outside. There was a compound wall and an entrance gate to mark this division. Within the compound, the front section can be said to be public in comparison to the rest. It was there that all the prestigious activities such as naming ceremonies, marriages and lineage meetings took place. The women's section was, on the other hand, physically and ideologically linked to the backyard. The expression for going to the toilet was 'going to the back of the house'. Defecation was done in the gardens or bushes at the back of the compound and everyday rubbish was also thrown there. These were the gardens where women spent much of their time. Females were therefore physically and ideologically closer to areas associated with mess and dirt. Women's daily chores in their compound units were also quite messy.

The sexual division of space between men and women was so strong that not even 'male daughters' might break the rule. A 'male daughter', when remaining in her father's compound, lived in her mother's *nkpuke*, wife's sub-compound unit which was a matricentric household, or in her own unit in the female section. It was hoped that she would produce a son who would occupy the *obi*. Not even 'male daughters' might tend patrilineage or family ancestral spirits and shrines; these resided in the *obi*, and the sight of them should provoke awe in women. As women's menstrual blood was believed to be polluting both to ancestral spirits and to men, a menstruating woman was forbidden sexual intercourse with her husband and banned from the *obi* areas. *Ino na ezi*, or *ino n'iba*, or *ino na nso*, 'in a state of taboo', were the expressions for being in menses.[4] These expressions were, perhaps, derived from the custom of isolating menstruating women in a little hut at the back of the compound, where they were supposed to remain until the menstrual flow ceased, after which a chick would be killed and the ritual of cleansing performed before they were allowed back into society. The penalty for a woman who broke the rule of trespass or sexual taboo while in her menses was severe. The fine was even more severe if her husband was an *ozo* titled man – a purified or holy man.

Even if the man was not master of the household economically, he was master of the family ritually. This was ensured through his control of the yam medicine (see Chapter 1). Even if women kept their own shrines, once a year the male head of the *obi*, usually their husband or his son or his brother, would go and consecrate the women's shrine (see Chapter 6).

General Beliefs about Men and Women

Men and women were talked of or judged according to the roles expected of them as full social adults, that is, according to their status as fathers and mothers.

What was stressed about men was their duty to provide for and protect their families. This culture did not stereotype bad men and no tales were told about men who were immodest about their physical beauty. This was not so with women: everyone knew the attributes of a bad woman. The expression *ajo nwanyi*, bad woman, immediately brought a picture to mind which contrasted with that conveyed by the term *ezigbo nwanyi*, good woman.

Bad women were those who failed in their wifely and maternal duties and sentiments. Such a woman did not care for her husband, and was bad-tempered. She usually ate the food without giving any to her husband. It was said about her that she hated her husband as a dog hated goat's food.[5] When her husband uttered one word, she uttered ten; she always fought him as if they were age-mates or equals. She always acted contrary to what her husband told her to do, and never heeded his presence. If her husband spoke out loud, she would scold him as if she were scolding a child. If he gave her money to go to the market to purchase food, she would refuse to go. If one of her children cried for food, she would beat him and send him outside. She would not sweep the compound, and cooked tasteless food, either putting too much salt in the sauce or not squeezing the bitterleaf before putting it in the sauce. She was always scolding and at odds with her neighbours. She was envious of her neighbours and would kill their fowl when they trespassed. If she had the chance to steal, she would do so. 'Always her mind burned her like pepper.' She always caused townsfolk to point their lips at her with distaste or in contempt. She gossiped and was abusive and adulterous. She indulged in *ikpa nsi*, that is, poisoning or killing people through sorcery. In short, a bad woman was one who enjoyed wrongdoing and her aim was always to break up her husband's household.

Just as much talked about was the mythical very beautiful woman, whose narcissism usually made her reject numerous suitors, only to end up choosing a demon or monster in the disguise of a wealthy man. It was stressed that a woman's beauty was not only physical, but must also be seen in her mind, good character and hard work.

In contrast to these bad women was the good woman, who was usually a good daughter, wife and mother. She looked after her husband, never refused him food and made sure that things worked out well in the household. She looked after her children, fed them, kept them clean and gave them good home training. She usually helped her husband financially through her own efforts. If her husband was unable to provide money for food, she was able to support the household through farming, marketing and trading. She was not quarrelsome, and always protected her children against any form of danger. If necessary she would even protect or defend them from their father. A woman's self-denial in relation to her children was expressed in the belief that mothers starved before their children. She did not eat before her children had done so.

Industriousness, which is what was meant by good character, was inculcated in a woman in her father's house, and would pay dividends in her husband's house. As for her female children, it was her duty to teach them not to copy all that men did, because a woman was like a breakable plate, *nwanyi bu efele owuwa*. A woman in her maidenhood should exercise self-control so as not to fall into the hands of men.

The likening of a woman to a breakable plate reflects indigenous ideas about male and female sexuality, which supported the socio-cultural significance made of the female biological process. It basically means that, because of biological differences, a woman is sexually more vulnerable than a man. A woman gets pregnant, a man does not. Since this culture stigmatized pregnancy before marriage,[6] the socialization of girls stressed sexual restraint and preparation for their future roles as wives and mothers. Socialization of boys, on the other hand, stressed masculinity, equated with virility, violence, valour and authority.

How They Made Them 'Men'

In the traditional society, sexual differentiation was not insisted upon in early childhood. All little children ran about naked. Little boys participated in what were regarded as female duties. Marked differences in socialization began in later childhood, when boys began to gang together and wander away from their sisters and the home. This was the beginning of three socialization processes into manhood and the qualities and attributes of masculinity. These processes and stages of male development were vividly remembered by Nnobi elders and middle-aged men, as most of the activities they described continued well into the first half of the 20th century. Youths were encouraged to participate in wrestling, hunting and masquerading.[7]

Formal wrestling took place in public, in village squares, and the 'strong' were praised and the 'weak' ridiculed. During wrestling, boys, young men and even the elderly paired up with their age-mates.[8] Hunting – ranging from small to large and dangerous animals – was also performed in age-sets; boys hunted the smaller animals with stones and catapults, men sought the larger ones, with guns and bow and arrow.

After the hunting stage, came initiation into a masquerade group, *ikpu mmanwu*. In these masquerades,[9] dead ancestors and spirits were incarnated and used as a law enforcement authority. Beliefs surrounding initiation into a masquerade group claimed that one had to travel to the land of the dead and come face to face with spirits before becoming a member. Women and little boys were made to believe that the masqueraders themselves were actually spirits which came out of ant holes, etc. Their fear of these masqueraders was therefore real and the masqueraders in turn terrorized women in particular.

What finally differentiated boys or youths from men, the ordinary from the gallant, were the dance societies in celebration of courage, valour and masculinity. These are not considered to have been secret societies, even though they had their own rules and membership to them was through initiations involving tests.

Igbenu-oba was, for example, described as a war dance of seasoned men such as brave elders, hunters and hard labourers – men considered to have performed violent or valorous deeds, *ife sili ike*. It was different from other dances in that being performed in an aggressive fashion it was considered to be dangerous. This dance, like many others in the same group, was performed at the funeral of a 'big man'.

Uninitiated men dared not join in the dance, let alone women. As with such war dances, their symbolic ferocity later earned them the disapproval of the new churches, hence their discontinuation. The men were expected to look very fierce and so they put white chalk marks on their faces and around their eyes.[10] While they danced, some carried human skulls and the skulls of animals they had killed.

Okpanga was another dance said to have been performed only by those who had done courageous acts, like killing a man in battle, and this was performed at the funeral of such men. *Abia* was also a dance performed for those who had perpetrated acts of valour, like killing a man during a war and bringing back his head or killing a leopard. For this reason, the words *abia* and *dike*, which means strong, were said to go together. In the *abia* dance, men carried human heads. As a Nnobi elder told to me,

Only men who had killed a man took part in this dance. What you should know is that, in those days, it was an act of valour to bring back a human head from war. It was not considered a sin or a crime. Human heads and skulls were usually displayed in great *obi*(s). Anyone who came back with a human head was met and welcomed with the *abia* dance. This was how he was congratulated. A male sheep would be killed and the blood spilled on the man's hand. These men were distinguished by the red feather they wore on their heads.

An event which appears to have been an open, general initiation into manhood and a general celebration of masculinity was known as *igba ikolo*. The word *ikolo*, war drum, suggests that the Igbo word for manhood, *ikolobia*, is derived from or associated with this event. Like the war dances, this occasion provided a forum for men who had proved their masculinity through violent acts to boast of their exploits and display their treasures, which included human and animal heads, lion and leopard skins, fangs, etc. In order to qualify for participation, youths were encouraged to prove their masculinity through violent and courageous ventures, such as killing wild beasts, or bringing back the head of a victim of war. After this, they were allowed and encouraged to boast of their exploits in no modest language.

Apart from the social celebration of coming into manhood, a man was also allowed the assertion of independence from the domination of a father. Once a man felt that he had come of age and wished to be independent of his father, he had the right to leave his father's home and set up his own; this was known as *ipu obi*. His father would then give him a machete and, depending on his means, a piece of land and the expenses for a wife.

Coming into Womanhood, *Igba Agboghobia*

In contrast to boys, when a girl showed signs of womanhood – menstruation and developing of breasts – her movements were curtailed and she was closely watched. She could no longer wander off into the forest to pick nuts and berries with other children. Her life was no longer the free and careless girlhood colourfully depicted by Nwajiuba.

Mothers had an ambivalent attitude towards the physical maturity of their daughters. On the one hand they were pleased, for soon their daughter would be married and have children with all the material benefits derived from in-law relationships (see Chapter 4). On the other hand, the period between a girl's maturity and marriage was a time of great anxiety for mothers. They worried that their daughters might have sexual relationships with men, or conceive before marriage; for a young girl to become pregnant before a marriage payment had been made was shameful. Her mother was usually blamed as it was her duty to warn her daughter against men. Since there was no contraception in those days, other methods of ensuring sexual abstinence were devised. Girls were told of lone men like wolves laying traps for them, also of gangs of young men roaming the wild, who could trap and rape them in the forest. The sight of a penis was said to be enough to make a girl pregnant – it did not have to enter the vagina to land her in trouble. Such tales were stressed and exaggerated. Punishment for a girl suspected of indulging in sexual intercourse before she was married was very severe, ranging from severe beating to red-hot pepper being put in her vagina. Girls were, therefore, taught to understand that sexual activity and promiscuity brought shame and punishment to females.

In the attempt to prevent pre-marital pregnancy, there were also various taboos and rituals surrounding a girl in her maidenhood. Apart from the waistbeads which increased in layers as the girl grew older, a waist charm was added to the beads. The expression used for the waist charm was *ido iyi*, placing someone or something under a state of prohibition or taboo. In the case of a girl, this meant forbidding anyone sexual intercourse with her. This waist charm would later be removed by her patrilineage wives during her marriage ceremony. Only when she became a wife did she qualify to tie wrapper.

The desire to break away from the natal home came as soon as the girl was able to run her mother's household confidently. She usually found that she was constantly being nagged at and overworked by her mother. She dared not be caught sitting down doing nothing, for there was always some work to be done, shelling nuts or grating cassava or pounding pepper or washing the bitterness out of bitterleaf used for preparing sauce. A woman sitting idly, *ino nkiti*, was looked on with disfavour.

This constant nagging and being told what to do was usually a cause for disaffection in mother/daughter relationships. Girls therefore welcomed marriage at the earliest opportunity, for it meant acquiring the right to possess things and have a home to manage alone.

For a male, full adult maturity meant self-assertion, adventurousness and self-sufficiency. He proved his masculinity when he participated in the war dances to display his treasures of war or from hunting wild beasts, boasting of his strength and courage, and wrestling with other brave warriors. He also proved his masculinity when he showed that he could fend for himself.

For a female, on the other hand, full adult maturity meant self-restraint in sexual matters, and less adventurousness in the pursuit of pleasure. Self-sufficiency for her came only with marriage. With marriage, too, independence, aggressiveness and thrift were encouraged in economic matters. Aggression and self-denial were also encouraged in the protection of children.

Ideas about the separate roles designed for males and females featured in songs about young men and young girls. Young men ate and used their energy in fighting. According to the songs, feasting was usually followed by fighting; the songs are full of boasting, challenges to other men for a show of force. Young men sang about daring confrontations with powerful spirits, fighting, wrestling, wooing young maidens, feasting, drinking and war. Sometimes they did not fail to ridicule old men, as can be seen from this song,

> If young men don't go to war
> Who will go to war – war!
> Old man who remains in the house,
> Bring money – war!
> To be a young man is to be fearless.
> If young men don't go to war
> Who will go to war – war!

The ideas stressed in songs about young girls were simple and to the point. When a female child was born, the women sang that a bag of money had been born (see p. 78). When she came of age, the song said simply,

> Bag of money has grown,
> She has grown.
> What is left?
> Nothing is left but to sell her.

This meant that there was nothing left but to marry her off!

Notes

1. The English word 'master' implies a male, whereas its Igbo equivalent, *di*, is genderless.
2. Similar terms of relationship in the domestic set-up are recorded for Onitsha society by Henderson (1972). He describes the terms husband and wife as implying

'a combination of masterful control and responsibility on the one hand, compliance on the other' (1972:215). Also in Onitsha society, as in most Igbo societies, as Henderson states, the term husband 'is used as a prefix to characterize persons having a high degree of control over some specific set of nonkinship activities; a man who has acquired exceptional mastery of farming may be called "husband (master) of yam" (di-ji), with the implication that yams respond dependably to his command. Similarly, when a man is characterized as a "wife" of another man (done only in certain nonkin relationships), this implies obedient "domestic" service.' (1972)

3. See the section *Ikpu-okwa* Festival and Patriarchal Ideology in Chapter 6.

4. This culture had a wealth of vocabulary for a woman in her menses. The first two words, *ino na*, in the three expressions mean 'being in'. In the first expression, *ezi* means 'outside'. *Iba* in the second expression means 'little hut'. *Nso* in the third expression means 'forbidden' or 'taboo'. The actual word 'blood' is therefore avoided, for blood is looked at positively in this culture. The closest of relationships and affections are viewed in terms of the closeness or oneness of blood, or in terms of springing from one womb.

For those interested in the analysis of menstrual taboo in terms of control and power over women, see Douglas 1966, 1975. My concern is more in line with Weidegar (1975): the demystification of the unclean notions of menstruation so that women can stop seeing their body functions as dirty and gain more confidence in themselves.

5. While dogs are essentially carnivorous, goats are vegetarian.

6. Since there was no status of illegitimacy, the stigma was not on the child but on its mother. Her patrilineage might incorporate the child, who would then take its mother's family name. Alternatively, the child's father might be required to make double payments before gaining legal rights over his child and its mother. He should not get the child without getting its mother as wife. Exceptions to the rule were mature first daughters, or daughters who, for various reasons, were allowed to remain in their father's home and bear children into their patrilineage.

7. These male socialization processes are described in great detail for Onitsha society by Henderson (1972). About these activities he writes, 'Within the hunting group, boys learn to stand up for their rights and to strive for excellence; they learn to wrestle while their elders criticize and praise them; they learn to divide meat according to ritual standards. When they encounter equivalent groups from other villages, they learn how to fight together as a unit' (1972:354).

8. While Nnobi, unlike Onitsha society, was not politically organized on an age-grade system, people nevertheless associated with their age-mates and joined their age-sets for recreational activities.

9. Henderson (1972) describes these masquerades as 'the collective incarnate dead'; that is, the 'ancestral ghosts of Onitsha community' (1972:348).

10. I was told that the frontispiece of Basden's (1966) *Niger Ibos* is that of an *igbenu-oba* war dancer, although Basden did not state this anywhere in his book. He describes the man as 'body and spirit', with the explanatory words, 'This man believes, and his fellow villagers thought likewise, that, after certain ceremonies, he was half man and half spirit and was treated accordingly'. Basden thus presented the man out of social context, which makes his observation meaningless.

6. Ritual and Gender

The contradictions in Nnobi gender ideologies are reflected in ritual beliefs and practices. On the one hand, there was a body of beliefs and practices embedded in a matriarchal ideology derived from the worship of the goddess Idemili. This generated and supported favourable female ideas and strong matrifocality in Nnobi culture. On the other hand, there were also beliefs and practices derived from a patriarchal ideology and expressed in the ancestor cult. These generated and legitimized anti-female beliefs and practices. Nnobi ancestors and ancestresses may have given birth to Nnobi people, but Nnobi people seem to have created their own gods and goddesses in terms of their own gender relations. Thus, the all-powerful goddess Idemili was domesticated and became the wife of a less powerful god, Aho. The worship of both these deities, and how the terms of relationship by which they are described reflect the terms of relationship in the family and in Nnobi ideology of gender, will be examined. Other ritual practices, which – contrary to social facts – supported the subordination of the female to the male will also be described.

The Goddess Idemili

The domestication or subordination of the goddess Idemili is implied in all her myths of origin (see Chapter 1). According to another myth, recounted to me by the present priest of the Idemili shrine, Eze Agba, Idemili requested her own domestication:

What we heard from our forefathers, going back to beyond eight generations, is that the idol called Idemili Nneogwu lived in water. One day, some master hunters took their dog and went hunting. When they got to the stream, they tied the dog to a tree in the bush in the water so that it would chase out an animal for them to kill, when Idemili suddenly appeared and looked like a human being . . . The dog barked at her three times, fell down and died. The hunter took his gun, and went to find out why his dog should bark and fall down and die. When he saw what it was, he stood staring. Then she told him to come to her, that she was a woman and had something to say to him. The hunter ran off, called the other hunters and told them about his experience, how the thing he saw said that she brought gain and not punishment. So the whole lot who went hunting went back to the water with him, where the creature repeated herself and then told them to report to their elders that they saw something in the water; that what they saw claimed that she brought benefit and not punishment; that they should come to her so that she would tell them what to do to be able to take her home with them. So, they went to the elders and reported what had happened. The elders in turn went to find out what it was all about. When they got there, she welcomed them and repeated the fact that she brought benefit and not punishment. She told them to bring her seven white hens, seven white cocks and one female cow and take her home with them. The elders went home and held a meeting, at the end of which they decided upon a levy, but those asked to contribute refused to pay.

The hunter who discovered her therefore went home and asked his first wife for help, but she said she had nothing and was not able to help. So he spoke to his junior wife, who promised to help. She made a condition that if she on her own were able to provide all that was demanded, when this thing came home, it would be in her possession. She then told her husband that she would summon her own people[1] to bear witness while she met the requirement; that she was ready to bear whatever consequences ensued; that if it was going to bring any benefits, then they would be hers. And so everything was done and she was brought out of water. When she was brought home, everything that was demanded was again done, involving cow, goat and fowls, and a house was built for her in the compound of this junior wife. This is why the shrine of Idemili is in Ifite. The *obi* of the junior son of Ifite provides the priest or messenger of the goddess. The main shrine of Idemili of Nnobi is in the stream, for she is a water spirit. She dwells in water. She also dwells on land, where market is held in her name. She also lives in the village sections where she is fed. She also has other idols under her.

The list of subordinate spirits and shrines associated with the goddess Idemili is endless. The important point here is that shrines dedicated to this goddess pervaded the whole of Nnobi. In accordance with her myth of origin, her most important shrine is in Ifite (see Appendix 2, Figure 3), one of the junior major patrilineages or wards in Ebenesi village. The second in importance is that in Ngo village called Idemili-Nwa-Onye-Ushi, followed by that in Awuda village called Idemili-Oli-Ewu. Their order of importance was indicated in the different rules which governed their veneration. In the more junior shrines, she was approached at least with hens and at most with goats, while she was approached at the main shrine at least with goats for less important rituals and cows for more important ceremonies.

Her importance was also indicated by the epithets applied to her. She was addressed as:

Oke Nwanyi – the great lady; *Eze Nwanyi* – female king; *Idemili Ogalanya Ngada* – Idemili with huge baskets of riches; *Nwanyi Odu Opka* – a woman wearing ivory anklets;[2] one who roofs her house with zinc, so that nothing can destroy her; *Ono na mba, mba n'akwalu akwa* – one who is worshipped abroad; *Eze Onyili Mba* – the unconquerable one; *Agadi nwanyi, nmuo nwelu okwu na ano na mpata* – old woman! Deity who has a shrine! Woman who sits on a special stool for *ozo* titled men!

The great respect in which Idemili was held extended to her priest and his wife. In the daily worship and 'feeding' of the goddess which continues until the present day, the priest sounds a horn-bell and runs to the shrine every morning. There, he throws the symbolic white clay and breaks kola. He eats his own piece of kola and throws Idemili hers, he then returns the way he came. On her special holy day, *Eke Okwu*, the ritual of worship is more elaborate. The priest throws the symbolic white clay in the veneration of the goddess, her associated female spirit Ogwugwu and her *ikenga*.[3] He then goes to her *obi*,[4] sits down and breaks kola while saying incantations and asking for life and good health.

In the performance of his duty, the priest of Idemili was expected to abide by certain rules. He should not climb a palm tree;[5] he should not wear a loin cloth but must tie a wrapper like a woman. His wife followed some of the rules observed by an *Ekwe* titled woman. She should not plait her hair, or tie a headcloth on her head; she should not carry anything on her head; she should always carry and dress herself gracefully. A priest of Idemili should observe all the taboos associated with the goddess. He should give her all the gifts presented to her by Nnobi people to keep her happy. It was his duty to approach her on behalf of others. People would promise the goddess a goat or a cow on condition that she fulfilled their requests.

Most of the activities which marked the traditional calendar were ritual ceremonies and festivals of thanksgiving to the goddess Idemili. The impression is of a society and culture completely coloured by the veneration of this goddess rather than the ancestors. In the yearly calendar for example, only one general activity was associated with the ancestor cult: the ritual of remembrance of the ancestors, *ilo nmuo*. Every other activity was in one way or another associated with the goddess Idemili.

The annual season for ritual activities and festivals was usually declared open in the sixth month of the traditional calendar, when the priest of Idemili performed the ritual called *olulu*, which marked the day upon which the goddess ate new yam and indicated that it was time for general eating of new yam and religious worship. Idemili therefore ate new yam before everyone else. On that day Idemili was ritually commemorated by the priest of Idemili in conjunction with Umuona ward. This was most likely with the priest of the Land Spirit in Umuona, who was the custodian of the yam medicine, without which new yam could not be eaten. The priest of Idemili, who for this occasion was referred to as the king of *olulu*, *Eze Onye Olulu*, would display new yam first in his compound, then in the market, to indicate that it was time for the eating of new yam (the Eating of the New Yam Festival). Once new yam had been eaten, the various villages and major patrilineages took it in turns to perform their religious worship and outing of their idols to market: *afia nkwu* (a festival when all the idols were dressed up and taken to the market-place).

For the outing of the idols, women and children decorated their bodies in fanciful designs with black vegetable dye. The idols were also decorated and dressed according to their sex. While children danced for money at the central market-place, girls were expected to attract suitors. The *igba ota* festival performed in the ninth month again provided a happy occasion, when villages went in turn to the central market-place and then to Idemili market. While women and children danced and ate cooked food, men shot guns in general thanksgiving to the goddess for good health and prosperity, and to plead for things in the future.

Etedenaghu was another annual ceremony which provided an occasion for the exchange of food by in-laws. This ceremony was really performed by women, as it involved giving gifts to a woman by her daughters' husbands. The gifts comprised a sample of farm products, especially tubers such as yam and cocoyam. The men were later invited to take part in eating what they had given and would also be given pounded food and sauce to share with their neighbours. This gift was also given to a child who acted as a baby-nurse; the gift would be given to her mother. *Onu*[6] was the annual harvest festival performed for the goddess.

By far the most important ceremony performed for the goddess Idemili, which Nnobi people are still proud of and have revived in a modern form, is what is called *ikwu ahu* or *odinke* festival. This was performed by men every seven, and by women every nine years, and was the occasion when Nnobi displayed cows.

To mark the beginning of this festival, priests of the three Idemili shrines performed a ritual which indicated the stopping of the normal hands of the clock and introducing the hand of the deities or spirits – replacing normal human time for ordinary activities with a holy period for religious activities. For this ritual, the three villages of Nnobi would approach the priests of the three Idemili shrines. The main Idemili shrine in Ifite would be approached with a she-goat. Others would be approached with hens. The priests would then pour libation and say that there would be no deaths and no sickness; may people's fowls and goats conceive and reproduce; may the seeds of kola-nut trees be plentiful so that their owners may be able to get money to buy a cow to kill for Idemili. Thus they would declare the festival open. Once the holy period was declared, funeral ceremonies were discontinued for the period of one year, at the end of which Idemili would be approached with a hen to remove the hand of the deities and restore normality.

As a preliminary to the festival, the priest of the main Idemili shrine would go to Afo central market and perform a dance known as *okpokolo* or *oke opi*. Others might then perform the dance. By this dance, a person declared the intention of buying a cow to kill for the goddess. To perform the dance and fail to kill a cow was considered an insult to the whole of Nnobi. The punishment was performing the ritual of appeasement for all the spirits and deities in Nnobi. This involved buying two sheep for each of them, and a cow for Idemili; the payment of money was also required.

After the cow had been displayed in the market-place, it was taken home and killed for mass feasting. By this ceremony, the rich fed the masses in return for titles. Meat and yam were cooked and people sat in a circle and ate their fill of meat. At the end of this festival, those who had killed a cow were given the title *ogbuefi*, cow killer. They would afterwards carry a cow's tail and a special cowhide fan. During special occasions, only such titled people could participate in the *oke opi* dance with other titled men and women.

This periodic festival at which cows were killed for the goddess was linked to her maternal and peaceful attributes, such as her abhorrence of bloodshed among her worshippers. For this reason, a cow was sacrificed instead of a human being. Today, her maternal role and its associated protectiveness are emphasized in what can now be considered legends. Before the departure of some Nnobi people to take part in the Second World War, the goddess is generally reputed to have demanded a rowing boat to take her children across the sea. This demand was met and, as the story goes, after the war, those who participated in it came back and recounted their experiences. Their claims included seeing the python lying beside them in their dreams; this meant that Idemili was guiding them. For this reason, they all took an animal to the goddess and thanked her for her protection. Similar stories were reported in connection with the Nigeria–Biafra war (1967–70), when it was believed that Idemili protected Nnobi. According to popular belief, this is why Nnobi was neither invaded, evacuated nor occupied. During this war, the goddess was believed to have turned into an old woman who wore ivory anklets. Thus she appeared in different towns, saving Nnobi people and bringing them back by miraculous means.[7] In her protective maternal role, the epithet applied to the goddess was *nku di na mba n'eghelu mba nni*, 'firewood in a land and still able to cook the food of those who are not of that land';[8] she is in Nnobi and still worshipped by surrounding towns. The implication is that she guards and aids her subjects, far and near.

While the annual ritual of remembrance of the ancestors appears to have been basically a male affair, the annual worship of the goddess Idemili was essentially female. In these two different patterns of worship, gender roles were symbolized. Symbols of worship also indicated gender and role differentiation. While male symbols were phallic, female ones were rounded. The male crop, yam, is phallic in form, while the female crop, cocoyam, is round.

Apart from the sticks and wooden figurines representing various deities and spirits in the ancestral shrine, a man also had a personal deity which was symbolized or represented by a tree called *oha chi*. To prepare this shrine, a long pole was painted white, the man would take some *oha* tree leaves, some oil-bean tree pods, white kola-nuts and a piece of white cloth. He would then stick the white pole under the *oha* tree and place all the other things there, and finally, he would kill a fowl there. One had to be possessed or called by the spirits to erect a shrine to a personal deity.[9] This usually happened when one founded a household and became independent. A woman's personal shrine, erected for the same reason as that of a man, was symbolized by a small pot.

Women's religious worship was called *ilo chi*, remembering the deity. Instead of 'god', I have deliberately chosen the genderless English word, deity, to translate *chi*, as the Igbo word *chi* is genderless and is used for both male and female deities. In this case, the deity that the women remembered was Idemili. The women's religious devotions commenced with private worship performed at their personal shrines in the sub-compound units. Group worship, referred to as *ilo chi Idemili*, remembering the goddess Idemili, followed. The ritual involved was described to me by Nwajiuba in January 1982, shortly after she had completed her own private worship.

Women's religious worship began with a ceremony called *ibu chi*, gifts for the ceremony, in which a woman's sons-in-law brought her yam and cocoyam, as, too, did her husband. If she had adult sons, they too were obliged to give her gifts. Those who did not have these food items were allowed to give her money instead. These items were placed on the ground where the woman would perform her sacrifice. The woman herself would pound cocoyam and cook the great sauce (*oke ofe*) containing everything. She would buy four fish, or eight if she had many in-laws. The *Agba Ekwe* titled woman usually bought eight fish – double the normal requirement. The woman would take out one fish for paying ritual homage. Apparently in this instance, she paid homage to her father, not to her husband. She would pound white cocoyam, cook the great sauce, put one fish in it and take it to her father's home. Her first daughter's husband would take one fish and other friends and relatives would come round for bits and pieces.

For the ritual itself, a woman placed four pieces of stick and one wine jar in her market basket. She dressed in her best, that is, the clothes she wore for going to the market, and took these things to her personal shrine, *okwu chi*, on the right-hand side of her compound gate, where, as Nwajiuba said, it protected her against evil spirits and wicked people. She would first place some food in the bowl on the shrine, and her children would eat the food as she put it in the bowl. The rest of the food would then be shared by everyone, in-laws and all. Finally, the food utensils were left on the shrine.

Next was the ritual in which a libation of wine was poured on the ground. Everyone present would drink the wine, leaving a little in the jar; the woman then placed her hands on the mouth of the jar, while the others placed their hands on hers. Together they would perform the ritual called *itu ya izu n'ato*, pouring the wine on the ground three times. At the fourth count, the jar was turned upside down, the wine all ran out, and the jar was filled with water. The ritual was repeated and then at the fourth time, the jar was left turned upside down. The food utensils and gifts were usually left on the shrine until the following day.

Here again, as with marriage and funeral gifts, we see the circulation of gifts through relationships forged through women. For the ceremony of a woman's religious worship, her daughter's husband might buy her a she-goat, or she might use a hen for the sacrifice. The first daughter of the in-law who bought her the goat would take the female issue of that goat. The goat's male issue would be sacrificed at the woman's personal shrine the next year. In her prayers, a woman simply said that wealth and prosperity, good health and no deaths were desired.

The public group worship of the goddess was performed at her shrine in Afo central market-place called *chi Idemili*. For this ritual, women would take goats to the shrine. The ritual of cooking and feeding the family, performed by mothers during the private worship, was performed by the wife of the priest of the main shrine. She would pound cocoyam and cook the great sauce for the shrine priest and the men. Other women would take their own food to the shrine and eat it there. In this worship, therefore, men acted as guests or participated in the sense of accompanying their wives to the shrine. They, too, offered what they could to the goddess and said individual prayers.

Ekwe titled women, because of their special status and relationship with the goddess, had an exclusive day of worship on which no one else might go to the shrine. After worshipping Idemili, each *Ekwe* titled woman performed a private ritual of remembrance associated with her title, known as *ilo Ekwe*. She did this at her private shrine, erected as a result of her possession by the spirit of the goddess.

The supremacy of Idemili, whether in her elaborate rituals of worship, her acknowledged status or her all-embracing administrative laws, and Nnobi women's identification with her, cannot be denied or underestimated. This being so, I asked the priest of Idemili, Eze Agba, whether this religion had any taboos against a menstruating woman, since the goddess is herself a woman. His reply was positive. It is important to note that Eze Agba, although Idemili's priest, tended the ancestral shrines of his *obi*. It is, therefore, difficult to separate the beliefs rooted in the ancestral cult from those derived from the goddess religion. His specification of this taboo was, for example, related to ancestral cult-associated rules and sanctions governing gender relations in the family and the patrilineage.

As *ilo chi*, remembrance of the goddess, was female, so *ilo nmuo*, or, more usually *igo nmuo*, remembrance of the ancestors, was male.[10] Women's involvement in the annual ritual and ceremony centred on cleaning and decorating houses, and cooking and exchanging food. Married daughters would take palm-wine, *nkwu nmuo*, to their natal homes. Daughters' children would also take palm-wine to their mother's natal home. While women cooked and served food, children visited relatives and friends. Girls danced and boys wrestled.

For the men, who were the central figures in this ceremony, it was the occasion for the general annual reaffirmation of statuses and roles through the paying of ritual homage in the family and patrilineage. Social juniors paid ritual homage to social superiors. On this occasion, even though a husband performed the ritual of general cleansing of abominations and evils in the family, a wife usually contributed a hen as homage payment to her husband. He would kill the hen in the *obi* section of the compound and sprinkle its blood in all sections of the compound, including the women's sub-compound unit. Thus his authority over her and her shrine was symbolized and reaffirmed. We shall see a parallel affirmation of male authority in the annual ritual festival associated with Aho, the hunter/father founder of Nnobi.

The Hunter/Deity, Aho

The conceptualization of Aho as the husband of the goddess Idemili reflects the contradiction in Nnobi gender ideology which ideally placed males in authority over females. The goddess is by all indications superior to Aho but, because she is also female, Aho has to affirm some form of authority over her regardless of her relative autonomy, as with males and females or husbands and wives in the family.

The goddess Idemili was acknowledged and worshipped by the whole of Nnobi and several other surrounding towns and villages, especially those along the Idemili River. In recognition of Nnobi as the original home of the goddess, these other settlements were said to have been ritually subordinate to Nnobi.

Her supremacy over other deities and spirits, including the ancestors, was stressed by the traditional ruler of Nnobi, *Igwe* Eze Okoli II:

Each individual in each village was subject to the orders of their own Idemili shrine, whereas there was one supreme central government and that was the goddess Idemili. Just as we go to church and call on the name of Christ, ancestor worship was one system of worshipping Idemili. The Idols worshipped originated from Idemili and derived their power from her. Before taking the *ozo* title, those involved would have given the priest of Idemili all his dues. The holy man who held the *ozo* symbol knew that it originated from Idemili.

This is why when a titled man commits an offence, it is the holy men who first come and condemn him, so that he will first appease them, then go to Idemili and appease her and then go back to the holy men, *ndi nze*, and begin to cleanse himself before the symbol of power is given back to him. When I first took the chieftaincy title, I was a boy. My father made us all chiefs; because of Christianity, we gave up the titles. After my father died, I was refused the right to take the chieftaincy title on the grounds that I had not taken the *ozo* title. I had to start all over again to do the cleansing ritual. All the ancient rituals were performed before I took the *igwe* title. Then they accepted that I was an *nze*. This is how I knew that all these idols were linked to Idemili.

In comparison to Idemili, Aho is recognized by all Nnobi as a hunter said to have emerged from the wild and married Idemili. He was not considered a deity and, therefore, was not worshipped by the whole of Nnobi. Only Umuona major patrilineage considered Aho a deity and worshipped him.

Succession in the *obi* (see Appendix 2, Figure 1) followed the principle of unilineal descent, whereby the first son replaced his father; hence Ebenesi is the most senior village in Nnobi. In its subdivision into patrilineages, Umuona is the most senior major patrilineage in Nnobi and said to have been the original site of the founding ancestor of Nnobi; hence the shrine to the Earth or Land Spirit of Nnobi was in Umuona and was tended by the person who held the first-son position in the first or most senior *obi* in the most senior minor patrilineage in Umuona. This was considered the first *obi* in Nnobi (see Chapter 3). The shrine to Aho was located in Umuona. Only Umuona performed the annual festival for Aho called *ikpu okwa*, in commemoration of his original emergence from the wild. Every year, during this festival, the priest of Aho who carried the main *okwa* mask re-enacted the original emergence from the wild and went round the whole of Nnobi cleansing it of abominations. At the end of this festival, the priest of Aho would go to the shrine of the goddess Idemili and symbolically 'undress' her by removing the palm-fronds with which her shrine was covered, an act known as *itopu omu* or *iwapu ogodo*. I see this as a symbolic expression of male authority. This ritual marked the end of the period of religious festivals, just as tying the fronds round the shrine of the goddess marked the beginning.

Ikpu Okwa Festival and Patriarchal Ideology

This festival was last performed in 1948. Most elderly Nnobi people clearly recollected the activities and beliefs associated with it. Indeed, one of those interviewed, an elder called Ezudona, had himself gone through some of the rituals required for the taking of the *ozo Aho* title associated with this festival. Ezudona has never been a Christian and still worships the goddess Idemili. Two other men whose vivid accounts are reported here were Nnajide and Eze Enyinwa, neither of whom has ever stepped into a church or been a Christian; they also worship the goddess.

The central figures in this festival were men with the title *ozo Aho* (one of the high *ozo* titles mentioned in Chapter 2), associated with the spirit of Aho. Like the *Ekwe* title, it was involuntary, but unlike the *Ekwe* title which may be taken by any Nnobi woman possessed by the spirit of the goddess, only men from certain patrilineages in Umuona took the *ozo Aho* title. A possible candidate would consult the priest of Aho as soon as he experienced signs of possession, which might begin in childhood. Through divination, the man would be told that Aho wished him to take his title.

Only those who had taken the title or were in the process of taking it carried the *okwa* masks during the festival. There were many taboos surrounding a man who had taken the title. For example, while eating, he was not allowed to mention the names of certain birds, such as *egbe, utugbe* and *ugene oma*.[11] He was forbidden to mention the word 'Nnokwa'[12] or to speak of the *ushie* dance.[13] All titled élites of the time had to observe similar protocol.

The *ikpu okwa* festival took place in the tenth month of the traditional calendar and lasted for one month. It began with the roasting of yam, a very male thing and, as with most Nnobi religious activities, ritual homage was paid. In this case, the head of yam was circulated (a yam is considered to have a head at one end and a tail at the other). Each male head of a household would send yam to his immediate social superior. Next was the looting ritual, when Umuona would invite all Nnobi major lineages in turn to eat roasted cocoyam. While a lineage group was in Umuona eating cocoyam, the whole of Umuona, including women and children, rampaged in their guests' compounds and gardens. This was called the gladness or joy of *okwa*, *onu okwa*. The aim was to collect things needed for the festival, such as young yellow palm-leaves, *omu*, from which the masqueraders' layers of raffia-like skirts were brushed out. They also looted other petty foodstuffs such as coconuts, garden eggs (aubergines) and vegetables. They could drink any palm-wine left on the trees but could not loot any major economic item such as yam, cocoyam or livestock. The guests at Umuona in turn might do a bit of looting on their way home; this would go on until Umuona had exchanged looting with all the other major patrilineages in Nnobi.

Next came the wrestling ceremony, whereby Umuona invited the different major patrilineages in turn for a wrestling bout[14] which was performed before the *okwa* masks could be carried on the head.[15]

The masks were decorated in secret; this was the responsibility of a particular patrilineage in Umuona where the title *nwunye nonu*, wife (*nonu*) was taken. Even though this title was held by a man, he was referred to as wife here in the sense of being in a domestic or service relationship to those holding the *ozo Aho* title. He and his patrilineage were responsible for preparing the *ukpe* dye which was rubbed on the masks. He was also responsible for decorating the body of the priest of Aho (who carried the main mask) with camwood dye, *ushie*. Several days before the masquerade began, those intending to take part in it would spend each night performing a ritual called *iti nkpu Aho*, that is, the night call to Aho to emerge from the wild.

Fully decorated in dyes and young yellow palm-fronds, the masqueraders, led by the priest of Aho, retraced the primordial route of Aho. They would emerge from a piece of forest in Umuona called *Agbo Aho*, go to the shrine of the Earth Spirit of Nnobi in Umuona, and then proceed along the route to the shrine of Udide.[16] From there, they would visit patrilineage shrines in the ancestral *obi* of each minor patrilineage in Nnobi to perform the ritual called *igwo ngwolo* ('the sitting position of the lame'). At each shrine, the priest of Aho would sit in this position while yam, cocoyam, money and kola-nuts were counted out for him in eights. He then invoked blessings on that shrine, purifying it and warding off evil spirits. He continued thus until he had visited all the lineage shrines throughout Nnobi. After that he proceeded to Aho's open space and the shrine where the wrestling competition involving the whole town would take place.

For this competition, the titled men and women of all the different villages and patrilineages gathered in Aho square, each taking their individual chairs, and the *ozo* titled men wearing their eagle plumes. They usually sat in a circle, apart from other common spectators. The main masquerader, the priest of Aho known as *isi Aho*, and other masqueraders known as the children of Aho, *umu Aho*, would place themselves in the centre of the circle formed by the titled. The priest of Aho would again take the sitting position of the lame in the centre of the circle, hitting his hands and feet on the ground and boasting of his powers. As he did this, people would strain forward to see what he was doing, while they were whipped indiscriminately by the children of Aho. Then a ritual involving the cutting of ritual marks on the chest, *igbuchi obi*, would be performed on fearless young men. They would lie down in front of the priest of Aho and he would cut them twice on their chests with a knife and rub medicine on the cuts. This indicated that in future Aho would protect them.

The priest of Aho, carrying the main *okwa* mask, would then engage in ritual embrace with his wife in a dance exclusive to *ozo* titled men, *ushie*, for the whole *okwa* performance was exclusively male. For this reason, the priest's wife would have undergone a ritual which would give her male status to enable her to participate in this dance with her husband. She therefore wore a string anklet, like *ozo* titled men. After the priest had embraced his wife four times, he stood in the middle of the open space with his legs apart and all pregnant women present crawled between his legs to pick yellow palm-leaf, *ikpa omu*. Each woman would hold one strand from behind and one from the front and break off tiny pieces. The women took them home to cook in sauce and eat, and were not expected to touch any other medicine until their babies were born.

Like the deity Aho, who punished by whipping, *okwa* masqueraders carried whips with which they indiscriminately but gently whipped spectators. After the performance in the open space in front of the Aho shrine, the whole masquerade would pass through Nnokwa to Agu Ukwu Nri and retrace their steps back to Nnobi and the Afo central market-place, where the masqueraders continued their indiscriminate whipping. During this occasion, old women would go to be whipped, in the belief that in this way Aho took away any illness in their bodies. Finally, the priest would go back to the shrine of Aho. He would shake his body vigorously and shed the beautiful palm-fronds from his body on to the ground. This was described as an incredibly beautiful and amazing sight. He then disappeared into the virgin forest of Aho – into the wild.

The composition, outlook and rituals of the *okwa* masquerade were extremely male oriented. Because of the maleness of this ritual symbolism the titled man who had to perform the typically female domestic duty of preparing dyes and colourful decorations had to be called a wife. The mask itself was carved from strong, heavy wood in the shape of a mortar for pounding, hence its name *okwa*. The assertion of patriarchy and male dominance are symbolized in three rituals in particular: the visiting of village and patrilineage shrines to sanctify them; the pregnant women crawling between the legs of the priest of Aho to pick young palm-leaves; and the final ritual of undressing the goddess.

I was given two explanations of the purpose of the pregnant women's actions. According to one it was to avoid having a baby who would sway its head from left to right or rock its head like the *okwa* mask carriers.[17] The mask was so heavy those carrying it involuntarily swayed their heads from side to side. Ezudona, who had spent most of his life and wealth taking the *ozo Aho* title, was more secretive and evasive. According to him, no one knew the reason – it was the custom, but, perhaps, it was intended to avoid difficulty in childbirth. Apart from the assertion of male dominance, Aho might also be claiming the power of procreation. He publicly embraces his wife four times – a gesture never performed in public under normal circumstances – and pregnant women crawl in between his legs. Both these activities have sexual connotations.

Patriarchy versus Matriarchy?

At the beginning of the season of ritual festivals, the priest of the Idemili shrine, in conjunction with Umuona, decorated the shrine with young yellow palm-leaves (*omu*). When the Aho festival ended, at the close of the period of religious activities, the Aho priest untied the palm leaves from Idemili's shrine. As he arrived for this ritual spectators laughed and teased the goddess, singing that her husband had arrived. This ritual was known as *ito omu*, untying young, yellow palm-leaves, or *ito ogodo*, to untie a woman's wrapper or undress her.

The Umuona people gave two reasons for the performance of this ritual: 1) that Umuona was the head of Nnobi, the ancestral home of all Nnobi and, therefore, had ritual prerogative; and 2) that Aho was Idemili's husband and, as such, first protected his wife from public view at the beginning of the season of festivities by covering her, and at the end (as a husband might say in English, 'the party's over, time to undress'), he 'undressed' her.

At the beginning of the *okwa* festival, before the commencement of the yam roasting ritual, the priest of Aho would take yam to Idemili as night food, *itu nni anyasi*, the yam a husband customarily gave his wife as his contribution to the household's daily food. Some saw this as a bribe or payment for a wife's sexual service and associated the expression 'night food' with sexual intercourse, which usually took place at night. The Nnobi saying claiming that when a wife knows no yam is left she answers her husband's call reluctantly or sharply may support this. However, it is also possible to see giving yam to Idemili in the context of paying ritual homage, as in Umuona at the beginning of the *okwa* festival. In this case, Umuona was not only acknowledging Idemili's ritual seniority but also her antiquity with its embodied matriarchy. Umuona was also acknowledging the goddess's male status because, like a fully fledged independent male, she had an *obi* and an *ikenga*, as was mentioned by her priest, Eze Agba, earlier in this chapter. The whole Aho cult may therefore symbolize the incursion of a patriarchal people on an indigenous matriarchal society.[18] The fact that in the worship of the goddess, women took ritual homage to their father and not to their husband, as in the worship of the ancestors, may support this thesis. Their fathers may not always have been heads of their natal homes. Possibly, a female was.

Interestingly, although Aho is seen as Idemili's husband, and their relationship conceived of in terms of husband and wife in the household, Aho is not seen as the superior or more powerful deity, even by Umuona people who, alone, worship him. Instead, he is seen as a man struggling to maintain a male authority over a very wealthy, independent and popular woman. This idea is expressed in another myth claiming that Aho was Idemili's husband. Idemili, being very industrious, soon became a great woman; rich, powerful and much more popular than her husband, Aho. In line with the belief that the way to humble an arrogant woman is to marry a second wife, Aho married Afo. Idemili, in her anger, closed all the rivers, including that of Aho and Afo, and said that only her own river would continue to flow.[19] Aho, in male indignation, ruled that thenceforth, all important activities in Nnobi would take place at Afo's place. *Afo* is one of the days of the week, the main market day and the name of the central market-place. Indeed, most festivals and activities take place there.

When I put it to the present priest of Idemili that Aho is said to be Idemili's husband, he became quite indignant, and said:

No, he is not! Who was there when he went and took her for wife? You should ask them to say who witnessed the day that Aho took palm-wine to go and get Idemili. Who was there when *alusi nmuo*[20] originated? All I know is that my own father did not tell me this. Umuona is just boasting. It is only people who claim that Aho is Idemili's husband. These are things which people came to the world and began to say. Have you ever seen where people accompanied deities to go and get other deities for marriage? It is when talking about customs that people tell these stories.

In response to this denial by the Idemili priest, Umuona people maintained that Aho gives yam to Idemili just as yam is given to a wife by a husband in the secular family.

Spirit Possession and Gender Ideals

Ideal gender roles were not only conceptualized in the relationships between the deities, but in spirit possession by various deities, and the associated titles for the possessed. As possession by the goddess Idemili symbolized the climax of economic success, possession by a lesser goddess, Ogwugwu,[21] symbolized female disorder and failure. *Ogwugwu* title was therefore the antithesis of the *Ekwe* title. For men, possession by the spirit of Agwu symbolized male failure.

Women, as wives, had access to economic assets from which they would eventually build up wealth and power, therefore, as wives they were possessed by Idemili to take the *Ekwe* title.

Ogwugwu, however, possessed daughters; the signs manifesting possession by her were usually directly opposite to those signifying possession by Idemili's spirit. Signs of possession by Ogwugwu's spirit usually appeared from girlhood, becoming conspicuous at marriage. A girl or woman so possessed failed in anything she did. Her crops would fail, fowls would die, hawks take her chicks. She might fail to conceive or suffer high infant mortality; her household was usually in disarray.

When these signs became manifest in girlhood before marriage (as they invariably did) there was nothing to be done, as an unmarried girl was considered a traveller unaware of her destination. She would therefore appeal to Ogwugwu to have patience, saying that she was still on the road and could not erect her shrine there. She would promise that as soon as she reached her destination – married – she would have her own home and could build a shrine there.

Possession by Ogwugwu can therefore be seen as a mechanism of social control for girls to train them in the ideals of woman-, wife- and motherhood. If signs of possession continued after marriage, the woman's husband would accompany her back to her natal home to perform the ritual of appeasement. On her return to her marital home she would then erect a personal shrine to Ogwugwu.

Like *Ekwe* titled women, Ogwugwu initiates, entitled daughters of Ogwugwu, *Ada Ogwugwu*, belonged to an exclusive society and shared payments made by new initiates. Their title was not political but carried great prestige. Like other men and women compelled to erect personal shrines as a result of spirit possession, *Ogwugwu* titled women also worshipped at these shrines during the period of annual religious remembrance and worship of the goddess Idemili.

The male counterpart was possession by Agwu. Like Ogwugwu, the spirits of Agwu were associated with patrilineages. Possession by the spirit of Agwu served not only as a check against social deviation in men, but also ensured succession to certain hereditary positions and professions in the patrilineage. First sons were, for example, more prone to possession by Agwu; so also were those in line to succeed fathers or other relatives in the *dibia* profession. Most men in important social positions would have appeased the spirit of Agwu either in childhood or later in life, and would, therefore, have an Agwu shrine. Possession by the spirit of Agwu was symbolized by personal disorder, signs of mental imbalance or breakdown, and general tendencies towards irresponsibility. Such a man basically fell short of 'manliness'. Early appeasement could check this tendency, but in hopeless cases, possession by Agwu excused social deviation in men. Such a man, though treated with contempt, was pitied and excused. In most cases, however, it was believed that the 'madness' would disappear as soon as the man took on whatever responsibility he was running away from.

Ritual Homage

The payment of ritual homage, *ibu ihu*, through the circulation of certain items, was the traditional manner of acknowledging both age and social seniority in the family and the patrilineage. Between towns, ritual superiority or political domination qualified for acknowledgement in this way. Associated with this practice was the idea of male superiority, for this homage was never paid to a woman, unless she had officially been accorded a male status.

Homage practice basically concerned who received what when an animal was killed. Men killed and dissected the animals, women carried the parts to the appropriate recipients. As the purpose of the gift was to acknowledge both age and social seniority, a man's children, male or female, took homage gifts to him. A wife was also expected to take a gift to her husband whenever she killed a fowl in her marital home. If, for some reason, she had to have an animal killed in her natal home, she was expected to give a homage gift from this animal to her father.

In a polygynous family, the oldest son of each wife received this gift from his siblings to acknowledge age seniority. In acknowledgement of social seniority, if their father was still alive, all the first sons of all his wives took homage gifts to their father. If their father was dead, then the first son of the first wife, who would have replaced his father in the *obi*, received the gift. He in turn would take his gift to whoever was in first-son position among his father's brothers. The same procedure would be repeated among the father's brothers in this order of ascendancy, until the patrilineage head received the last gift. He, himself, gave homage to no one, but would offer his meat to the sun before eating it.

When a goat was killed, the kidney, the head of the liver, a rib and a shoulder were taken as homage gifts. The recipient would then give a small piece of meat to the wife who brought the gift from her husband; he also cut a piece of the rib received and returned it to the giver. If it was a fowl, the homage gift would be the wings, the giblets, the neck and the posterior; the recipient would give the neck to the giver's wife as payment for carrying the gift. In acknowledgement of homage received he would return a gift of yam to the donor.

A person who did not have an animal from which to make this gift was instead allowed to give one head of tobacco and some kola-nuts. In this gesture of 'respect' shown to social 'superiors', first fruits or seeds of any tree planted were also given as homage gifts. Even children had early education in the giving of this gift. They were instructed to send the first spring water they fetched to the person to whom they should pay homage. In addition to the water, they should also give four seeds or a kernel of palm fruit.

Even though women as females did not receive homage gifts, the special or privileged position of the first daughter was indicated by the fact that a brother in first-son position and also the occupant of his father's *obi* would give his oldest sister the privilege of cutting palm fruits from a particular tree in their *obi*. As long as she cut the palm fruits, she was obliged to take a fowl to be killed in her father's *obi* during the annual remembrance or worship of the ancestors. She would then give the appropriate parts as a homage gift to her brother, who in return would give her back the neck in acknowledgement.

In the case of women heads of an *obi* or family, only those who had officially been accorded male status received a homage gift. Nwajiuba, for example (see Chapter 1 and Appendix 2, Figure 1), would receive homage gifts from the *obi*(s) which make up the minor patrilineage of Umu Okpala as she had officially been made male and occupied the first-son position. In contrast to Nwajiuba, the first-son position of the minor patrilineage of Umu Ochom (see Chapter 2 and Appendix 2, Figure 2), would not receive homage gifts, as their founding ancestress Ochom was not officially accorded male status. He would take homage gifts to the Umu Oshuga patrilineage, whose founding ancestor was the brother of Ochom. In the case of Ochom, unlike Nwajiuba, it was not as a result of a shortage of men that she remained in her father's *obi*. The story is that because she was very ugly she could not find a husband. She remained at home and conceived, so her brother Oshuga gave her a piece of land on which she lived and founded a lineage. Even though the patrilineage of Oshuga ranks third in the order of seniority of Amadunu minor patrilineages, the Umu Ochom patrilineage founded by the sister who was female must always rank last.

Even in the case of Nwajiuba, although homage gifts were given to her in principle, I could not verify whether she herself received them since, as a woman, she could not tend patrilineage spirits. In ritual matters, Raphael Ezeani, a senior male in her patrilineage, acts as her messenger. In practice, he tends the patrilineage ancestral shrine and the shrine to the Earth Spirit. In this capacity, he is referred to by Nwajiuba as a messenger.

The general payment of ritual homage marked the beginning of the period of religious worship which also coincided with the period of the festival when new yam was eaten. Thus, there was an annual reaffirmation of status differences in addition to the daily reminder of role and gender differences in the family and in the patrilineages through such practices and customs as the breaking and sharing of kola-nuts.

In common with giving homage gifts, the rules governing breaking and sharing kola-nuts symbolized authority, status and gender differentiation in Nnobi. As a general rule, a woman should never break kola when a male was present,[22] be it only a little boy. The man should bless and break it. A man should not eat kola split by a woman. A woman should not pick up a fallen kola-nut pod, but must ask a male to pick it up for her. In male company, whether in the family, the patrilineage or a general gathering, the most senior male present, either by age or by social seniority, should break the kola. The pieces of kola would then be taken in order of seniority. Women took kola last.

No ceremony or ritual could begin without breaking and sharing kola which was the first thing offered to a visitor. It was in fact the medium of worship and invocation of blessing or saying of incantations, *igo oji*. A junior or an inferior could not invoke blessings on a senior or superior.

When women only were present, the breaking and sharing of kola also symbolized status differences between them. Daughters, as males, should break kola when in the company of wives. The daughter could, however, touch the kola and give the most senior wife present authority to break it.

Thus, again, as shown in previous chapters, there were contradictions in the structure of ideologies, which acted as a system of checks and balances. Some practices which had roots in patriarchal concepts reinforced strict sexual dualism in social organization and male dominance in gender relations. Others, derived from matriarchal concepts and beliefs, including some flexibility in gender construction, gave women access to power and authority in the political structure.

Is it finally possible to say how men and women behaved towards each other in the olden days? Any categorical statement of the kind of interpersonal relations existing between men and women in the traditional system might prove misleading. Relationships varied enormously in this multiplex society, and were in a constant state of interaction. The quality and patterns of relationships between men and women can be deduced from marriage rules, style of architecture and the choices open to women. I believe that the old pattern of segregation in domestic arrangements encouraged autonomy and respect between husbands and wives. For example, (see Chapter 2) Akueshiudu could refuse to give her husband food because he did not contribute meat or yam for the meal. Her co-wife Ifeyinwa could overshadow their husband and still be adored by him. Eze Okigbo, who was also in a powerful position, could openly challenge his wife's effort to overshadow him. None of these incidents led to divorce.

Sex was not forced on a woman; she was constantly surrounded by children and other people. Men did not enter the women's quarters freely or casually. Avenues were open for 'politicking' and there is a particular kind of romance in insinuations, innuendoes, bribery to sweeten the heart or words to poison it, as the case may be. The sanctity of motherhood meant that women were treated with respect. One woman might desire an intense relationship with her husband, another might see marital obligations as a necessary but loathsome duty. Some might abandon their relationship with their husband and shun 'men and their trouble'. Indigenous architecture and male/female polygyny made these choices possible. The very young wife who might have been dominated in a polygynous marriage had positive models in the traditional powerful women, whose ranks she could aspire to enter.

In any case of violence, relatives were at hand to defend their sister, daughter or mother. Women were therefore better protected in this system. Indeed, there were many choices open for a woman with imagination. Nevertheless there were still women who remained at the beck and call of husbands as there were husbands completely dominated by wives.

The relationships between men and women certainly did not include anything like the 'recreational sex' which reportedly takes place in Western societies today, where in spite of their monogamous orientation, women are said to be very promiscuous (Greer, 1984). They shudder at the thought of polygyny, immediately equating it with oppression of women, simply because wives have to share a man sexually. Facts may yet associate the spread of sexually borne diseases with monogamy, since in this situation, one partner does not know with whom the other might be sharing sex.

Notes

1. Members of her patrilineage.
2. Very wealthy women wore ivory anklets.
3. *Ikenga* was yet another item kept by men of independent status among their enormous collection of ritual objects. Women's shrines to their personal deities were simple in comparison. In traditional society, the more power one claimed or acquired over others, the more protective or validating cult objects one kept. Heading an *obi* and keeping an *ikenga* appear to have been connected, according to the explanation given to me by the priest of the Idemili shrine:

A man who leaves his father's *obi* and builds his own house has to be possessed before having an *obi* in which he will erect a shrine for his ancestors and Idemili, so that when he needs to perform sacrifice to Idemili, he need not take it to the main shrine. The thing being sacrificed may be killed and eaten in his house. *Ikenga* is what he will have in the shrine of the ancestors. Not just any man may keep an *ikenga*. A man has to be possessed to be able to keep an idol representing this spirit. It is the ancestors who will demand that one should keep an *ikenga*. Once a man has a house and an *ikenga* in it, he is of equal status to his father. *Ikenga* spirit usually possesses first sons. If the man has been possessed for three or four decades, from 60 years, he is forced to erect an *ikenga*. All these involuntary possession victims are given something like goat's horn. When the person dies, the priest of the particular deity repossesses the horn.

4. Again, having an *obi* indicates the male status or classification of the goddess Idemili.

5. This is possibly due to the classification of the priest of the goddess as female, since females should never climb trees.

6. In the recent trend of cultural revival, this traditional harvest festival (*afia olu*) has been resurrected. This is an annual call to all Nnobi citizens everywhere to return for general cultural celebrations and thanksgiving services in the various churches.

7. It is interesting to note that these claims were made by Christians.

8. This is meaningful in the context of overpopulation in a land tenure system where most of the land is owned by localized patrilineages and individuals with genealogical connections. It is therefore nearly impossible for a 'foreigner' or one with no genealogical links to have access to land from which to cut or collect the firewood essential for cooking.

9. These personal shrines appear to be linked to the goddess religion, as they were erected outside the *obi* and distinct from the ancestral shrines, which were in the *obi*.

10. The words *chi* and *nmuo* distinguish both rituals since *chi* means deity and *nmuo* means spirit. While spirits are not deities, deities, like people, have spirits.

11. *Egbe*, hawk, which was the sign on the *okwa* mask, belongs to the kite family, and so, possibly, do the others.

12. The Nnokwa taboo is associated with the story of how the neighbouring town Nnokwa 'opened up rain' on *okwa* masqueraders returning from Agu Ukwu Nri when they were passing through Nnokwa. 'Opened up rain' means using rainmakers to induce rainfall. As the story goes, only a certain old man called Eze Odije survived. When this old man noticed it was raining, he took his mask off his head and put it on his shoulder. The water trickling down from the mask therefore did not enter his mouth and so he did not die. All the other men died, as *ukpe*, a poison used for painting the masks, got wet and ran into their mouths. After that incident, *okwa* was always carried on the shoulder.

13. *Ushie* or *ufie* was an exclusive dance performed only by *ozo* titled men.

14. Young men selected by each major patrilineage to represent it took part in this wrestling competition. Victory was a cause of great jubilation.

15. It appears that the masks were carried on the head locally and on the shoulder for external visits.

16. Aho's local routes are still well known by most elders in Nnobi today. In 1982, I asked Mr R. O. Madueme what Aho used to go and do at Udide. He said that Aho used to go to meet Udide who was perhaps his girlfriend. 'The deity Udide, I think, is a woman, isn't she?' he asked.

17. Nnobi people believed that objects or people's physical characteristics

strongly influenced babies in the womb. Consequently, pregnant women avoided looking at 'ugly' or deformed people for fear that their babies would resemble them.

18. The fact that figurines of all the other deities in Nnobi which have their shrines elsewhere, including Aho himself, are represented in the main Idemili shrine supports this thesis.

19. A lot of the shrines are located in dried up rivers.

20. Deities.

21. Some claimed that Ogwugwu was the second daughter of Idemili. She is a goddess of fertility.

22. A 'male daughter' in the position of Nwajiuba was an exception to the rule. During my fieldwork in 1982, Nwajiuba and her wife, who was pregnant at the time, visited me. There were also some elders who came to visit my father. So we all sat together, as they knew I was collecting information on Nnobi customs. My father, as the host, produced kola-nut for the guests and respectfully offered it to Nwajiuba. She simply touched the kola and gave it back to my father to break. After saying incantations through the kola, he broke it and again offered it to Nwajiuba so that she could take the first pick. All the men present picked from the plate before Nwajiuba's wife and myself, as women in the company of men had the last pick.

Part Two:
The Colonial Period

7. Colonialism and the Erosion of Women's Power

The post-1900 period saw the invasion of Igbo hinterlands by the British. This was followed by the violent suppression of indigenous institutions, the imposition of Christianity and Western education, and the introduction of a new economy and local government administration through the warrant chief system. These new institutions, with their linked ideologies and cultures, greatly affected the structural position of women in modern Nnobi society. Whereas indigenous concepts linked to flexible gender constructions in terms of access to power and authority mediated dual-sex divisions, the new Western concepts introduced through colonial conquest carried strong sex and class inequalities supported by rigid gender ideology and constructions; a woman was always female regardless of her social achievements or status.

Christianity: A New Gender Reality in the Religious Sphere

Christianity first reached Igboland through the Delta States. The first contact with Christian missionaries was in 1841 in Aboh. By 1857, a permanent Christian mission had been established in Onitsha (Isichei 1976:160; Nwabara 1977:47). Once a strong presence had been established at Onitsha in the form of a large trade and commercial centre on the banks of the River Niger, missionary contact with Igbo people in the hinterland soon followed. By 1883, Bishop Samuel Adjai Crowther, one of the early evangelists, was reported to have gone to Obosi to dedicate a new CMS church (Nwabara 1977:51). It was at Obosi, a town on the Idemili River not far from Nnobi, that Eze Okoli, who later established the CMS church in Nnobi, was said to have been converted to Christianity in 1908 (*Abalukwu*, Vol. 1, September 1975:13).[1]

Apparently, when Christianity was first introduced in Nnobi, it was not seen as a thing for the masses. Consequently it did not at first gain ground. Those privileged few who sat together to discuss the new doctrine were elders, *ozo* titled men and *ukozala* title holders. Women do not seem to have been involved at this stage. This is understandable, as the privileged women who would have had access to Christianity or were qualified to sit in the company of titled men, would have been the *Ekwe* titled women. The fact that their lives were centred on the service of the goddess would have made it impossible for them to welcome the new religion. Other writers on the Igbo in general have also commented on the unwillingness of elderly women to be converted during the early period, and also their resentment at missionary propaganda and attacks against indigenous religious cults (see Ifeka-Moller 1975:141 and footnote 61 for other references in support of this claim).

Indeed the earliest recorded mass protest movement by Igbo women was the Nwaobiala – the dancing women's movement of 1925. The basic demand of the movement, which was dominated by elderly women, was the rejection of Christianity and a return to traditional customs. Nnobi is mentioned as one of the three towns where a military escort was sent to restore order, as women there burnt the market, blocked the main road and piled refuse in the court house. Children were withdrawn from school and the market was boycotted (see Mba 1982:68–72).

This resistance to conversion has been sustained by a few people in Nnobi. Eze Agba, the present priest of Idemili, does not go to church, nor does Nwajiuba, the 'male daughter', who is head of the first and most senior *obi* in Nnobi. Together with a few other elderly people, they practise the indigenous religion – the worship of the goddess. The Christians refer to them as 'pagans' or 'heathens', but they call themselves *ndi odinani*, the custodians of the indigenous culture. The youngest of them are middle-aged. All their children and grandchildren are Christians. Ironically, a new resistance against Christianity now springs from the Western-educated élite, who were in fact brought up in the church and educated in mission schools. They are now strong supporters and admirers of the indigenous religionists and preach the doctrine of cultural revival while condemning aspects of Western culture and dominance.

The early missionaries made the mistake of associating themselves with commercial firms, giving the local people the impression that Christianity and commerce were linked (Nwabara 1977:48–9). The Nnobi 'big men' therefore first saw Christianity in terms of material benefit and soon dissociated themselves from the missions when no positive results seemed to be forthcoming. Similar initial failure was also reported by evangelists in other parts of Igboland at the end of the 19th century. Isichei, for example, quotes one of the early missionaries as saying, 'A thankless task among a thankless people . . . Religion is only merited for material purposes' (1973:153).

The two men who were able to win a following for the church were those who could prove that some benefits – material or otherwise – could be derived from Christianity. They did so with the active support of the colonial government. They were Eze Okoli, whose name is connected with the establishment of the CMS church in Nnobi, and who became a warrant chief and later a paramount chief (see *Abalukwu* Vol. 1, September 1975:13). The other was called Okanume, but was better known as Ome ihe Ukwu, 'one who does great deeds'. He brought the Catholic Church to Nnobi.[2]

Okanume never became a monogamist as prescribed by Christianity. He still lived as a 'big man'. He inherited the wives of his father, Eze Okigbo, and married two more wives himself. After he died, his son Anadi took his position in court as chief but married only one wife. His son John Okigbo also married only one wife. As the Catholic Church later incorporated male titles into their church, John

Okigbo is both an *ozo* and *ichie*[3] titled man.

While the Catholic Church in Igboland has now accepted the taking of the *ozo*[4] title, in the Anglican Church the dialogue continues, as do the frustration and bitterness of wealthy men. The idea of incorporating female titles is not even considered in the debate.

By the first two decades of the present century, with the firm establishment of both the Protestant and Catholic Churches and their schools, Christian and Western ideas and cultures were being introduced into Nnobi with the support of British political allies, namely the warrant chiefs. Church and school were synonymous. Classes were in fact held in church buildings and no one was admitted into the school who had not been converted to Christianity. This practice later led to bitter quarrels between the colonial government and the missionaries, with the government insisting on the separation of education from religious instruction (Nwabara 1977:62–3 and footnotes).

The first lessons and teachings focused on condemnation of indigenous religion and beliefs (Nwabara 1977:53, 56; Isichei 1976:161–2).

In Nnobi, people were told to stop worshipping indigenous religious symbols which the Christians interpreted as idols. The Christian doctrine claimed that God created all persons and all things, and that, unlike the goddess Idemili, God was a 'he' and not a 'she'. No wonder that the colonial anthropologist, Reverend G. T. Basden, a member of the Church Missionary Society and a universal reference on Igbo indigenous culture, describes the goddess Idemili as a he and a god (Basden 1938:41–3). He writes, 'There are five Ide-Millis, each with his distinctive status and functions' (1938:41). The male image persists in his imagination in spite of female symbols like water (stream) and roundness (pot): 'All these five gods have but one patronal head, namely, the python (Ekke)' (1938:43).

A male image again invaded the imagination of the Igbo professor of history, J. C. Anene, when he referred to the Earth spirit, present in all Igbo communities, as a god and not a goddess (1966:12–13). Another male historian made the correction by saying, 'Anene's terminology would be more accurate if he used "the Earth Goddess" in place of "the god of the land"' (Afigbo 1972:17, footnote 41). The famous Igbo novelist, Chinua Achebe, also a product of Western education, is no less guilty of the masculinization of the water goddess, whom he describes in his novel *Things Fall Apart*, as the 'god of water' (1958:144).

All activities which centred on the goddess were condemned and replaced by those rooted in the belief in and doctrine of a patriarchal Christian god and his son Jesus Christ.

According to the Nnobi elder Ikebeotu, at first there were conflicts between Christians and followers of the indigenous religion. This was also the case in other Igbo communities (Nwabara 1977:50–51, 55). In some cases, the Christians were punished by isolation or ostracism. By far the greatest conflict centred on the Christian practice of killing the python, which is a totemic symbol of those who worship the goddess Idemili. To kill a python was a taboo, the breaking of which carried a heavy penalty. The frustration of those involved was heightened by the fact that when these cases were reported to the District Officer, he would tell the villagers to leave it to the particular deity to deal with the offender.

A particular incident which took place towards the middle of this century is vividly remembered in Nnobi today. This was the case of a man called Nathaniel, but better known as Natty, from Ngo village, whose action had so incensed the women as to provoke a demonstration of indigenous female militancy.

This man, out of Christian fanaticism, had killed a python. When news reached the women, they demonstrated their anger by bypassing the local court, controlled by equally fanatical Christians, and marching half naked to the provincial headquarters, Onitsha, to besiege the resident's office. He pleaded for calm and patience and asked the women to go home, saying that he would look into the case. The women considered this a feeble response, so they returned to Nnobi, went straight to the man's house and razed it to the ground. This was the indigenous Igbo female custom of dealing with offending men (Harris 1940:147; Green 1964: 196–214; Leith-Ross 1939:109; Van Allen 1972). Two weeks after the incident, the man is said to have died. A song about this case is popularly known in Nnobi, and was sung to me by Mr B. Emeh. It goes like this:

> *O no n'ezi gbasika – o!*
> *O no n'uno gbasika – o!*
> *Naaty gbulu eke – o!*
> Those on the street, out of the way!
> Those inside the house, out of the way!
> Natty has killed a python!

This is reminiscent of the song sung by lineage daughters as they made their way home bringing back the body of a sister who had died as a wife elsewhere (see Chapter 3).

The violence which occurred as a result of disrespect for indigenous taboos by Christians is also recorded in other areas which experienced missionary activities (see Nwabara 1977:50 and footnotes). Chinua Achebe, who was in fact born in Nnobi,[5] records the conflict between Christian and non-Christian villagers in *Things Fall Apart*. His account of the incident involving the killing of the royal python by an over-zealous Christian is particularly significant as it is reminiscent of the fate which befell Natty in Nnobi. As punishment for the crime committed by Okoli, he and all the other Christians were outlawed by the village. Achebe wrote,

> Okoli was not there to answer. He had fallen ill on the previous night. Before the day was over he was dead. His death showed that the gods were still able to fight their own battles. The clan saw no reason then for molesting the Christians. (1958:147)

Christian disrespect was directed not only against the totemic symbols; they are also said to have been fond of killing and eating animals sacrificed to the goddess. Again, the DO's response to the complaints was nonchalant. He would tell the people to leave it to the goddess to show her power. In this way the Christians hoped to expose and confirm their claim of the impotence of the 'idols'. The missionaries would also take in twins and their mothers and bring them up in the church. These social 'outcasts' in fact formed the early Christian congregations. These claims by Nnobi people are also confirmed by the findings of the historian Elizabeth Isichei, who writes, 'The bulk of the first Christian converts were drawn from the poor, the needy, and the rejected: the mothers of twins, women accused of witchcraft, those suffering from diseases such as leprosy which were seen as an abomination.' (1976:162).

In the opinion of the elder, Samuel Ikebeotu, Christianity soon gained many followers as they picked on those things or laws or customs which people found difficult, unjust or irksome but tolerated for fear of retribution. At the same time, this staunch believer and avid church-goer claimed that the church and Christian denominations are to be blamed for Nnobi's backwardness and lack of unity today. This opinion is also shared by historians of Igboland (see Isichei 1976:170; Nwabara 1977:56).

Not only did Christianity condemn the goddess religion, but it also banned the associated *Ekwe* title. In a short space of time, the focal symbols of women's self-esteem were shattered. At the same time, women found themselves divided in their families, their patrilineages and the town by the different Christian denominations to which they belonged.

Changes in Marriage Practice and Gender Relations

In Part One, it was shown how in the traditional society, a flexible gender system meant that male roles were open to certain categories of woman through such practices as *nhanye*, 'male daughters', and *igba ohu*, 'female husbands'. These institutions placed women in a more favourable position for the acquisition of wealth and formal political power and authority.

Under colonialism, these indigenous institutions – condemned by the churches as 'pagan' and anti-Christian – were abandoned or reinterpreted to the detriment of women. The *Ekwe* title, which was both a social and a political acknowledgement of female economic success, and therefore a reward for female industriousness, was banned. Indigenous customary laws associated with the institution of woman-to-woman marriage became confused as a result of its reinterpretation according to canon law and Christian morality. To illustrate changes in marriage practice and gender relations, and their economic and political effect on the women involved, a case study of one *obi* through three generations, from the period just before the colonial invasion to the present day, follows.

As most of the participants in this drama are still alive, and the settlement of the dispute did not meet with the approval of most of those concerned, I have used fictitious names in telling what is a true story.

a) Okenwanyi's husband had two wives:

$$\blacktriangle = \bullet = \bullet$$
Okenwanyi

b) Okenwanyi herself had nine wives:

Okenwanyi

c) The first wife of Okenwanyi's husband had one son called Okonkwo, while Okenwanyi herself had one daughter called Nwadiuto and a son called Emeliena:

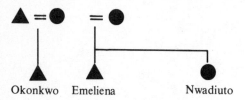

Okonkwo   Emeliena   Nwadiuto

d) On the death of his father, Okonkwo, as first son, succeeded his father in the *obi*, and inherited his father's wife Okenwanyi, who is his 'stepmother' in English terminology. They had a son called Maduabuchi. Maduabuchi, as the first son of Okonkwo, succeeded Okonkwo in the *obi*:

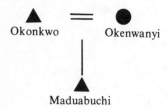

Okonkwo   Okenwanyi

Maduabuchi

e) One of Okenwanyi's nine wives ran away and had three sons and a daughter. The boys were called Kaine, Osita and Nkemka.

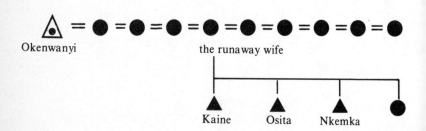

Okenwanyi   the runaway wife

Kaine   Osita   Nkemka

f) Okenwanyi's own son, Emeliena, married Ada Eze and they had many sons and daughters. The first son was called Obiora, the second, Nwokem:

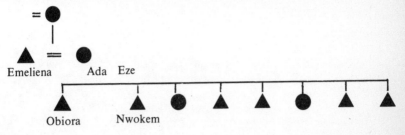

g) Ada Eze herself married one wife:

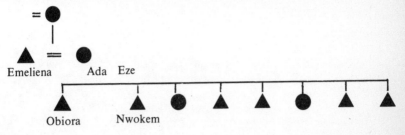

Ada Eze

Origin of the Problem: The Indigenous Institution of 'Female Husband'

Okenwanyi was one of the wealthiest and most popular women in Nnobi in the latter half of the 19th century. She overshadowed her husband, who died without leaving much to be remembered by. Okenwanyi was then inherited by her husband's first son, Okonkwo, who succeeded his father in the *obi*. He was born to Okenwanyi's co-wife. Okenwanyi herself had two children by her husband, a boy, Emeliena, and a girl, Nwadiuto. By all indications, Okenwanyi's stepson, Okonkwo, who became her husband, must have been a very young man, as he did not seem to have had much control over her, though she bore him a son called Maduabuchi.

As was the common practice with wealthy women in those days, Okenwanyi had several wives. Some of them were said to have gone away and others stayed and had children. One wife who went away remarried in a neighbouring town and bore four children, a girl, who was sold, and three boys, namely, Kaine, Osita and Nkemka. Okenwanyi's son Emeliena and his wife Ada Eze had five sons and three daughters. Their first son was called Obiora and their second, Nwokem. Nwokem, who is now an old man, and a Christian, commenting on the children born to the wife who went away and remarried, said,

It was through Okenwanyi that these people were born. It was nothing to do with Emeliena, my father. A woman brought in a fellow woman, and she bore them. That woman had left before Ada Eze, my mother, was even married. My mother did not even know her.

125

The Problem: Reinterpretation of the Institution of 'Female Husband'

Okenwanyi's husband had two sons before he died. Okonkwo, as the eldest son, succeeded his father in the *obi* and this made the other son, Emeliena, the head of a subordinate *obi*. Following the principle of unilineal inheritance, Okonkwo's son Maduabuchi superseded his father's brother Emeliena and succeeded his father in the *obi*. All this time, no problems were posed by any issue from Okenwanyi's wives, as she had redistributed them to various husbands and had collected marriage payment, except for the wife who ran away, and the money paid to acquire her was not reclaimed. The problem arose when colonial rule was imposed, and the warrant chief system of local administration was applied in Igboland between 1898 and 1929 (see Chapter 8).

Maduabuchi, through the influence of the son of his father's half-sister Nwadiuto, was made a warrant chief. Through various proclamations by the colonial government, warrant chiefs and their native courts acquired various judicial, legislative and executive powers which had hitherto been diffused in the indigenous political system. Laws were passed which upheld their economic position and political authority. The chiefs even had powers of conscription, as stated in the Roads and Creeks (Rivers) Proclamation, 1903. About this proclamation, an Igbo historian writes,

> Once instructed a warrant chief had the right to call out any man between the ages of fifteen and fifty and any woman between fifteen and forty years old residing within his area of authority to work on the road or waterway or part of it for a length of time not exceeding six days in a quarter. (Afigbo 1972:96)

Maduabuchi, like other corrupt warrant chiefs of his time, found the space provided by his father's *obi* too confined for his new lifestyle, so he built a big, two-storeyed house elsewhere, which he used as a court. As he acquired a lot of what had hitherto been communal land, he found that he needed a lot of manpower. His mode of transportation was said to have been a truck, pushed along by a few men. It was in this context that his action of reclaiming and bringing back home the sons of the wife who ran away was understood. As one of the 'cheated' sons put it to me,

When Maduabuchi became chief and needed a lot of manpower, he went and collected back the sons of the runaway wife and used them as slaves. Then, when my father Emeliena died, he brought up the case. Ada Eze, my mother, was alone then. Her oldest son, Obiora, who should succeed my father in his *obi*, was in an urban town then. When she heard that the case was coming up, she sent for Obiora but, before he arrived, Maduabuchi and his fellow chiefs had taken a decision on the case. He put one of the sons of the runaway wife in his own *obi*, as he no longer had use for it since he had vacated it and gone elsewhere to build a court. The other son of the runaway wife was put in my father's *obi* without waiting for my eldest brother, Obiora, to get back. As the decision arrived at was not in her son's favour, my mother was very hurt and very angry. Obiora went back to the urban town, got rich, came back, bought a massive piece of land and built the first three-storeyed house in Nnobi. This was near the only tarred road, which was the major road, too. Everyone went to look at it. My mother was happy again. Others thought that if they took the *obi* away from us, we would become useless. In fact, the taking away of the *obi* from us because our father was dead, and the unhappiness of our mother, made us very determined to succeed. All five sons had left home and gone to find employment in the urban centres. Soon after our senior brother finished his own house, I sent him money to build mine, also along the major road. Before long, our youngest brother came home, bought a piece of land and built his own house, also by the major road. So we all had somewhere to live. The females had all gone to their husbands' homes.

When discussing this case with those involved, I concluded that there was a conflict of opinion in their interpretation of the status of the woman who ran away. The woman had been married to another woman and, in fact, the literal translation of the term used for this practice, *igba ohu*, is 'buying a slave'. As explained in Chapter 2, this term was restricted to woman-to-woman marriage and not man-to-woman marriage, but both types were governed by the same customary laws. This might in fact explain why Nnobi and other related areas have no slave settlements, even though they participated in the slave trade. Nnobi indigenous institutions made no provision for the status of a slave. Instead, there was the institution of *osu*, cult slaves or those dedicated to the goddess Idemili. Those of the 'injured sons' who referred to the runaway woman and her sons as slaves, did so from Christian and Western influence. In this, they were challenged by other members of their patrilineage, including one of the injured sons, who insisted that the runaway woman was a wife and that therefore her sons had right of inheritance. According to this son,

The man who was put in the *obi* was not born from that *obi*. His mother bore him elsewhere. Emeliena did not father him. Everybody knew that. The question then became whether she was married, or bought by a woman. Either way, she was a wife in that *obi*. Native law stipulates that, as long as brideprice was not reclaimed, any children born to her inside or outside this *obi* belong to this *obi*. It was on this understanding that our people went and brought back the children she bore from somewhere else. Not demanding back the brideprice was a serious mistake on our part.

It is in fact only because of the difference of opinion on the status of the runaway woman that the 'injured sons' were unable to chase out the present occupants of the *obi*. The man who was put in this *obi* had married two wives. As the quarrel intensified and life became uncomfortable for him in the *obi*, he returned to his biological father's town. When he left, only one wife agreed to leave with him – the other stayed behind. As he had left voluntarily those involved were glad that the problem had been solved, not knowing that the wife who had remained behind was pregnant. When she gave birth, the baby was a boy; and he therefore succeeded to his father's position in the *obi* – thus the problem remained. He in turn now has a son, like himself, born in the *obi*, and this son will succeed him.

The other reason the present occupants remain in the *obi* is that the houses and homes built by the 'injured sons' have now overshadowed the original *obi*. The disputed occupants of the *obi* have in fact served as servants to some of the 'injured sons' and have been set up in business by them. But as everyone involved knows, if the 'injured sons' desperately wanted to be rid of the present occupants, they could do so easily by applying new meanings to old institutions and they would be supported by the church, birth certificates and the law court.

The effect of this case on the mother of the 'injured sons' also reveals the helplessness of women against modern institutions. Ada Eze was described as a very popular woman, who commanded great respect. All the women from her father's *obi* were said to have commanded much respect, as he was a very powerful titled man. They were also proud, and other women looked up to, and listened to them. As one of her sons recounted,

Before this case, I remember my mother as a very happy woman. She married very early and was married to my father only because he too was from a great *obi*. Our mother was hard-working. She alone used to cultivate all that land that we owned with Maduabuchi. It was from it that she fed all of us. As my father died early, and his *obi* was usurped, my senior brothers had no assets. The little education I had, was sponsored by my mother and my most senior brother, till I won a scholarship to go to secondary school. In those days, after school, I used to go to meet my mother. At the close of the market day, she would wait for me and I would go and help her head-load her goods back to the house. She belonged to all the women's associations in Nnobi at that time. I used to see them come to our house for all kinds of meetings. She also belonged to the Women's Council. Obiora, her first son, killed her a cow, hence she was an *ogbuefi* titled woman. He bought her coral beads. He also bought her ivory anklets and bracelets. In those days, these were the highest ornaments one could buy for one's mother. The day that the anklets were being paid for, I was one of those who cried at seeing all our money being heaped into the basket.[6] As the basket was being carried away, we burst into tears. It was only on the day that she wore the ornaments, and we went to the market to celebrate with her friends, that we danced for joy. It was after the case of who should be in our *obi*, when it was decided that the son of the runaway woman should be in our *obi*, that she became a very disappointed woman. We tried our best to make her go to church like the rest of us, but she refused. Obiora bought everything that would make her happy so that he could convince her to go to church, but she refused. She did go for a few days and then fell back. It did not make any sense to her. When discussing with someone, one had the impression that she had been to school. Certain events helped shake her faith. The events were: the behaviour of church-goers; some did not speak the truth; the things she saw with her own eyes that were being done by church people; their lies and hypocrisy and, worst of all, the outcome of the case of who should be in our *obi*. This helped shatter her faith. She felt that Maduabuchi, the brother of her husband, knowing that the presence of the sons of the runaway woman would deprive her sons of their position, should not have brought them back, or when he no longer had need of their service, he should have taken them back to the town where they were born and claimed back the original brideprice, since the town would have been pleased to have them back as they knew their father there. That problem would have been resolved ages ago to the satisfaction of everyone.

There were all kinds of interpretations as to why Maduabuchi had 'cheated' Ada Eze's sons of their rightful place in their father's *obi*. One was the pride and arrogance of Ada Eze who, according to customary law, should have been inherited by Maduabuchi at the death of her husband. As Maduabuchi had become a staunch Christian and officially a monogamist, one can only guess at some of the conflicts that would have arisen. Ada Eze's father, a very powerful man, had been disgraced by the colonialists, while Maduabuchi, a 'nobody', had been made powerful by them. From my knowledge of the viciousness and power of Nnobi women's tongues she could not have left him in peace. Her husband, Emeliena, was also known as a very powerful and knowledgeable *dibia*, a profession which the church Maduabuchi was identified with condemned, though he was said to have continued to use the services of a *dibia* in secret, especially in his quarrel with Ada Eze.

The basic argument against Maduabuchi was not that he had flouted customary law, but that he had slighted Ada Eze, a woman of such high status. He could have avoided the problem of succession, as one of Ada Eze's sons pointed out, by sending the men back to their father and claiming compensation from him. But the colonial government gave him the power with which to belittle a woman of Ada Eze's status, a thing he would not have dared do before the coming of the White man, as he would have had Ada Eze's powerful father to contend with.

As the case of Ada Eze and her own wife will show, it was customary for a woman's son to inherit her wives, thus giving the sons born to her wives equal status to those born to her son. The second son of Ada Eze stated that as his mother was a very wealthy woman, she acquired a wife. According to him, it was Ada Eze who married the woman before she was inherited by Ada Eze's son, Obiora.

Two explanations were given to me as to why Ada Eze acquired a wife. 1) was a matter of status and prestige: she was a very wealthy woman and an aristocrat, therefore she acquired a wife; 2) was a matter of necessity. Things had changed. All her sons had left to seek employment and live in the urban centres. The daughters had left for their husbands' homes, some of which were not even in Nnobi. Consequently, she was alone and without help; therefore some of her children, especially the daughters, decided that she should acquire a wife. Her last daughter, now a woman in her sixties, recounted how they went to a neighbouring town to acquire a wife. According to her, it was a quick business and very little money was paid to acquire rights over the very young girl.

Complications arose later when the girl grew into womanhood and no arrangements had been made to allocate her to a man, as Ada Eze was a widow. The girl's family insisted that she should be inherited by Ada Eze's son, or else they would claim her back. But Ada Eze's son was a Christian and already had a wife, with whom he had been joined in holy matrimony. As the girl's family insisted on taking back their daughter, Ada Eze's son decided to take her, and she became an additional wife. In this case, a son, and in fact an only son, had already been born in wedlock, and therefore his succession to his father's *obi* was guaranteed. Other issues from subsequent marriages would have equal status, but junior to the first-born.

In the case of Okenwanyi, the sons born to her wife were equal in status to her own. They were also born before her sons' sons, and therefore had first right of succession in the event of her own sons' vacating the *obi*, which is what Maduabuchi did when he went elsewhere to build a court. All the sons of Ada Eze's son, Obiora, were regarded as legitimate under customary law, even though it is common knowledge that the sons born to the inherited woman were not fathered by him. But under church law, all his sons are not legitimate; only the son born in wedlock was recognized as legitimate by the church. Obiora himself, as a punishment for collecting wives, was banned, not from attending church and giving donations, but from taking holy communion. This became the church sanction for polygyny. It also seems that polygynists were not baptized in the early days of Christianity (see Isichei 1976:165, 181).

When I interviewed the inherited wife, she was proud of the fact that she had been the wife of Ada Eze. I made a comparison between Ada Eze and her daughter, who is known to me, and asked the inherited wife if the daughter looked like her mother. The very smart, agile, elderly lady hotly denied any such similarity. She used both the term 'our mother', *nne anyi*, and 'my husband', *di'm*, when she referred to Ada Eze, who had died in the middle of this century. According to her, Ada Eze was stout, but firm and dignified, wielding authority with confidence. Her daughter, on the other hand, according to this lady, is fat and flabby, bad-tempered and foul-mouthed. 'My husband was never like that! No, they are not alike!' she said. This lady still runs errands for the daughter of Ada Eze, whom she had served as a child. In any case, Ada Eze's daughter is her classificatory husband as a senior daughter in the patrilineage into which she is married, and therefore her superior (see Chapter 3).

Not only has the institution of 'female husband' and the associated practice of inheriting wives been affected by canon law and Christian morality, but the very practical traditional practice of widow inheritance has also been rejected by the Christians and educated élites. Ada Eze's son Obiora, for example, died some years ago and left three widows; two other wives had died before him. Traditionally, these women should have been inherited by his brothers, but this has not been the case even though the youngest wife is of child-bearing age; the wife of one of Obiora's brothers died recently, leaving him a widower. When, during fieldwork, I raised the point that customary law allowed him to take at least the youngest of his dead brother's wives, the idea seemed to him repugnant! Yet Okenwanyi, the mother of his father, had been inherited by her stepson, by whom she bore Maduabuchi. Indeed, this fact has now become a 'family secret', and I learned of it from other members of the minor lineage, and even then, it was admitted only by the elderly men in the family; it was too 'embarrassing' to be spoken of by the other, educated, Christian sons. According to Christian morality and marriage laws, such a practice is abominable and unlawful. It is clearly stated in the Bible, 'The nakedness of thy father's wife shall thou not uncover: It is thy father's nakedness' (Leviticus 18:8). (The man who gave me the information has never, in fact, been to church. He still worships the goddess Idemili.)

If the son who rejected the inheritance of his brother's widow sought support for his position from the Bible, Leviticus would provide it: 'Thou shalt not uncover the nakedness of thy brother's wife: it is thy brother's nakedness' (18:16). This is repeated in Leviticus 20:21, where the punishment for breaking this law is stated: 'And if a man shall take his brother's wife, it is an unclean thing: he hath uncovered his brother's nakedness; they shall be childless.' This verse was quoted by the Tudor

King Henry VIII of England, in his debate with the church when he wished to discard his wife by levirate, Catherine of Aragon, and marry Anne Boleyn (see Palmer 1971:45–50). The church, opposing him, found support in Deuteronomy, where it is stated that God did permit levirate:

> If brethren dwell together, and one of them die, and have no child, the wife of the dead shall not marry without unto a stranger: her husband's brother shall go in unto her, and take her to him to wife, and perform the duty of an husband's brother unto her. (Deuteronomy 25:5)

In the case of Henry VIII, and in Hebrew culture, levirate served a male interest of continuity of the lineage, as is stated in Deuteronomy 25:6: 'And it shall be, that the firstborn which she beareth shall succeed in the name of his brother which is dead, that his name be not put out of Israel.' In Igbo culture, widow inheritance was a means of retaining property, including wives, in the lineage, as well as ensuring social continuity and guaranteeing economic security for elderly women. This point was also made by Basden, who, after stating that wives were inherited as part of the property of a deceased man, wrote, 'If the women are old, they remain quietly as members of the compound under the new owner, and are rarely disturbed' (1938:268). As access or right to farm land was linked with the status of wifehood, widow inheritance ensured that wives did not lose their means of subsistence. It also ensured that elderly and therefore no longer sexually attractive or biologically reproductive women did not find themselves without husbands or homes, but could remain viable members of the complex compound or extended family.

As Obiora's wives have not been inherited by any of the lineage men, but remain in his compound fending for themselves and their children, since Obiora's son lives in an urban town with his church-wedded wife, these women may take lovers and even have children by them, and not be rebuked by anyone. One does not ask a widow who is the father of her child in Nnobi culture or elsewhere in Igboland. Such widows, in the past, had a good chance of accumulating wealth, which would be converted to wives and then more wealth and titles, as they were free from marital and domestic responsibilities. This is the case with a few wealthy trader women in urban centres today. Having accumulated wealth, they may acquire wives in the names of their sons or male relatives. Since Nnobi no longer has titles for women, women can no longer seek formal political power for themselves through title-taking as do wealthy men in Nnobi today.

The last *Ekwe* titled women died before the middle of this century, by which time the customs associated with the title had changed. From my observations during fieldwork, Christianity did not seem to have deterred men from accumulating as many wives as their wealth allowed them. This was not the case with wealthy women. A 71-year-old elder, Chief Akudolu, talking about his father and one of his wives who was an *Ekwe* titled woman, said that his father was a wealthy man who had nine wives known to him personally; there had been others but some had died and some had left his father. One of these wives was an *Ekwe* titled woman. When I asked the elder if this woman had bought wives, he said,

No, she did not buy wives. By the time she took the *Ekwe* title, people had become enlightened. It is not long since she died. It was way back in the past that they bought wives. She herself did not buy a wife, but married wives for all her sons.

Overwhelming evidence shows that women in Nnobi and in Igboland in general were neither more comfortable nor more advantaged from an economic point of view under colonialism. They had lost their grip on the control of liquid cash; men had invaded the general market, and women were becoming helpless in their personal relations with husbands. But, most important of all, pro-female institutions were being eroded both by the church and the colonial administration.

Notes

1. Information on the introduction of the Church Missionary Society (CMS) church in Nnobi is drawn from articles in *Abalukwu* magazine and discussions with people in Nnobi, notably Samuel Ikebeotu, in August 1980. Born at the close of the 19th century he had been a schoolteacher. He started going to church in 1909 and first attended school in 1910. Though an old man he is still alert and agile and at present is a leading member of the clergy at St Paul's Church, Ebenesi, Nnobi. In 1980 he gave a sermon based on a detailed eyewitness account of the coming of the CMS to Nnobi. Throughout my fieldwork this sermon was widely quoted in Nnobi.

2. John Okigbo, titled Chief Eze Anyidiaso Okigbo, whom I interviewed in January 1982, gave me information about Okanume and the coming of the Catholic Church to Nnobi. He is the grandson of Okanume and a titled member of the *Igwe*'s council. Okanume was also made a warrant chief by the colonial government.

3. Titled members of the *Igwe*'s (traditional ruler's) council (see Chapter 9).

4. The Catholic Church, in approving the taking of the *ozo* title by its members, insisted on expurgation of the 'pagan' aspects of the rituals involved. During fieldwork in January 1982, I attended an *ozo* title-taking ceremony and was surprised when some Anglican relatives who took me to the ceremony claimed that what we saw was 'paganistic'. They were disgusted by the fact that a Catholic reverend father came and gave it his blessing. The man taking the title belonged to the major patrilineage of Umuona, and consequently, the participants were all from there. The priest of the Aho shrine, Ekechukwu, received the man into the *ozo* title, while the Umuona elder, Ezudona, again, a non-Christian, capped him. The Aho shrine priest used the *abosi* leaf (believed to have a cleansing, purifying power) for 'washing' the man's tongue. Thenceforth, the man was expected to speak nothing but the truth. For the same purpose, he passed an egg and the *abosi* leaf over the man's body and over his tongue. Next, he placed the egg on the ground and the leaf over it. The *ozo* candidate was then instructed to step on the leaf and squash the egg. I was told that in the past, a chick would be used instead of an egg; the candidate had to sit on it to kill it. It was the use of the old symbols that my Anglican relatives objected to, without appreciating that they symbolized righteousness. The title taken by the *ozo* man was *Igbo-fu-ego*, when an Igbo person sees money . . . This is a short form of the saying, *Igbo fu ego, ogholu aku*; the insect called *aku*, like moths, is attracted to light. The analogy therefore is that the Igbo and money are like moths and light. The implication, I think, is that Igbos turn

money into a fortune; they are enterprising. The *ozo* title is voluntary and achievement-based. When a man becomes financially successful, he seeks power and prestige by buying the *ozo* title.

5. When Achebe was born, his father was a schoolteacher from the nearby town of Ogidi.

6. The introduction of European money caused general inflation and the devaluation of cowrie shells, the local coinage.

8. The Erosion of Women's Power

Western Education and the Invisibility of Women

As Christianity introduced a male deity, religious beliefs and practices no longer focused on the female deity, but on a male God, his son, his bishops and priests. While women formed the great majority of the congregation – the body of the church – a few men, the clergy, constituted the headship of the church. These new gender relations and realities were also being generated through the early patterns of Western education.

The enrolment figures quoted in Nwabara (1977), drawn from the *Annual Report of the Department of Education* for the year 1906, demonstrate that boys had a head start over girls in the early years of Western education in Igboland. In the Eastern Province Nwabara quotes: 1,592 boys and 132 girls for the 12 schools managed by the United Free Church of Scotland; 213 boys and 109 girls for the four schools run by the Roman Catholic mission; 538 boys and 184 girls for the nine schools belonging to the Niger Delta Pastorate. By 1900 the government itself had one, boys' only, school. This sex imbalance in the schools was also true of the Central Province of the protectorate under which Nnobi was grouped. The enrolment figures for the 19 government schools were 1,038 boys and 116 girls; for the 21 Roman Catholic mission schools, 1,550 boys and 11 girls. The Church of England's one school – the Onitsha Industrial Mission – was for boys only.

Two of the mission schools provided opportunities for advanced education in vocations usually considered male, such as carpentry, tailoring and printing. Thus initially only males had access to higher education. When the need arose to train indigenous West Africans as teachers, men were the first to be trained. Men also served as learner-clerks and were trained for government services and trading with European firms (Nwabara 1977:60–62).

Male bias was therefore a strong feature of government educational programmes as well as mission policies and education. Had the government's attitude to women been more progressive, great possibilities for women might have been found in the government schools, where at least education was not dependent on conversion and religious instruction. Mission schools were, however, far more numerous than government educational institutions.

The *Annual Report of the Department of Education* for the year 1909 gives a figure of 4,302 boys to 279 girls for the government schools in the three provinces of the eastern protectorate. The number of mission schools kept well ahead of government schools. In 1911, for example, in the Central Province, the government had 28 schools while the missions had 45. In the Eastern Province, the government had 22 schools compared to the 107 run by the missions. The *Annual Colonial Report* of 1911 recorded a figure of 1,160 boys to 20 girls in 29 schools.

This pattern of higher enrolment of males continued in the first half of the present century, as figures for government and private schools between 1929 and 1938 indicate (see Nwabara 1977:68–9; Nnobi was in Onitsha province). However, the figures in Table 2.2 of edition 4 of the *Statistical Digest* (1973) of the East-Central State of Nigeria, show that by the early 1970s, the number of girls enrolled in primary schools was quickly catching up with that of boys. (In these Tables from the *Statistical Digest*, Nnobi falls under the Idemili division.) Table 2.3 shows a comparatively higher enrolment for girls into secondary schools in more recent years, especially in the urban towns. Girls, however, seem to drop out after completing secondary school, especially in the rural areas; in Idemili Division, no female intakes are recorded for the sixth form. The explanation could be that in the rural areas girls marry much earlier, and immediately after marriage devote their time and energy to the subsistence sector and domestic responsibilities. This explanation is supported by figures in Table 2.6, which records high enrolment figures for girls up to the age of 20 in the urban town of Enugu, and much lower figures for girls in some rural towns. Figures for Ezzikwo and Nkanu indicate that in some areas of Igboland girls were still not sent to school in 1973.

While boys were prepared for government, trade, industry, church and educational services, girls were prepared for domestic services and taught cooking, cleaning, childcare and sewing.

By the 1970s the pattern of male–female education had changed very slightly with a few females trickling into what had hitherto been considered male disciplines. Table 2.32 of the *Statistical Digest*, for example, gives enrolment figures for the University of Nigeria, Nsukka, which show that women still monopolized the department of home economics, except for one man admitted in 1972 among 30 women, and three more in 1973 as against 34 women. This interest of men in cookery can be understood in the context of urban Nigerian society where hotel catering and management are booming enterprises. In the public sector, cooking is a paying vocation.

Even though Igbo women have been described as keen traders, the figures show that very few go to university to study business administration. In 1973 enrolment for language studies was 58 women to 48 men, while enrolment figures in the department of education show male predominance. In the engineering faculty, enrolment figures for 1970 and 1971 record only three women, in the department of architecture/estate management. By 1973, however, five women were enrolled for engineering as against 515 men, while 11 women and 174 men were enrolled for architecture/estate management; one woman and 76 men enrolled for surveying.

In the fields of law, medicine, science and social sciences, the enrolment figures for females are very low indeed. Table 2.34 in the *Statistical Digest* shows the pattern of male–female enrolments over the period from 1964 to 1974. Very few people compared to the total population had access to university education by 1974 and still fewer females than men had university degrees.

Judith Van Allen tried to find some answers to the questions of why men had preference in the 'modern' development schemes, why it was mainly boys who were educated and why they were given a different education from girls. In response to these questions she writes,

> At least part of the answer must lie in the values of the colonialists, values that led the British to assume that girls and boys, women and men, should be treated and should behave as people supposedly did in 'civilized' Victorian England. Strong male domination was imposed on Igbo society both indirectly, by new economic structures, and directly, by the recruitment of only men into Native Administration. In addition, the new economic and political structures were supported by the inculcation of sexist ideology in the mission schools. (1976:80)[1]

Material presented in Part One shows that strong male domination and ideology did exist in the formal, traditional Nnobi social and ideological structure, but at the same time the flexibility of its gender system mitigated sexual dualism. This was not the case with the Victorian ideology transported into Igboland by the British missionaries and educationalists. It was from their ideologies that the expression 'a woman's place is in the home' was derived. This slogan has ever since been a popular topic for school debates in Nigeria. Other notions of womanhood embedded in Victorian ideology also idealized the virtuous and frail-minded female incapable of mastering 'masculine' subjects like science, politics and business (see Rogers 1980). These were some of the prejudices held against women by the colonialists and missionaries and carried over into Igboland (Van Allen 1976:80–81 and footnotes).

The significance of these prejudices, the masculinization of religion and government, is manifest in the exclusion of women from the colonial political administration in Nnobi and elsewhere in Igboland. The political and economic frustration felt by the women led to mass demonstrations and rioting by women all over Igboland at various times from 1928 to 1980.

The Exclusion of Women from the Colonial Local Administrative System

As we have noted, with the introduction of Christianity and Western and Victorian ideologies, women took a secondary position in the fields of education and religious leadership. The same process of masculinization occurred in political representation in the local government system, in Nnobi and all other Igboland communities. During the colonial period, those who wielded power – such as warrant chiefs, court clerks and court messengers – in the local communities, were all men.

The colonial government in its classification of indigenous Igbo political systems had incorrectly included Nnobi among those communities with traditional constitutional monarchies (Afigbo 1972:141–2). It is, therefore, not surprising that when the British colonialists came to Nnobi as part of the military expeditions in Igboland (1900–1919) to break the resistance of the natives and destroy their guns

(Nwabara 1977:97–155), the name of Eze Okigbo was given to them as they insisted on meeting local kings, even where there were none. In Nnobi oral tradition, the British military expedition has come to be known as 'the gun-breaking war', as this seemed to have been very important to the invaders.

Eze Okigbo, the 'big man' in Nnobi at the time, had heard shocking stories about the activities of White men and had sworn never to set eyes on them. He therefore declined to meet them when they invaded Nnobi, and was consequently taken by force to the central market-place and publicly whipped. He went back to his *obi*, took poison and died.

After the death of Eze Okigbo, the system of government in Nnobi changed, as it did everywhere else in Igboland, after the military expeditions and firm establishment of colonial presence and rule. Ignoring the different indigenous political systems, from 1891 to 1929 the colonial government established a universal system of local government throughout Igboland in the form of the warrant chief system. The most detailed account and analysis of this system appeared in Afigbo (1972). Describing it he writes,

> The British selected certain natives who they thought were traditional chiefs and gave them certificates of recognition and authority called warrants. The warrant entitled each of these men to sit on the native court from time to time to judge cases. It also empowered him to assume within the community he represented, executive and judicial powers which were novel both in degree and territorial scope. (1972:6–7)

Eze Okoli, the First *Igwe* of Nnobi,[2] and the Birth of a New Era of Male Domination

As warrant chiefs had already been appointed in the neighbouring towns of Obosi and Nnewi, politically ambitious men in Nnobi were aware of this new short cut to power. The death of Eze Okigbo was followed by a state of emergency in Nnobi while there was competition for leadership among the wealthy men who fought for powerful positions in the new local government structure.

Chief Solomon Eze Okoli was a wealthy and famous *dibia*. This placed him among the most privileged and powerful in Nnobi; hence he was able to defeat opposing forces in his support of colonial invasion and rule. His father, Eze Ebube Akunma, had also been a very rich man and, as the only surviving son, Eze Okoli succeeded him at his death. In no time, he himself achieved great wealth and influence. Unlike Eze Okigbo, who was in his declining years when the White men came to Nnobi, Eze Okoli was in his prime, alert and shrewd. He quickly assessed the political climate and made choices which placed him in a favourable position for power.

Solomon Eze Okoli, to put himself in an advantageous position in his bid for power, took private lessons in speaking, reading and writing English. This won him the respect of administrators, district officers, and court clerks and interpreters. He also gained favour with the missionaries as he became a Christian convert and actively aided them in the spread of Christianity in Nnobi. By supplying the colonial government with troops in the Cameroons and accommodating British troops in Nnobi during the military campaigns of the Royal Niger Company Army (1900–1912), he was equally favoured by the colonial administrators. His loyalty and support were rewarded by making him a warrant chief and opening the Obiaja court in Nnobi in 1915.

Chief Solomon Eze Okoli later became a paramount chief in 1918, following the Native Authority Ordinance of 1916, when certain native court areas came under 'Sole Native Authorities' who later became paramount chiefs. This was as a result of Lugard's venture to bring local government in the Eastern Provinces into line with the system in the Northern Emirates, regardless of differences in indigenous political systems (Afigbo 1972:140–42).

Chief Solomon Eze Okoli, a paramount chief, backed by the colonial government, went through a brief imperialistic career himself setting up 'hegemony', according to his son, over 13 towns which he named *Mbailinito*. He had his native court and the district officer's rest house and court in an area of Nnobi called Obiaja, which had been designated as crown land.[3] Again, in keeping with the practices of the warrant chiefs, Chief Eze Okoli made his son president of the district court for the Thirteen Towns in Idemili Division. The communities which made up the Thirteen Towns were Nnobi, Awka-Etiti, Alo, Oraukwu, Nnokwa, Abatete, Umuoji, Uke, Nkpo, Oba, Ojoto, Obosi and Akwukwu. Interestingly, Nnewi, the 'daughter' of Nnobi, never came under her 'hegemony'.

Solomon Eze Okoli had become so powerful that he could influence the appointment of other chiefs and headmen in Nnobi. Through his influence a chief was appointed for each quarter of Nnobi, Ebenesi, Ngo and Awuda. Having established himself, relatives and friends in the powerful seats of local government, he then set out to develop Nnobi and the other towns under his authority. He established schools and churches and built roads between the towns. He built himself a palace in which he set up a court, and employed a court clerk called Augustine Ezenabo. He appointed chiefs in the Thirteen Towns who were given warrants by the district officer. When the colonial government embarked on its plan to introduce direct taxation in the Eastern Provinces, Chief Eze Okoli was among those warrant chiefs escorted on a tour of the areas already taxed in the Western Province (Afigbo 1972:224). The climax of Chief Eze Okoli's career was the award, while on this tour, in Lagos, of a certificate and medal of honour by King George V of England through the then commander-in-chief of Nigeria, Sir Graeme Thompson. He was then appointed a district head in Onitsha and paid as such.

Already the warrant chief system was deeply detested in Igboland owing to the corruption and high-handedness of the warrant chiefs, court messengers and clerks. The introduction of direct taxation and the appointment of district heads made matters worse. These and other social and economic factors led to a period of general unrest in the then Eastern Provinces, the climax of which was the Women's War which broke out in the old Owerri and Calabar provinces in 1929.

According to the views of the present local chief of Nnobi, the son of Chief Solomon Eze Okoli, who himself served as president for the Thirteen Towns,

The introduction of poll tax and the appointment of district heads in Igboland met with unpleasant consequences. In old Owerri province, the situation resulted in the women's riot of 1929. In Nnobi, Eze Okoli's political enemies quickly exploited this highly explosive situation in Igboland and antagonized him. They were held responsible for introducing tax revenue in Igboland. By that, Nnobi community in Idemili division suffered a major political setback which is yet very difficult to correct. (*Abalukwu*, September 1975:14)

According to information gathered from Nnobi and from references in Afigbo (1972), Eze Okoli was guilty of corruption and abuse of power. For this reason, he was dethroned in 1928 even before the Women's War (1929–30) and the consequent fall of the warrant chief system. With the introduction of direct taxation in 1928, the colonial government recommended a system whereby each village or ward was a tax unit, and the village or ward head the tax agent responsible for collecting tax gathered by compound heads, and handing it to district headquarters. In Onitsha Division, Chief Eze Okoli ignored the ward head and collected tax himself throughout Nnobi court area (Afigbo 1972:231 and footnotes).

As a result of British support and unchecked powers given to paramount chiefs, some of whom would not have been regarded as 'big men' by their local communities, warrant chiefs, interpreters, court clerks and even messengers began to adopt the lifestyle of 'big men', accumulating wives and wealth; they became a terror to the local people (Nwabara 1977:171–2).

In Nnobi, Chief Eze Okoli allegedly proclaimed that any child or animal born on *Eke* day (the goddess Idemili's traditional holy day) was his property; he also claimed the services of everyone on *Eke* day. The Roads and Creeks (Rivers) Proclamation of 1903 which was enacted on the assumption that traditional chiefs had the right to conscript or call out members of the community for communal labour supported his claims.

As government by warrant chiefs became autocratic and oppressive, in the words of an Nnobi elder, Mr R. O. Madueme,

People's eyes opened under this oppression and they began to question the autocracy of the chiefs. They said that the chiefs were not gods but people. In Nnobi people refused to go and work for the *igwe*. When he summoned them, they would not go to his palace.

This state of affairs soon led a group of Nnobi citizens to petition the resident at Onitsha that they no longer wanted the *igwe*, and in this they were actively supported by the Women's Council. So Chief Solomon Eze Okoli was dethroned.

Afigbo reveals that even though the other two provinces of Eastern Nigeria, Ogoja and Onitsha provinces, took no part in the 1929 Women's War in Owerri and Calabar provinces, localized violent opposition, especially by women, to direct taxation had occurred in Ogoja and Onitsha provinces as soon as it was introduced in 1928 (1972:232–5).

It is therefore correct to state that those areas which did not participate in the 1929 riots demonstrated their own opposition to taxation in 1928. Afigbo (1972:224) also made the point that, according to information gathered during his fieldwork in Ogoja and Onitsha provinces, women there were officially told that

139

women's riots in Owerri and Calabar provinces in 1929 were in response to a local chief imposing taxation on them. This was not true, and consequently, as these women were dealing with their own oppressive chiefs, they saw disturbances in the other provinces as localized.

Women throughout Igboland were actually demanding the removal of the warrant chiefs and closure of the native courts and European firms (Perham 1937). Women had no place in the colonial government or law courts, and were rapidly losing out in the new economic structure. As Afigbo put it,

> The point is that nobody in the upper reaches of the administrative pyramid, where official policy was made, realized the need to go fast with reform. To learn this lesson they needed the shock of mobs of irate women tearing down native court houses, snatching Warrant Chiefs' caps and hurling themselves in desperation at trained troops armed with rifles and machine guns. (1972:245)

Even when reforms were made in 1933 as a result of the women's struggle, women's demands for a place in the judiciary and government were ignored as they seemed absurd to the British who were ignorant of, or so ethnocentric they could not accept the fact of indigenous women's organizations and their place in the traditional political structure (Van Allen 1976:74).

In 1933, the British therefore legitimized a new sexual politics based on a very rigid gender ideology which Igbo men were to manipulate effectively in their monopolization of power in the public spheres during the post-independence period.

Women and the New Cash Economy

Writers on the Igbo in general have expressed two views on the effect of colonialism on Igbo women's economic position. Ifeka-Moller, for example, emphasizes the economic ascendancy of Igbo women from 1880 to the early 20th century. This she attributes first to the expansion of the overseas trade in palm-oil and palm kernels, and later, when colonial government was established, to the spread of petty commodity production and the emergence of a new cash economy and the large-scale trading corporations. The combination of these produced a new generation of traders and, as she put it, 'the important novelty was that many of them were women' (1975:136–7).

My Nnobi data, however, do not support such a late emergence of wealthy trader women, nor her view that the exclusion of women in the colonial formal political structure is a continuation of the traditional system of political domination by men. She writes, 'The formal political system, which was under male management, did not shift towards integrating women as chiefs or priests as their economic influence grew' (1975:134).

The case studies reported in Chapter 2 reveal the economic and political prominence of women in indigenous Nnobi society, owing to their participation in the production and sale of palm-oil and kernel much earlier in the 19th century.

The institutions of the *Ekwe* title, the availability of the *ogbuefi* title, the existence of *dibia* women, the ritual and political roles of daughters, the practice of 'female husband', are indications of formal political power and authority for women, sometimes based upon the idea of achievement and reward. It was under church and colonial rule in Nnobi that women suffered a reverse in their economic and political power.

Both Okigbo (1965) and Judith Van Allen (1976) support the view that it was colonial rule, a strong cash economy and European firms that undermined women's economic and political power. Pax Britannica, as well as increasing the involvement of women in long-distance trade, also established European firms and factories with a monopoly over certain commodities and a pricing system which disadvantaged women competitors. No doubt there emerged a few very wealthy women in urban towns, who acted as middlewomen for the European firms, but for the great majority of them, as Van Allen put it, 'the accumulated surplus remained small, often providing only subsistence and a few years' school fees for some of their children' (1976:78–9).

Okigbo (1965), in a structural analysis of the social consequences of economic development, locates the reversal of Igbo women's economic ascendancy over their husbands in changes in traditional methods of production and consequent changes in relations of production. Not only did women lose some degree of economic independence and their monopoly over the processing and sale of certain food items, they also lost their power of applying economic sanctions in both the domestic and the public spheres as men found a new independence in work or trade relations with European firms and businesses. A process was thus set in motion which affected power relations in the communities.

The economic history of 19th-century Igboland marked the transition from slave trade to palm-oil trade. During the slave trade period the British trade frontier had been the Delta States, which supplied the middlemen, while the Igbo interior produced the victims (Isichei 1973:44–60). With the abolition of slavery and the British blockade of the Delta ports, European merchants shifted from exporting slaves to exporting palm-oil (with which European factories made soap); palm kernels were also used in the manufacture of soap as well as margarine and cattle-feed (Isichei 1973:62–7).

As we saw in Chapter 1, women's centrality in the production and sale of palm-oil and kernels in traditional Nnobi society gave them a considerable advantage over their husbands. The introduction of pioneer oil mills mechanized the whole process of extracting the palm-oil and cracking the kernels. This, of course, meant a much higher oil yield which necessitated bulk buying by the agents of the mills and the channelling of most of the village's palm fruit to the mills. The main centre of production was therefore shifted from the family to the mills. At the same time, wives lost the near monopoly they enjoyed in the traditional method of production and the independent income they derived from it (Okigbo 1965:418). Instead of wives selling the palm-oil and keeping some of the profits, husbands now sold direct to the oil mills or their agents, and collected the money.

It is therefore in the context of the threatened loss of economic independence and power for women that Okigbo places the women's rioting in the Ibibio area between 1951 and 1952, when the erection of a pioneer oil mill there was under consideration (1965:419).

It was Ibibio women, together with Igbo women who fought the 1929 Women's War. Even Ifeka-Moller, for example, writes, 'With one exception, all the recorded cases of women's protest movements in the nineteen-twenties testify to the catalytic effect of economic discontent' (1975:134 and footnote).

Nnobi women, with their men, succeeded in removing the paramount chief imposed on them by the colonial administration, in 1928, long before their sisters started rioting in 1929 in other parts of Igboland, for the same end.

Women experienced the pinch in their pockets when male taxation was introduced, they also experienced economic difficulties associated with payment of their childrens' school fees. In 1958, the Eastern Region government's reintroduction of school fees in classes above infants II (see Nwabara 1977:72–4; Mba 1982:125–30) provoked a mass demonstration by Igbo women, still remembered vividly in Nnobi where women marched throughout the town and central market-place.

As in Ifeka-Moller (1975), there are contradictions in Mba's (1982) assessment of colonialism's effects on Igbo women. She points out that women were excluded from the colonial administrative system; that traditionally exclusive female activities were invaded by men. Yet, of the 1929 Women's War, she claims that Igbo women were not against the White man and that they

> did not want the white man to leave because they felt that their interests had been served by colonialism – as they understood it. The change it brought about in their economic activities and their increased legal rights under the native courts system, despite the abuses of the chiefs, were to the advantage of women. (1975:90–91)

The enraged women were well organized, objective and disciplined. They attacked, not the heavily armed White man, but his symbols of power and oppression such as courts, factories, foreign goods in the markets and the warrant chiefs. The song the women sang to Okugo, the warrant chief who became the focus of agitation, shows clearly what they thought of the White man. They told him that but for *nwa beke*, petty White boy, they would have crushed him like peanuts. This is recorded by Nwabara (1977:188). His translation of the Igbo is different from mine. He writes, 'If it were not for the white man we should have killed chief Okugo and eaten him up.' In other words, they were constrained by the military might of colonialism.

Mba's views on marriage and divorce, stemming from her Western bias, are ethnocentric. Polygyny is consequently condemned as she claims that changes in customary laws of marriage, that is, the institution of monogamous marriage by colonialism, benefited women by giving them greater security in marriage and making it easier for them to obtain divorce. Evidence from Nnobi presented in Chapter 7 indicates the contrary, and as I have also illustrated, others, such as Basden (1938) and Leith-Ross (1939), who was herself a widow at the time of her research in Igboland and therefore had a personal interest in making comparisons, saw advantages in the traditional polygynous marriage system. These advantages included the possibilities of autonomy within marriage, especially for elderly women; the embedded supportive systems in terms of childcare and domestic help which facilitated mobility and therefore encouraged women's economic and political activities.

As we shall see in Part Three, under the new institutions inherited from colonialism, Nnobi women became more constrained, less mobile and generally poorer. Men, on the other hand, became richer, gaining new wealth and new ideologies which they employed in the gender war, reinforcing their determination to marginalize women's position.

Notes

1. In July 1982, M. E. Amadiume found that, based on a random selection of equal numbers of male and female students of different ethnic groups from all the faculties in the university, 'students subscribed to the arbitrary idea of "masculinization" and "femininization" of careers' (research for MA in Education Guidance and Counselling, University of Jos, Nigeria). She also found that women students in what were considered traditionally men's fields ('female deviants') were subject to being stigmatized and to general curiosity, largely because of the belief that too much education jeopardized a girl's marriage opportunities. Amadiume wrote: 'Where she registers for a "feminine" course, especially one that qualifies her for teaching, she may be "pardoned" and will attract ready suitors. For an "acada" girl [woman graduate] . . . registering for a course in a non-traditional field, the general feeling among the males and even the females is that marrying such a girl will be tantamount to bringing "another man" into the family – a situation which will seriously jeopardize harmony in the family.

'Nicknames and ridiculous comments are often used to antagonize such female deviants. The male deviant . . . such as [in] the home economics department, is considered as probably lacking in ambition and not a match for his fellow men. He himself might even wonder if his attraction to such careers could be a sign of sexual abnormality.'

2. Information on Chief Solomon Eze Okoli is derived from interviews and discussions with various people in Nnobi, most of whom knew him, or were related to him. A short account of his life and activities by his son, Edmund Eze Okoli, the present *igwe* of Nnobi, appears in *Abalukwu*, Vol. 1, September 1975:13; see also Afigbo (1972). According to the accounts of Solomon Eze Okigbo's life I received, he was similar to Elizabeth Isichei's 'new men' who emerged in the history of many Igbo communities in the 19th century (1976:104–7); Chief Idigo of Aguleri's background (Isichei 1976:16) in particular is similar to that of Solomon Eze Okoli as recorded by his son (*Abalukwu*, September 1975). Both men were *dibia* and became wealthy through that profession. Both acquired knowledge and influence from having travelled widely; both stood firm against local opposition in the pursuit of friendship and favour with the British colonialists.

3. Igbo native law and custom recognized individual, family and communal ownership of land (see Chapter 1). The principle of communal ownership best suited the colonial government, and other methods of land tenure in Igboland were quickly denied. Following both the Native and Public Lands Acquisition Proclamations of 1903, the colonial government assumed the right to acquire any lands for public and government purposes (Nwabara 1977:34–9).

Part Three:
The Post-
Independence Period[1]

9. The Marginalization of Women's Position

The mass demonstrations and rioting by Igbo women from 1928 to 1930 against exclusively male and anti-female colonial institutions finally led to the collapse of the warrant chief system of local government. In seeking reforms in the colonial system of local government, various ordinances were passed between 1930 and 1960, when independence was granted to Nigeria (Nwabara 1977:203–15). Even after the general unrest, women's demands to be incorporated into the ruling administrative bodies (revealed to the Commission of Inquiry set up in 1930 to hear evidence of the riots in the southern provinces) were not seriously regarded by the colonial government.[2] Consequently, when, after a series of unpopular ordinances aimed at native court reforms, the idea of democratic representation and consultation finally occurred to the colonial legislators, leading to the promulgation of the Eastern Region Local Government Ordinance Number 16 of 1950, a guaranteed place for women in government bodies was not written into the law. The emergent county councils and district councils became political institutions monopolized by men, especially the decision-making processes. Decisions on, and the imposition of levies for community projects such as the building of schools, churches, maternity homes, assembly halls, roads, piped-water and electricity systems, police barracks and post offices etc., were made by men. Women, even though also liable to pay the levies, became an unwaged labour force for bush-clearing, carrying sand and wood, and fetching water, and in general became the public cleansing department and an entertainment group to dance for local chiefs and politicians.

Male control of the machinery of local government was confirmed in Ordinance 18 of 1959, which provided for the formation of a provincial assembly in each province of Eastern Nigeria (Nwabara 1977:212); this was a consultative and deliberative body above the native council. Its duty was to advise the government on such local matters as development projects or allocation of funds through provincial commissioners. In the structure or composition of local leadership, no seats were given to women.

A few months before independence, on 1 July 1960, the Eastern Region Independence Local Government Law shifted control of legislative, judicial and executive powers from colonial officers to Nigerian men; electoral regulations were made; the functions and rights of different levels of local government bodies were defined.

In filling government administrative offices, preference for and dominance of men was either stated or implied. The position of women was therefore marginalized in all social fields as a result of the rigidity of gender embodied in Western ideologies and institutions.

Women and Local Politics

As a result of the ban on the *Ekwe* title, women lost a prescribed and guaranteed position at the centre of local government; today there are no titles in Nnobi available to women. In the local ruling council (the *igwe*'s council) seats are reserved for certain titled men such as the *igwe* himself, who must always be a man, and the *ichie*(s), but there are no guaranteed seats for women. As in the church, women in local government again form the masses, not the paid leaders. We find that leaders of the women's organizations are used simply to enlist women's support for male-dominated political parties and their male candidates.

The modern political history of Nnobi is about men, their rivalries for power and their organized efforts to suppress and control the women's organizations. The backbone of the women's organization was finally broken in 1977, when leaders of the Women's Council were arrested and detained on charges of subversion. The Women's Council was then put under the supervision of the male-dominated and controlled organ of local government, the Nnobi Welfare Organization.

Local Government Bodies

With the removal of most local chiefs, following the Women's War, the colonial administration encouraged local communities to set up self-help projects. The organizations which initiated such projects were called Patriotic Unions, Improvement Unions or Welfare Organizations. The first such association was set up in Nnobi in 1942 by an Onitsha-based business man, Frederick Egbue. It was called the Nnobi Patriotic Union and was intended to see to the welfare of the home town. It fell casualty to local politics, sabotaged by some individuals still loyal to the deposed local ruler.

Not until 1946, following the rapid spread of Improvement Unions all over Igboland, did another Onitsha-based Nnobi man, Samson Ezenagu, set up the Nnobi Improvement Union. This organization then took over the leadership of Nnobi under a chairman, secretary and representatives from various branches in the urban towns, who began to help in the administration of Nnobi. When Samson Ezenagu died, another man, Richard Anoliefo, took over the presidency, then yet another man called Michael Ogochukwu. No woman has yet been either chair, president, secretary or treasurer of these Unions which later became known as Nnobi Welfare Organization (NWO).

In 1951, NWO, under the presidency of Richard Anoliefo, reached a unanimous decision to have the *igwe* of Nnobi reinstated. It was thus that, in 1951, Chief

Solomon Eze Okoli again became the *Igwe* I of Nnobi.[3] The *igwe* appears to have been a purely ceremonial head during his second term of office, as the administration of the town was really carried out by the Welfare Organization. When the *igwe* died in 1955, his first son, Lawrence, was invited to take over the office, but he declined; his junior brother, Edmund Eze Okoli, was then made *Igwe* II of Nnobi in 1957.

The NWO had an all-male central executive comprising a president general and a secretary general. Officers of the central executive were to be elected at proposed general meetings of all Nnobians[4] residing outside and in Nnobi. Like other ethnic associations described by Lloyd (1967:195–202), the NWO had branches in all the towns in Nigeria where Nnobians reside. The central focus, however, was the home town where general meetings were held with each branch expected to send two representatives. Each quarter of Nnobi was also expected to send representatives, and finally the Women's Council was also expected to be represented. In its composition, therefore, the NWO can be said to be democratic.

As well as the NWO there are two other, exclusively male, ruling bodies in Nnobi: one is the *igwe*'s council. The *igwe* himself is the local chief, known by the title *igwe*, a title not indigenous to Nnobi which did not have overall male chiefs (see Chapter 3). There were *ozo* or *eze* titled men associated with specific lineages or quarters and a few 'big men' who obtained overall recognition through influence, power and wealth. The only generally recognized male title was the *eze ana*, usually taken by the *isi ana* of Nnobi, the priest of the Earth Spirit. This title was, however, hereditary and could be taken in only one *obi* in Nnobi: that which holds the *okpala*ship (first-son status). The title had ritual and first-share prerogatives, but was not a kingship title. Only the female *Ekwe* had had overall political power in the sense of vetoing rights in public, or constitutional, assemblies (see Chapter 3). As the church banned the female title, colonial rule brought about the introduction of a ruling male chieftaincy in Nnobi. Eze Okoli took the title of *Igwe* of Nnobi when he became a warrant chief.

As a result of a new identification with chieftaincy and kingship titles, it became necessary for interested parties in Nnobi to re-examine and reinterpret the indigenous political systems. Some recognized successive generations of *eze*, kingly, titled men in the *obi* of Eze Okigbo in Awuda as past dynasties (see Chapters 2 and 3). Since in the Igbo political concept, kings did not crown themselves, king-makers were not sought in Awuda but were found elsewhere, in Ebenesi. Ebenesi was then given the status of traditional king-maker; for that reason, it did not produce the kings, but crowned them (*Abalukwu*, December 1976:7).

When the first *igwe*, who was from Ngo, died, the argument was whether to make the *igwe*ship a hereditary office or to rotate it between Awuda and Ngo, leaving Ebenesi as the king-maker, or for the three quarters in Nnobi to hold the title in rotation. This threatened to erupt into a serious political issue in Nnobi, thus it was felt to be safer and easier to invite the son of the first *igwe* to take up the *igwe*ship. The method of filling the *igwe*ship and *okpala*ship is still a dangerous and unresolved political issue in Nnobi today.[5] In the dialogue and debate concerning filling these political offices, no thought is given to the possibility of female candidates or parallel female offices.

The *igwe*'s council therefore comprises the *igwe* himself, the *okpala* (elder son) and 18 *ichie* titled men elected by their wards. In addition, the *igwe* nominates three special *ichie* titled men, usually one in each village. The *ichie* titled men and the *okpala* act as advisers to the *igwe*; when all of them meet together this is referred to as *igwe*-in-council. They deal mainly with traditional matters as well as native law and custom.

The other administrative body, the local government, is an official government body composed of elected and nominated councillors and other local administrators, all of whom are male. For administrative purposes, Nnobi is divided into 36 wards, with 12 wards in each quarter or village. Usually the ward nominates a candidate who stands unopposed. But I was told that where there are two contestants, each candidate enlists the female members of his lineage on the day of the election; otherwise, only male ward members meet to elect a ward councillor. There has never been any female candidate for councillorship. The local government council is an independent body; its members usually consult and co-operate with the NWO as well as the *igwe*-in-council. They are, however, able to give orders to the other two bodies in their capacity as an arm of government. Funds and government development projects are channelled through them.

By far the most powerful of all the governing bodies was the widely representative and self-supporting NWO. Most community self-help and development projects were initiated and supervised by the NWO, which made and collected levies for these projects, but liaised with the *igwe*-in-council and sought its sanction for major projects and associated levies. Thus, when committees for specific projects were set up, final decisions were taken at a joint meeting of the NWO and *igwe*-in-council. Where projects concerned women, such as the market-place, the Women's Council was invited to the meetings. Therefore, for local administration and government at all levels, an all-male caucus made initial decisions and suggestions and only later apparently attempted wider consultation.

Women and Local Political Issues: 1946–60

As the NWO had the mass support of Nnobians, who saw it as their invention and not government-linked, it found itself dealing with religious, cultural, economic and political problems. During this earlier period of the NWO, Women's Council members claimed they were always invited to its meetings.

The main religious problem at the time was the divisive effect of Christian denominations and the neglect of 'idol' shrines and squares. Rivalry between Anglicans and Catholics was apparently so intense that members of these denominations did not intermarry. The problem was then taken to the NWO which ruled that Catholics and Protestants should be allowed to intermarry. From my observation, Catholics still refuse to marry non-Catholics all over Igboland. Regarding the neglected idol squares, which were covered in grass and weeds, the NWO ruled that women should tend and sweep these squares and open spaces.

Apparently, even as early as this, the NWO had begun to undermine the customary autonomy of the Women's Council by means of laws or rules concerning some indigenous ceremonies which brought mothers material benefits through their daughters, for example, the *Etedenaghu* gifts (see Chapter 6). It was not really compulsory to make this gift. For example, a son-in-law was not duty-bound to give this gift after the birth of his first child. But knowing the strength of local gossip and innuendo – a communication sphere controlled by women – it seems likely that most sons-in-law did give this gift.

The influence of Christianity did not immediately end this custom; instead, the Christians put it at Christmas, and it became part of the Christmas gift exchanges. In the words of Mr R. O. Madueme, however, 'This festival became so luxurious that people even started taking goat and textile material, taking so much that it took seven to eight people to carry the gift. This was not how it used to be.' The problem was taken to the NWO, which then made rules to control the quantity of gifts to be given.

But the organization itself, under the leadership of Michael Ugochukwu and Clement Anyaeche, his general secretary, soon found itself dealing with the problem of alleged embezzlement of money.

As a result of suspicions and general dissatisfaction with financial activities of the NWO, Nnobi elders were said to have ruled that no one should pay the levy demanded for the installation of pipe-borne water in Nnobi. They called for a commission of inquiry to which the whole of Nnobi, at home and in the urban centres, were summoned. Findings were read in public.

Accounts of the proceedings of the commission of inquiry, apart from exposing male monopoly and dominance, reveal the personal and vicious nature of local-level politics, not only in Nnobi but in all other Igbo communities. It shows the relative autonomy and isolation of rural communities in terms of development programmes and finance, and also reveals the supreme judicial powers of the rural community over its members, whether at home or elsewhere.

Women and Local Political Issues: 1960–82

In the early history of the NWO it is possible to claim that its formation and its leaders were motivated by necessity and patriotism, in common with other such bodies and improvement unions which emerged in all Igbo communities in that period (see Isichei 1976:217–23). Founded mainly in the 1930s and early 1940s, mostly in urban centres, Isichei compares their evolution to similar organizations formed by workers in large industrial cities of England during the Industrial Revolution in the early 19th century. Like the workers in England, Igbos in urban centres sought security, friendship and mutual aid, but strongly focused on their home town. Neglected at the national level of development programmes, individuals took it upon themselves to do things for their home town which should have been done by government, and thereby sought reward, fame and power. In electoral politics they became favourite candidates, hence the link between wealth, its conspicuous display, and political power.

As men competed for control of the NWO and local events in Nnobi, and for prominence in local and national politics, some elements in Nnobi society and the NWO sought to subdue and control the Women's Council.

Nnobi Home Welfare Organization: 1977

As the history of the NWO has shown, most of its early founders and leaders were urban based. Many of them were wealthy male traders living at Onitsha. In 1977, urban control of the NWO became a burning issue. On 11 April 1977, what seems to have been a rival organization, the Nnobi Home Welfare Organization (NHWO), was formed. Their quarrel with the NWO was based on the claim that it financed and generally catered only for the funerals of Nnobians who died away from home, bringing the body home for burial. They resented the fact that although all Nnobi citizens, male and female, paid contributions and levies to it, the NWO did not concern itself with the funerals of those who lived in Nnobi.

NHWO membership is drawn from Nnobi males living in Nnobi. As the leader said in 1982, this all-male, growing organization is now poised to take over the NWO's duties.

The general resentment against the NWO's leadership arose from the fact that most of its leaders were urban dwellers outside Nnobi, and thus had no right to dictate to Nnobi people.

The lack of a large membership has not deterred the NHWO from such ambitious proposals as, for example, building lock-up shops in the central market. Meanwhile, the NHWO was busy learning a dance to perform at the funerals of their members. Their constitution included a rule that the wife of a deceased member should be given 200 Naira. The NHWO, as at January 1982, did not intend to admit women to its membership – in the words of its chairman, 'We did not invite them at all.'

The Arrest of Leaders of the Women's Council: 1977

The sexual duality of indigenous formal political organizations in Nnobi meant that women ruled over women while men ruled over men, but formally, males, sometimes including certain categories of woman, exercised overall authority (see Chapter 3). As these indigenous organizations are embedded in descent and kinship systems, colonial rule and influence could not eliminate them. Some of their legislative and judicial roles were transferred to government institutions, but they still retained control of routine management of life-cycle ceremonies of birth, marriage and death. The Women's Council, on the other hand, was still firmly in control of the daily affairs of the local women and sometimes extended this control to men. With the increasing male control of public politics and the concentration of legislative, executive and judicial powers in the hands of such modern, male-controlled organizations as the NWO or government-approved councils like the local council and the ruling *igwe*'s council, a clash with the Women's Council over the exercise of rights and duties was inevitable. What was not anticipated was the form this clash took in Nnobi: police arrest and imprisonment of elderly women in 1977.

The event which precipitated the arrests was the judgement of a case involving two women who had fought at a public water pump. In accordance with tradition, the offending women were invited to the Women's Council's meeting, their case was heard and a fine was imposed. They were not told to pay the fine (14 shillings) immediately but given a specific day on which to pay it. By the evening of the day when the fine was due, rumours that the leaders of the Women's Council had been arrested began spreading like a bush-fire.

When the leaders managed to discover the reason for the rumoured arrest they quickly denied having fined the women 14 shillings each, but claimed instead that they had been told to bring some kola-nuts. Members of the Women's Council quickly hid the papers in which minutes of the meeting had been entered. However, the president and the vice-president were arrested, taken to prison and released the following day.

The frenzy and confusion engendered by these arrests are best conveyed by the words of one of the participants, Nwajiuba.

The following day, all members of the Women's Council were instructed to go to Onitsha. Men had come back and had held a meeting, after which everyone was told to assemble at Afo market-place, dressed in their best. The 'pagans' were allowed to come fortified with all their sorcery. Nnobi was shaking with uncertainty that day, swaying backwards and forwards. The men provided transportation and we were all taken to Onitsha. When we reached Onitsha, we all got off the buses and sat down waiting to be told which court to go to. The women were restless and sitting under shades. Three women went from each ward, therefore there were 108 of us. We were then told where to go. When we got there, instead of the war we went for, we were served food and drinks. The leaders had settled things with them. We do not know what decision they arrived at!

Nwajiuba's account is corroborated by that of Chief R. O. Madueme, who was elected by a public meeting to travel to Onitsha and bail the women. Even several years after that event, he did not fail to stress that he had nothing to do with the arrests.

No one seemed willing to commit themselves as to who had authorized the arrests. I was told they were based on what is known in Igbo as *akwukwo nnunu*, bird's letter, that is, an anonymous letter, written to the police in Onitsha. This letter was said to have alleged that representatives of the Women's Council had behaved in a wilful manner to the *igwe*; that their institution was too powerful and they were like a state within a state. The complaint was made that they fined people indiscriminately; that if a man had the slightest dispute with his wife, the Women's Council stepped in to fine him. It was therefore claimed that their government was upsetting Nnobi. An example was cited of a particular man who quarrelled with his wife and was fined £25 by the Women's Council. I was told that it was on the basis of these reports that the police travelled from Onitsha to arrest the women.

Even in 1982, this incident was talked about only in whispers. The leaders told me they knew who was responsible for their arrest though they would not mention names, but claimed to have booed him a few times and made it impossible for him to enter the market-place. Obviously, the person or persons had considerable standing and recognized authority in Nnobi, or the police would not have heeded the request to arrest the women. Interestingly, for fear of women, those concerned had to resort to secrecy.

I was told that after the arrest, the women became vigilant and cautious, stating that if they were arrested again they were determined to find out who was responsible. Consequently, they devised a method whereby any woman who was fined was warned against revealing it, and told that if the facts leaked out, she would be held responsible for the consequences.

The arrest of the Women's Council leaders is a landmark in the political history of Nnobi for several reasons. The confidence of the women was broken. For the first time in their history, the women thus assaulted found themselves denied their effective militancy in self-protection and struggle against the men. Instead of demonstrating solidarity in resistance to men, women were being organized for mass action by certain men, while their leaders were collaborating with others, as Nwajiuba confirmed when she said that the leaders had settled the matter with the men without consulting the rest of the women, who were not even told what decisions were arrived at. The women therefore lost confidence in their leaders.

After this arrest, meetings and activities of the Women's Council were banned until 1978. Then, in December 1977, the elected general president of the NWO invited the women to Eziehulu Hall and told them that they could start meeting again. This move followed pressure from individuals in Nnobi who had been embarrassed by the arrests and the ban on Council meetings. Therefore, when a new executive for the NWO was elected in December 1977, it was bombarded with questions about the reinstatement of the Women's Council. In a paper entitled 'The Task before the New Executive' (Amadi Obi, *Abalukwu*, April 1978:20), the writer said: 'When I talk about the market, I remember the "Inyom Nnobi". I wonder how we can rule without our women. This noble women-body should be reorganized without further delay. Their services are essential.'

The need for the reinstatement of the Women's Council was put more directly in an interview with the general president of the NWO, Mr B. C. B. Eruchalu:

> *As you are aware of the fact that Inyom Nnobi is no more functioning, what is your intention about them?*
> My humble answer to this question is that you cannot rule a nation without women. Men alone cannot answer Nnobi. It is only my foremost job to reorganize the Inyom Nnobi and get their organization functioning because they are another militant wing in our community, whose job is to be reckoned with, such as maintenance of law and order, general cleanliness of our town, orderliness in our market, communal labour, maintenance of our customs and traditions, training and care of our children, collection of authorized development levies. These are the main duties which Inyom Nnobi can perform for the interest of our town. (*Abalukwu*, April 1978:9)

Having thus spelt out the need for a female labour force and financial contributions from women, saying nothing about incorporating women into its executive, the NWO reorganized the Women's Council. The women said they were simply invited to Eziehulu Hall and told to start their meetings again. Their method of representation in the Council was changed. They were told to choose representatives, two Christians and one 'pagan' from each ward. If there were no 'pagans' in the ward, then three Christians would represent it. The women reported that they were given what, to them, was *mpempe akwukwo*, a piece of paper, which they were to observe. It was in fact a constitution, even though the majority of the women's leadership was illiterate. The NWO substantially reduced the range of offences for which fines could be imposed. In short, it placed the Women's Council under its guidance and supervision.

New Gender Realities which Contributed to the Arrests

Differing opinions were expressed by Nnobi people on the arrest of the elderly women leaders of the Women's Council. Men and women who looked at the matter from the perspective of traditional attitudes towards women expressed their shock and disbelief, commenting that pandemonium would have broken loose in Nnobi had this happened before the colonial period. The thought of it, they said, made them shudder. To them, the arrests and detention amounted to sacrilege, *alu*. There were elders, including both men and women, who said they would have held the same opinion, but their views had been coloured by their distrust of the leaders of the Women's Council. These leaders, they felt, were corrupt and used their powers dishonourably, conspiring in secret and fining people unjustly in order to enrich themselves. They therefore saw the arrests only as a sanction against excessive use of power, but did not feel that the women should not have or use power.[6]

The opinion expressing outright condemnation of the women echoed the supposed content of the anonymous letter to the police. The women were a government of their own and were becoming uncontrollable. Their objections reveal the near-supreme power enjoyed by the Women's Council and the pervasive nature of its communications network which in a modern situation could be considered an invasion of privacy. They were accused of having ears and spies everywhere. The sheer audacity and militancy of the women come across in the language they are said to use, such as the threat to uproot water pumps and break down people's houses.

Clearly, in the minds of Christians and Western-influenced élites, such 'maleness' and 'headstrongness' were unfeminine. In their opinion, all women ought to bow their heads to their husbands. The biblical story of creation was cited and woman was seen as a helpmate. One should respect and hold sacred what is written by God: for God said that a woman shall be under her husband and obey her husband (see Genesis 2:21; 3:16).

There is a new politics of control of meaning in this changing society: in the reinterpretation of gender relations, some looked to the Bible and Hebrew culture; others distorted facts about traditional culture in defining the proper status of women *vis-à-vis* men. Their interpretation of indigenous gender relations was usually full of contradictions as they tried to insist on control over women. In this situation of plurality of cultures, interpretation and meaning become a political issue in social relations. Those in positions of power seek to impose their own interpretations of culture, or of aspects of a particular culture according to what suits them best.

Nnobi men appear to have discarded aspects of their traditional culture which guaranteed women full participation in the political structure. They have proceeded to monopolize the modern institutions of government, seeking to justify new forms of male dominance borrowed from other cultures, while 'feeding' themselves and their women alien gender ideologies. Had they sought justification in the traditional culture, they would never have entertained the idea of arresting and detaining members of the Women's Council. Had the women not been baffled and inhibited by modern institutions, they would have acted spontaneously as their mothers did over the Natty case only 40 years previously when they marched to Onitsha (see Chapter 8). Instead they waited for leadership from the men who would hire buses, organize food and drinks and negotiate with the police. But on the other hand, women in Nnobi have had no practice in dealing with modern public institutions: leadership in organizations which would have given them the necessary experience – such as the local government council or the executive of the NWO which deal with modern developments in Nnobi – has so far been monopolized by men.

The Collapse of NWO: 1980

Officially, every Nnobi adult of taxable age automatically belonged to the NWO, it was therefore seen as an organization of the people. It was, however, run by an all-male executive which, before the alleged fund mismanagement crisis of 1958, was elected annually. Following this crisis, as a result of the findings of the commission of inquiry, the NWO executive was dissolved. A steering committee comprising representatives from the various branches of the NWO and initially set up to settle the dispute within the NWO, took over the functions of the dissolved executive. This unelected, all-male committee took it upon itself to handle the affairs of Nnobi from the early 1960s, throughout the period of the Biafran–Nigerian war (1967–70), until 1977.

A few community self-help projects were carried out during this period. In 1954, Nnobi built itself a maternity hospital and in 1958 its first secondary school for boys, followed in 1959 by one for girls. In 1961, for the first time, pipe-borne water was supplied in Nnobi though serving only a few people and areas. Most people had to fetch pipe-borne water from the public tap at the central market-place or from the iron-gated homes of a few urban-based wealthy individuals. In response, the section of Nnobi which did not get water refused to pay when contributions for the building of a police barracks were called for. The NWO issued a two-week ultimatum for payment but the people still refused and consequently did not get pipe-borne water during the next phase of development (*Abalukwu*, April 1976). The police barracks was completed on 8 June 1976. The people then had to beg the government for policemen to fill it. On 18 June 1977, the Nnobi post office was completed (*Abalukwu*, September 1977).

The number of self-help projects undertaken during this period indicates that the NWO must have handled a considerable amount of money collected through levies. By 1977, the steering committee was under great pressure from the people to render accounts to the public (*Abalukwu*, September 1976). But the most controversial issue was the claim that the method of collecting and paying in levies was defective. Individuals made their own personal calculations to try to estimate the amount of money handled by the NWO. From the figures derived from lineage registers during the still-born election for *okpala*ship, it was calculated that there were 6,000 taxable male adults in Nnobi. The normal minimum levy of 5 Naira on each adult male would give a sum total of 30,000 Naira. In addition, females usually paid 2 Naira. There was thus concern at the amount of money in the hands of individuals rather than banks.

It was later revealed (*Abalukwu*, Vol. 7, April 1978) that the administrative wing of the NWO had, at the general meeting of 31 December 1977, made it known to Nnobi people that 'it had looked for auditors for THREE GOOD YEARS to audit it without success'. The reading public was told, 'It is no longer a secret that Nnobi operated, at least, from 1970 to 31st December 1977 without a bank account.' The sum for building the post office was then revealed: 50,000 Naira had been handled by individuals!

Discrediting the elder, male-dominated steering committee, younger and more educated men called for the setting up of a committee to draw up a new constitution for the town, to be followed by a general election. They demanded that in the new NWO, women, youths and social organizations should have seats in the executive committee.

As a result of public pressure, a general meeting of the NWO was called in December 1977. The steering committee was disbanded, a general election was held, and an executive committee was elected. The call to include women in the executive committee had not been heeded. The list of elected officers published in *Abalukwu*, Vol. 7, April 1978 shows that again an all-male executive committee had been chosen to run the affairs of all Nnobi people.

I was told that there were no female officers because no women stood for election. Nevertheless, this executive drew up a constitution for the Women's Council and placed it under its supervision.

The general president thus spelt out the blueprint for a male-monopolized local government in Nnobi. Safeguarding his own position, he expressed his personal bitterness against the manner in which, as he implied, Nnobi had framed, humiliated and punished those they had appointed to serve them.[7] He crystallized this message by a proverb used in his maiden speech: 'Nnobi people are fond of sending rain after a child they have sent on an errand with a parcel of salt!' (*Abalukwu*, April 1978). In 1980, he was himself caught in the rain carrying a parcel of salt when the organization he was heading collapsed.

The editorial of *Abalukwu* of April 1978 had warned the newly elected NWO executive committee of the dangers of lack of information. It also pointed out that Nnobi people were becoming more enlightened and therefore more inquisitive about the running of their affairs, especially the use made of their money. Despite this advice there was again a problem of accountability in 1980, and as a result of action by Awuda, the most junior quarter or village of Nnobi, the central executive of the NWO ceased to exist.

The NWO had demanded payment of the highest levies ever heard of in Nnobi. All Nnobi men both living at home and away were requested to pay 20 Naira, while women at home and away were to pay 5 Naira. People apparently paid the money dutifully, then awaited the development and improvement projects for which the money had been collected. Nothing seemed to be happening. Unrest followed.

Awuda then openly demanded that unless the money was accounted for no more levies would be paid in Nnobi.

I was told that the NWO was basically a government based on representation of four groups, the three which make up Nnobi – Ebenesi, Ngo and Awuda – and the fourth, the Women's Council, which was regarded as a branch of the NWO and consequently was entitled to send representatives to all meetings. Decisions of the meeting were said to be based on consensus or on majority vote; the nearest to a veto would be a walk-out by one group. It was in this way that Awuda was able to bring the NWO to a standstill: it ceased to function when Awuda boycotted its meetings. If the NWO was made up of four groups, they seem not to have had equal powers: I was told that a walk-out by the Women's Council would have been ineffective. Indeed, the leaders of the Women's Council complained that they were hardly ever invited to meetings.

As the problems of the NWO were based on suspicion and rumour, and not on proved embezzlement of funds, a panel was set up to audit the accounts of the organization from 1970 to 1980. At the same time, a much wider body, called a peace committee, was appointed to look into the whole affair and come up with a new constitution; the NWO would then start again as a newly constituted body. This committee, meant to represent all sections of Nnobi, was again male-dominated.

It was after the NWO lost its credibility with the public that the Nnobi Home Welfare Organization, formed in 1977, threatened to take over its functions. If women's position in the NWO was peripheral in the NHWO they had no place at all. When I put it to the NHWO chairman that women still had a seat in the *igwe*'s council and the NWO, he replied:

A seat in *igwe*-in-council and the welfare organization? Is it the dissolved welfare organization or our own welfare organization? I do not see where they have power for we did not invite them at all. The main welfare has been dissolved, so no one should say they have a position in the welfare until an election has been held.[8]

The Response of the Women

Representatives of the Women's Council, during my discussions with them in January 1982, said that they were no longer invited to NWO meetings. They maintained that previously they had been informed when NWO meetings were to take place. Their chairwoman sat at the front table with the chairman, and other members sat with the men. But now they were invited only to work, for example, clearing the bush before the post office could be built and clearing and cleaning the old native administrative court where visitors were received for the launching of the new Obiaja local government, of which Nnobi was made the headquarters.

The women, aware and resentful of their political exclusion, nevertheless did nothing about it. Asked why they tolerated the situation, they said they were now directed by the NWO. Some maintained they were excluded from the decision-making process and the men monopolized everything; others pointed out that they had a seat in the *igwe*'s council and in the NWO. Obviously, as a result of the 1977 arrests, they were afraid of being implicated in protests.

Yet I learnt that not long ago, the Women's Council had clashed with a special market committee appointed by the *igwe*'s council to take over the policing of Nnobi market. This committee had been appointed without the consent of the Women's Council. The *igwe* himself admitted that the women had made life impossible for those sent to reorganize and police the central market. When reminded of this incident, the women confirmed that they had refused to co-operate. 'We said that men should also take over the sweeping of the market. Yes, that they should begin to sweep the streets and open space. In no time, the market-place was covered in weeds and grass. The market became bush.'

A compromise solution was the appointment of market masters jointly by NWO and the Women's Council. The market masters were to be responsible for the allocation of market stalls and for policing the market with baton and whistle. The general tidiness of the market was left to the Women's Council. But as an Nnobi research student remarked, the market masters were still unable to cope owing to what he termed 'millions of insults received from the illiterate market women' (Ezeani 1980:32).

As Ezeani observed, even in 1980, the market-place was still very much the women's domain.

> Apart from the itinerant bulking traders, butchers and shopkeepers on the periphery of the market, the trade is almost totally dominated by women. Many of these women are obliged to bring their infants and pre-schoolers, who spend the day in the market's dark, dank and unhygienic environment. (Ezeani 1980:30)

Women were, therefore, still able to act in a situation where they were not dependent on a leadership; that is, when they felt offended on their home ground – the market-place. There, women could act individually or collectively by making life difficult for any threatening or intruding elements such as market masters with their batons and whistles. This was not so with wider political issues in Nnobi. On the affairs of the NWO, for example, I found members of the Women's Council quite ignorant, uninformed and helpless. For example, they had no idea that the peace commission of which they were a part had been assigned to write up a constitution for Nnobi. The constitution in any case would be discussed and written in English. These women were uneducated, illiterate in the English language and ignorant of Western legal terminology.

Notes

1. Information on the modern political history of Nnobi is based on findings made during fieldwork in Nnobi between 1981 and January 1982. Among those interviewed were people who had participated in the various improvement unions

over the years and who have themselves been political activists both in Nnobi and in the urban towns. Such men include Mr R. O. Madueme, an experienced schoolteacher, clergyman and politician, in his seventies; Mr B. B. O. Emeh, a business tycoon in his fifties and a notable political figure both in Nnobi, the state and the federal political levels. Information was also received from Chief Akudolu, a 71-year-old Onitsha-based trader. He was one of the founder members of Nnobi Welfare Organization. Another Nnobi elder, Eze Enyinwa, a member of the *igwe*'s council, was also interviewed, the 'male daughter', Nwajiuba, and members of the Women's Council.

2. The findings of the Commission of Inquiry were published in the same year as a Blue Book, *Nigeria: Report of the Aba Commission of Inquiry.*

3. The government of the then Eastern Region had established a House of Chiefs in 1951 and appointed the anthropologist G. I. Jones to look into the traditional political system and advise on methods of determining chieftaincy. In order to have representation in the House of Chiefs, there followed a general revival of kingship and chieftaincy titles. Businessmen quickly claimed chiefly titles (see Nzimiro 1977).

4. A modern term used in Nnobi today.

5. If Nnobi had traditionally been centralized under a single monarch, there would not have been so much confusion and controversy over filling these two political posts; prescribed rules would have existed to guide these matters. On 25 September 1976, for example, a planned election for *okpala*ship fell through as a result of poor turnout, unclear regulations concerning the registration of votes, qualification of voters, approval of candidates, etc. (*Abalukwu*, December 1976:12).

6. Following is the transcript of a discussion held with leaders of the Women's Council in which they described some of their methods of punishment.

What kind of punishment do you mete out to those who break your rules?

We send a message and ask the person to come to our meeting. When she arrives we tell her where she has defaulted and what her punishment is. If she defies us then we ban her from the market and from fetching water from the public tap in the market. If she proves stubborn and attends market then we go to her shade and carry out what we call *isi nta* or *isi ahihaa* (picketing). We prevent her displaying her goods, fetching tap water. She will not enter our market or pass through Nnobi.

How is isi ahihaa *performed?*

We go to her shade and sing: *ahihaa, anyi ahawu haa – oo/ekweghewuu – oo, anyi ekweghewuu – oo/don idoo,* chorus, *iidoo!/don idoo*, chorus, *iidoo!/nde ni weta okpili ka anyi na ha tie – ee.* Chorus, *iidoo!*

[This song is not easily translatable; it expresses the women's total disapproval and determination. The imagery is that of a tug-of-war, hence the warning, 'We are about to pull.' The concluding line is, 'Bring your batons or clubs, let's exchange blows!']

The person quickly takes her things and runs. In fact, it is at the sound of the first word *ahihaa* that she runs.

Do you really do this today?

Yes, of course! We still do it even now [wild uproar and laughter]. We did it to your in-law. [I did not press to find out which of my in-laws they did it to and why. I thought it best to let sleeping dogs lie!] If he comes to the market we boo him. Yes, we still do it.

It seems to me you still have some power!

Indeed! The men respect us. We do not walk in their house and they do not walk in ours. A man may want to quarrel with his wife, but when he remembers that he does not have the energy or power to face Inyom Nnobi, he desists. When husbands and wives quarrel, we repair the quarrel. We settle the matter. We work for peace in the family. People do not like to confront Inyom Nnobi.

7. Conflicts within the NWO and cases of peculation are not peculiar to Nnobi. Similar problems are reported in the history of such improvement unions in other Igbo towns (see Isichei 1976:220). Dr Isichei does not seem to see the provision of basic social amenities as the responsibility of the wealthy Nigerian government to its tax-paying masses. Otherwise she would not question the choice of priorities of local people in building what she terms 'empty prestige projects'.

8. By January 1982, during my last period of fieldwork in Nnobi, and even from correspondence in August 1982, I learnt that the committee was still sitting and that there has been inefficiency and disorganization in the NWO but no proven embezzlement.

10. Wealth, Titles and Motherhood

We have seen in Chapters 3 and 4 how in the indigenous Nnobi society, women organized themselves in their capacity as wives and mothers and sought structural power on that basis. As wives and mothers, they had access to essential economic resources – land and market. Those who were successful economically, or showed signs of charismatic leadership ability, could take titles and become political and ritual leaders, for example, *Ekwe* titled women. As wives and mothers, women had an exclusive formal organization with specific rights involving the fertility and marriage of daughters. Motherhood was therefore economically and politically rewarding. We find that in the colonial and post-colonial Nnobi society, though the material situation of women has changed, women still cling to their social and cultural status as mothers, and seek power in that capacity even though no provision is made for women as mothers in the seats of power. No title is given to women as a reward for motherhood that would guarantee them a seat in the *igwe*'s council alongside titled men.

Women's New Poverty

We therefore find that although the economic position of women had changed, the ideologies which supported the economic centrality of women had not changed. Matrifocal notions and the ideology of hard work were still associated with females. While women in general fed their children and paid much of the school fees, wealthier women, instead of accumulating wives for themselves, paid brideprice for male relatives, sons or husbands. In this respect, the local ruler in Nnobi, Edmund Eze Okoli, *Igwe* II, was able to tell me in August 1980,

Women take a more active part in farming, the production of foodstuffs, and marketing. It is to their credit that we eat today. Men are mainly traders and business men. It is women today, because of what they inherited from the goddess Idemili, who do all the work.

If it is to the credit of women that the people of Nnobi eat today, Nnobi has certainly not rewarded these women with titles as it has the men. Moreover, as most of the women themselves pointed out, they worked very hard but found they had little to show for it in terms of profit. The local chief confirmed this when he said that there was no woman in Nnobi today rich enough to take the *Ekwe* title, as in the past. This was not the case with the men: on the contrary, more men – mostly traders and business men – were taking the *ozo* title than ever before.

This comparative lack of wealth among women was raised during a discussion with Women's Council members in January 1982. Most names mentioned were those of Igbo women, other than Nnobi, living in the urban centres. The name of a Nnobi woman living in an urban town was then mentioned, but some of the women refused to recognize her as a very wealthy woman, as she simply had a large provision store and a dressmaking shop, where she employed a few hands. Other women mentioned, also in the urban centres, were in business with their husbands, and wealthy only because their husbands were rich business men, contractors or traders. The leaders of the Women's Council eventually concluded that women were no longer wealthy in Nnobi, being fully occupied by the sheer struggle for subsistence.

While men were involved in various businesses and contracting work, most Nnobi women were still basically farming housewives. They cultivated subsistence crops on the family farm plots, and sold their surplus at the market-place. According to the 1973–74 *Rural Economic Survey Report of the East Central State of Nigeria*, over 78% of the rural population were farmers. The 1977–78 *Rural Economic Survey Report* (Table 7) indicates that 72.5% of the rural population of Anambra State were farmers; 42.7% of the population were women involved in farming: 16.5% were solely farmers; 2.6% were part-time farmers; 0.1% were farm labourers; and 23.7% were farming housewives. The figures for men were 29.8% involved in farming: 23.9% were solely farmers; 5.5% were part-time farmers; and 0.4% farm labourers. Nought point eight per cent of women in the rural areas were solely housewives. For women who are solely housewives in Idemili and Nnewi local government areas (under which Nnobi is entered) the entry is nil. In the same Report (Table 1) the rural population of Anambra State is estimated as 3,615,900: 1,931,300 females; 1,684,600 males. The total population for Idemili and Nnewi local government areas is 454,100: 241,300 females; 212,800 males. Of the total number of households (72,000), 59,200 were farming households (Table 17), which was 82.2% of all the households. Most farm plots were less than 0.05 hectares; 205,710 were less than 0.05 hectares, 47,400 plots were between 0.05 and 0.099 hectares in both Idemili and Nnewi local government areas (Table 30).

Farms in these areas would, therefore, not be regarded as big enough to qualify for government loans or grants. This is confirmed by entries in Table 36 of the same 1977–78 Report, which show that Idemili and Nnewi areas, which are not regarded as agriculturally productive, received no loans from financial institutions. Family accounts, rather than financial institutions, provided the money for farming. Table 32 of the 1977–78 Report also reveals holder–owner type of tenure, derived from inheritance rather than allocation or purchase, although Tables 32–35 in the 1973–74 Report indicate that some farms in the Idemili division were purchased, leased or received as gifts; 88% were, however, acquired through inheritance.

Men's New Wealth

Unlike women, who were strongly motivated by the ideology of motherhood and the associated principle of self-sacrifice, in male organizations such as the patriotic unions, improvement unions, clubs and age-grade associations, the salient motive was competition for power and distinction.

Okigbo points at the individualization of activities as the most important change in West African societies in the 20th century (1965:420–23). Isichei (1976), on the other hand, following the history of the improvement unions in Igbo societies, makes the point that as a result of the ethnic unions, vertical bonds of locality replaced horizontal class identification. At the same time, however, there were signs of a growing class identification among Igbo élites which was not based on the common bond of the shared home town, for example, the emergence of the *okaa* society in 1963, described as 'an exclusive association of wealthy men', which included business men, professional men and civil servants (1976:221). Although Isichei, perhaps misinformed by her source, describes *okaa* society as comprised exclusively of wealthy men, numerous wealthy matrons were known to have been members. They were referred to as *okaa* madams, or *okaa* was prefixed to the commodity each individual woman controlled (see Introduction).

In the case of Nnobi, and Nnobi citizens living elsewhere, a process of multiple alignments appears to have taken place. There was the NWO, to which, in principle, all citizens of Nnobi belonged. This identification was based on a vertical bond of locality irrespective of horizontal class loyalties. There were, on the other hand, individual Nnobi citizens, both men and women, who belonged to several associations in the towns where they lived which had no relevance to daily politics and administration in Nnobi, except in terms of prestige. At the funeral of a member, for example, fellow members would visit the deceased member's home town and honour him or her by conspicuous display of wealth. They would, for example, flood the streets with symbols of prestige such as cars, food, money and drinks. Any other benefits were individually derived, such as shared loans and businesses.

On the whole, new associations in Nnobi and elsewhere in Igboland have called themselves age-grade societies, contrary to Okigbo's claim about the lack of importance of age in the new associations of the wealthy and educated élites. Similar associations or organizations formed by women have, however, named themselves after the female-linked role of motherhood, the most numerous and widely spread being those of the church. Women in the Catholic Church call their association the Christian Mothers and those in the Anglican Church, the Mothers' Union. Another organization, of successful business women, with a universal Nigerian membership including a branch in Nnobi, calls itself Sweet Mother.

The Age-Grade Associations and Local Politics

The early 1970s, the period after the Biafran War, saw the spread of age-grade clubs and societies all over Igboland. There were three such social clubs in Nnobi.

Membership of the Oganiru Middle Age-Grade of Nnobi, launched in 1973, is drawn from Nnobi men and women born between 1945 and 1950. This club is essentially dominated by male traders, as is another club called Igwebike Age-Grade of Nnobi, which draws its membership from those born between 1938 and 1944. By far the most powerful of these clubs is the Abalukwu Social Club of Nnobi. Although it was started in 1973 by a few youths in Enugu in the lower grades of the civil service, successful business men and women and other reputable professionals became honoured members. By 1975, the club had branches at Aba, Lagos, Onitsha and the home town, Nnobi. The opening up of branches in other important Nigerian towns with Nnobi residents followed gradually.

The Abalukwu Social Club, whose motto is 'love, unity and development', describes itself as 'purely a social club devoid of any taint of politics' (*Abalukwu*, September 1975:7). Its most important mouthpiece is the *Abalukwu* magazine which, in 1975, stated its commitment to the preservation of Nnobi culture.

It is in an attempt at cultural revival that these age-grade societies of Nnobi and other such clubs elsewhere in Igboland began the practice of ordering a periodic mass return of members living outside the home town. Those who fail to return are usually fined very heavily.

Clearly, although they see themselves as solely cultural associations, these age-grade societies are informal political groups. In the attempt to gain prestige and power in the home town, they compete with one another in identifying themselves with development projects. They build recreational and meeting halls, construct roads, bridges and health centres, and award scholarships. The main object is to sound their own trumpet, praising individual financial contributors and announcing the exact sum donated by each person. This is usually done on the grand occasion referred to as launching. Launching has come to provide a political platform and arena for wealthy business men, contractors, traders and civil servants ambitious for political power. A would-be politician is usually selected on the basis of the size of his financial donations during local events. This platform is invariably monopolized by men, except for a few wealthy women given prominent positions as they too may perhaps donate large sums of money.

Abalukwu Social Club is the richest, largest and most popular of such clubs in Nnobi. Its membership is drawn from all élites: academic, business and the civil service. Although the club's captions usually read 'sons and daughters of Nnobi', membership is almost exclusively male. Daughters are usually mentioned in connection with advertisements for launching occasions when there is a need to raise money. This really means an invitation to prominent Nnobi daughters to show their patriotism.

During these occasions, the word 'daughters' has become all embracing and stands for all women, including wives. The irony is that the mass of Nnobi daughters/wives are basically petty traders and foodstuff sellers who would not venture near these launching events, knowing that they are occasions for the display of wealth. If they did, they would remain inconspicuous onlookers in the background, applauding the rich. Not only do these significant occasions inhibit and exclude the less wealthy, especially the mass of women, but the entrance fee is also very high. The financial undertakings of the club require the raising of a lot of money, hence the frequency of launching occasions. Their bereavement payment to members and to families of deceased members is also very high. Abalukwu Social Club has undertaken to build a large cottage hospital in Nnobi, and this is near completion. It will be the first and only hospital in Nnobi.

As wealth determines prominence and power in the informal associations, so also does wealth ensure not only nomination for, but success in, political careers. We therefore find that successful politicians are not women but men who have demonstrated evidence of wealth in their local towns. They are men who would, for example, build schools, factories and other visible symbols of modern development. They are also men who act as brokers, entrepreneurs and middlemen, having knowledge of and access to state and central government departments responsible for development plans for the local areas. Such men therefore claim credit and reward for completed government development projects in the local areas. Their reward usually takes the form of titles or nomination as candidates in electoral politics. We thus find that political campaigns are fought not so much on ideological principles, but on the basis of concrete material gains and necessities such as water, roads, electricity, schools, health services, etc.

Contemporary Women's Associations and the Politics of Motherhood

The strong guiding principle of women's organizations, which are controlled by the ideology of motherhood, has been suppression of self – self-sacrifice and concern for order and peace. This was only one aspect of ideas associated with motherhood in the indigenous culture. As shown in Part One, motherhood had its social rewards and was known to motivate aggression and competition in economic pursuits, and militancy in self-defence or in the pursuit of public peace.

The suppressive and inhibiting aspects of the ideology of motherhood are prominent in the modern women's organizations, which are now basically church-linked and controlled. They have been encouraged by the very male-biased and patriarchal family laws of the Old Testament, especially the Levitical laws which carry strong anti-female notions of pollution. Church women do not therefore see themselves as possible clergy members. For many of them, exclusion from public politics has become acceptable in terms of the church's patriarchal laws, which place women directly under the authority and rule of their husbands, and demand their obedience and servitude. This would explain the attitude of the present leaders of the Women's Council, their ambivalence and contradictions as they are torn between traditional, positive female aggressiveness, and modern negative female subservience. The attitudes and opinions of the present leaders of the Women's Council were tested on two issues. One was their position with regard to the quarrel within the NWO and its disintegration described in Chapter 9, and the other was the question of title taking for women.

Unlike the competitive attitude and ambitious hopes of the NHWO *vis-à-vis* the NWO, Women's Council leaders saw their role essentially as peace makers, as it was the duty of mothers to settle disputes and ensure harmony among their children.

They therefore spoke of the executive members of the NWO and their dispute as if they were naughty, quarrelling children. According to the Women's Council spokeswoman, their intention was to call upon the men to speak up and say what the quarrel was about, and ask them what benefit they derived from quarrelling. According to the women, they themselves do not quarrel.

Even though the women identified competitiveness as the root of the quarrel in the NWO, in their view this sort of thing originates in lack of respect. According to them, men do not understand respect, hence their tendency to override one another and seek fame as individuals.

In the discussions the women gave the impression that they were aware of the mediatory role they were supposed to play in the traditional concept, but in reality found themselves powerless. They were, for example, aware that Nnobi men had commented about the role the Women's Council would, traditionally, have played in the present political stalemate. As the Women's Council was virtually excluded from the decision-making process, the leaders were unaware of the details of the dispute, neither were they being consulted in the peace moves. It is therefore not surprising that they had done nothing about summoning a meeting with the men; they lacked the confidence. After all, they had been disgraced, imprisoned and put under the leadership and supervision of the NWO. Consequently, it was God that they looked to for peace. As the women said, 'By the grace of God, if the men are to be at peace with one another as the women are, then Nnobi would really be blessed.'

This trust in God and dependence on canon law and Christian ethics governs the attitude of the Christian leaders in so far as the idea of title taking for women is concerned. While being aware of the connection between wealth, title and political power for men, the Christian women dismissed any suggestion of equivalent titles for wealthy or prominent women in Nnobi, saying, 'No, we will not participate in such things. We will not take titles with them for we are church-goers, we are Christ's people.'

It was put to them that nowadays, a successful, rich man has the opportunity to buy himself prestige and power by taking the *ozo* title, but wealthy women seem no longer to have any social rewards or power through title taking, as they no longer take the *Ekwe* title. There now seems no way to indicate that a particular woman is very wealthy or economically very successful. What, today, is women's social reward for hard work, comparable to the *ozo* title for men?

The reply was that the *Ekwe* title was involuntary and not taken only because a woman was rich. They did not accept the suggestion that signs of wealth were followed by possession but, on the contrary, in their opinion, it was possession that brought wealth, because in order to take the *Ekwe* title much money was needed. The call (possession by Idemili's spirit) to the title itself produced the necessary money to take it. Yet they admitted the fact that *Ekwe* tended to run in lines of descent. The women's spokeswoman, a leader self-appointed by sheer audacity, a very aggressive and charismatic woman, pointed out that the mother of her mother's mother (great-grandmother) had taken the *Ekwe* title and was also related, by marriage, (husband's grandmother) to another outstanding representative of the Women's Council. Another prominent representative, a non-Christian who still dressed in the indigenous manner[2] and was called Agba Ekwe, said that she

167

was the reincarnation of a titled *Agba Ekwe* woman, hence her name. The point here is that in present Nnobi society, none of these women is wealthy, but all have leadership qualities, hence their prominent positions in the Women's Council. In the indigenous society, it is most likely that their vigour and resourcefulness would have led them to wealth, titles and position in the ruling structure.

Today, the *Ekwe* title is felt to be contrary to the teaching of the Christian church. As far as the Christian women were concerned, the rituals involved in conferring the *Ekwe* title, such as giving the title-taker prestige and acknowledging her superiority by crawling on all fours between her legs, made the title-taker appear like a god. In the words of the women,

Were we to participate in these things we would not carry Christ's cross. As far as women are concerned, it is the cross of Christ that we will carry. We are steadfast in our resolution. Let the men do what they like. You see our understanding of the *Ekwe* title taking is different from your understanding of it. In the past, when a woman took the *Ekwe* title and the women crawled under her, they took her as their *chi*. From our understanding now, we believe that no human being should be worshipped except *Chineke*.[3] This does not mean that we do not respect people. But to worship a person as a god! No! This is what we mean by faith in Christ. The Bible says it is a sin to worship someone like a god.

It must be noted that this was not the attitude of the non-Christian representatives of the Women's Council, who were excited by the idea of a revival of female titles. It was, in any case, apparent that the 'pagan' women were so far dominated and intimidated by the more 'enlightened' Christian women, that in public gatherings they ended their prayers in the Christian manner, 'in the name of Jesus Christ our Lord'. When asked why they did this, they laughed and said it was the fashion.

The Christian women were intimidated by their commitment to the church, but their attitude to title taking evinced some degree of ambivalence. The suggestion of honorary titles, in particular for services to Nnobi, was very exciting to those who might qualify for them. The argument put to them was this,

Listen, let me defend myself. You know that the Vice-President of Nigeria, who is an Igbo man, is called Ekwueme, and you know that this name is also a title. It is a title given by people of a town in appreciation of what someone has done for them. *Ekwueme* means one who fulfils his promises. He proposes and carries out his proposals. I see no reason why Nnobi should not have similar titles to give to women as a reward and encouragement for hard work. Take this leader of yours, for example. You appreciate and praise her dynamism and efforts. Why should she not be rewarded with a title? Say, something like *odozi obodo*, which means one who keeps the town at peace or works for the well-being of the town. In which case, she would feel happy and rewarded to continue her good work. Perhaps you all now understand what I've been driving at. I do not suggest that you worship another human being, indeed, I'd be the last person to suggest such a thing.

This idea was welcomed by most of the women; they even suggested that, since I had access to those in power, I should put it to them!

The women were totally unaware that a constitution was being drafted for

Nnobi, thus their organization had no opportunity to make the suggestion. Discussions with those entrusted with drafting the constitution revealed that a section of it would include the revival of certain male titles, but expunged of rituals offensive to Christianity.[4] Revival of female titles was not included, and only one or two men had considered reviving the female *Ekwe* title. The present Chief of Nnobi said women in Nnobi today are no longer rich enough to take the title.

The Christian women, in rejecting the *Ekwe* title, were not opposed to title taking as such, as they maintained that they did participate in one kind of title taking: membership of the select committees of the Catholic Christian Mothers, or the Anglican Mothers' Union. They described these select committees as equivalent to the *ichie* titled men of the *igwe*'s council, that is, the equivalent of the superior elders among *ozo* titled men, known as *ndi ushe* (respected elders). The Anglicans' Mothers' Union, for example, has a large membership, with a few select women as leaders who make decisions for the rest of the members. The leaders are selected on the same principle as in the Women's Council, which is made up of representatives from the various wards of Nnobi. The same principles of formal organization used at descent level and town level are carried over to the church organizations.

The Women's Council, for example, is a representation of all married women in Nnobi, as, too, are the church unions' organizations. Whereas the indigenous organizations are descent and town linked, the church unions are branches of a wider, national body. Steady, for example, describes the Mothers' Union of the Anglican Church as 'a worldwide body that sets itself up as the guardian of Christian marriage and morality' (1976:230). Leadership in the indigenous organizations was based on titles and seniority but today, seniority alone is the qualification, and in the church it is the wives of clergy, lay readers or prominent men in Nnobi who tend to assume leadership positions. This is despite the existence of more highly educated, élite Nnobi Christian women who, however, live in the urban centres. The educated élites in these areas are often elected as chairpersons[5] of the various local branches. Home-based leaders maintained that these branch chairpersons were under their jurisdiction. As the spokeswoman of the Women's Council said,

The real head of Nnobi women is the head of the Women's Council at home. Those in the diaspora respect us. Even if they fight in their branches, we meet here, consider the case and write to them and admonish them for spoiling our name. Therefore we do not neglect those outside Nnobi. If we were to dissociate ourselves from them just because they are on the road, they would wander away and actually get lost. We are therefore doing things quite sensibly. When they default, they are fined in their branches and at home. An offender outside Nnobi can in fact be summoned back to Nnobi where her case is judged, if she proves too powerful for the branch leaders. The strongest committee is usually from those at home. The annual general meetings last for three days and the educated women are not really powerful or in control of things at these meetings. We at home control them. We admit that we learn a few things from them, since they are educated and can read, write and keep books.

Because the *Ekwe* title had conferred unopposed leadership of the Women's Council, which is now assumed by the church women's leaders, 'pagan' women believe the title is being taken secretly by these women in the church. How else, they question, did they become Women's Council leaders? But, as only Idemili's priest can sanctify the *Ekwe* title and the priest does not attend church who, then, sanctifies it?

The indigenous women's organizations were political with some form of representation at every level of the political structure; church unions are non-political. Membership of church unions is open not simply to women as wives and mothers, but only to women who have been married in church; even they are screened to ascertain they are of good character.

Women who organize bazaars, thanksgiving services, harvest festivals and fund-raising activities for the church are predominantly motivated not by political ambition but selfless service to the church. While men use such occasions to donate generously, display their wealth and gain individual prominence, women are expected to work hard, unnoticed and seeking no reward, like good mothers for the benefit of their children and in the service of Christ. Thus, most of the money for church maintenance and activities is raised by the efforts of women.

By extension all charitable work has become a female concern. The thrift and industriousness of Nnobi women in their management of the subsistence economy has been transferred to fund-raising ventures for the church. Sections of the church women's associations, for example, buy chairs and cooking utensils which are hired out to the public at great profit during occasions such as marriage, birth or funeral ceremonies. The proceeds are usually reported at the annual general meetings. Some of the profits are invested in other profit-yielding enterprises, some used for entertainment, and the remainder donated to the church or charitable organizations. The focus is therefore not on self-aggrandizement, unlike the male organizations where individuals are motivated by power and prominence.

The organization Sweet Mother was the only non-church-based women's association in Nnobi which came into focus during my fieldwork. Data were not collected on this association as it did not originate in Nnobi, nor does it as yet have any profound influence there. A non-Nnobi wife of a Nnobi man had just started this club, and the membership was still minimal. Sweet Mother, like many other such clubs, is a national organization of professional, business and trader women, which welcomes branches in any Nigerian town. Membership is open to women of any ethnic group, like the Christian Mothers and the Mothers' Union. Sweet Mother has its own uniform and other distinguishing symbols.

This association is important to Nnobi in so far as it could provide an alternative option for politically ambitious women, constrained by church rules and morality. Sweet Mother shares much the same principles as male associations and clubs. The high membership fee (including a specific number of cartons of beer) has kept membership very low; money must also be contributed periodically. A specific sum is paid to a bereaved member by her particular branch and by the national headquarters. This form of life insurance policy appears to be the main attraction of these associations. For this reason, some branches have an age limit on membership, fearing that, in order to avoid paying many years subscription, women may join only when they are so old as to expect to be members for their last few years, while their family would have the same claim to bereavement benefits as those of longer standing members.

At one level, therefore, the motivating factor is self-aggrandizement. At another, as its name – Sweet Mother – suggests, it is the ideal of motherhood, in common with church-linked associations, hence its involvement in welfare and charitable projects.

Another exclusively women's association mentioned during fieldwork was Okwesili Eze ('those fit to be kings'). Its name immediately implies a different orientation from the other motherhood-linked associations. Again, detailed data were not collected on this club, as there was no branch in Nnobi. Only a few individual urban-based Nnobi women were said to belong to it. This club is, however, relevant in so far as members can effect social change. Women who belong to this club, as its name suggests, see themselves as fit to be kings. Not surprisingly this is an exclusive club of extremely wealthy women. The popular belief was that only post-menopausal women were admitted into it. This may only be a way of ensuring that all members are free of domestic duties and childcare responsibilities. Most members, therefore, tend to be wealthy, divorced women or rich widows, mainly business contractors, factory owners and big traders.

As their rules of membership eliminate some of the constraining factors, these women emerge in full social, economic and political association and competition with men. They may be made chairpersons during ceremonial occasions; like men, they donate large sums of money during launching or fund-raising occasions. They play philanthropic roles like wealthy men, and in many cases buy or are given chieftainship titles by towns which have such provisions for wealthy women. It is from such women that state and federal governments choose for appointed offices. Such women stand ready for nomination as candidates by political parties, or failing this are made leaders of female wings of political parties. In Nnobi, such women find themselves alone or in a minority, but supposedly equal, in mixed-sex clubs and associations such as Abalukwu Social Club or Okaa Social Club (which was banned by the military government, but later reappeared as the People's Social Club when the ban on political activities was lifted in 1978).

In the contemporary socio-cultural context, we find that the persistent identification of women according to the traditional role and expectations of motherhood can lead only to their exploitation and their marginalization from the power structure. In local politics, it is the wealthy and the benevolent who receive rewards in the form of titles or political appointments. The mass of women, still limited to church-based organizations, preaching self-denial to other women and doing charitable work, cannot begin to see themselves as business tycoons, ambitious for political power and careers. The traditional unity of Nnobi women has been largely undermined by the Christian churches, not to mention the deleterious effect on their self-image and esteem of the denial of the goddess Idemili and the *Ekwe* title which she gave to women.

Notes

1. Table 5. Published by the Ministry of Economic Development.

2. Her body was decorated with black, vegetable dye and she wore ivory anklets and bracelets.

3. God the creator. I know of no comprehensive study of Igbo religions which links the hierarchy of religious symbols and manifestations to the concept of a supreme Deity. However, Igbo people know that such a concept is indigenous and predates contact with universal religions.

4. By August 1982, the proposal for honorary titles for men had already been put into practice. See Appendix 4 for a copy of the letter from the traditional ruler sent to those nominated for honorary titles (it includes my father, Solomon Amadiume). There is no woman among them. Yet the traditional ruler himself said to me and I quote him, 'Women take more active part in farming, the production of food-stuffs and marketing. It is to their credit that we eat today.'

5. I have used this expression to illustrate the new attempts in the West to demasculinize certain important male-linked roles in the English language and make them genderless, therefore open to both sexes.

11. The Female Element in Other Igbo Societies

In looking at gender in Nnobi society, I found that it was not enough to stress matrifocality or the importance of the female element in the domestic arrangement or kinship system. The consequences of this importance in the wider ritual and political institutions of the society had to be looked into in order to establish the place and role of women in the overall seats of power.

From evidence of the distinct prominence of matriarchal principles in this supposedly 'patrilineal' society, we can confidently challenge the rigid classification of traditional Igbo societies on the basis of principles of succession and inheritance based on descent. A brief comparative look at data from other Igbo societies reveals an underestimation of the importance of the female element, and consequently of the importance of women in the various social and political systems.

Whether classified by Forde and Jones (1950) or by Onwuejeogwu (1981), most Igbo areas have been presented as basically patrilineal. Basden (1938:268) referred to the presence of matriliny in Ohaffia as 'an isolated example'. For Forde and Jones (1950:52), the system was in fact 'non-Ibo'. It is now an established fact that there is a strong and predominant matrilineal element among the Cross River Igbo (Nsugbe 1974). Ohaffia, whether by the classification of Forde and Jones or of Onwuejeogwu, belongs to the Cross River Igbo category. Despite Nsugbe's convincing arguments establishing the predominance of matriliny in Ohaffia, however, Professor Onwuejeogwu lumps Ohaffia in with others, such as the Afikpo Igbo, who share cultural features such as a 'double unilineal system of inheritance' (1981:13).

It is from a gender perspective that Nsugbe's approach to the study of the matrilineal Igbo people of Ohaffia[1] has been most disappointing. His exclusive concern with principles of descent, succession and inheritance, at the expense of other dynamics of gender ideologies in the social processes of Ohaffia, leaves a lot to be desired in a work which gives a partial impression of the very prominent position of women *vis-à-vis* men in this Igbo community.

Nsugbe's data show that, although there was a very high valuation of the female gender, which was reflected in the ritual position of the matrilineage female head, secular affairs in the matrilineage and the wider public sector of the village appear to have been controlled and run exclusively by men through their various age-sets (1974:58–67). It is also solely in connection with the male secular office of village head that wealth, achievement and bought titles are mentioned (Nsugbe 1974:95, 98 and footnote 7).

However, a dual-sex political system appears to have been in operation in matrilineal Ohaffia, whereby the autonomous non-lineage-based village Women's Association, which dealt exclusively with the affairs of the adult women, in some ways duplicated its equivalent Men's Association (Nsugbe 1974:67). The leader of the Women's Association was known as *Eze Nwanyi* (female king), and held both secular and ritual office within the female sphere. She presided over the women's meetings and acted as the spokeswoman of the Association. During the planting season, she ritually declared farming open for the women (Nsugbe 1974:68). Unlike the more powerful male government association, which depended on a junior age-set for the execution and enforcement of its rulings, the Women's Association executed its own rulings. In addition, it could effectively oppose any unwelcome actions or decisions taken by the men, as it had the power to call for mass female non-co-operation and boycott (Nsugbe 1974).

Rights to patrilineal building land were patrilineally inherited. Land immediately beyond and adjoining these building lands was owned by the matrilineage, as was all the land beyond this, including frontier lands; most land, therefore, belonged to the matrilineage (Nsugbe 1974:86–8). Although residence in Ohaffia is said to have been patrilocal, according to Nsugbe the patrilineage was an endogamous unit, and as he writes, 'marriage of patrilineage relatives even as close as half-siblings which will be an abomination among patrilineal Igbo is permitted in Ohaffia' (1974:78). Again, Nsugbe quotes the Ohaffia themselves as saying, 'we take in marriage whom we bear, for amity' (1974:79). The matrilineage, on the other hand, is said to have followed the rule of exogamy and to have been named after their ancestresses (1974:73). It is on this basis that Nsugbe would not classify the Ohaffia system as double descent, even though residential land followed the rule of patrilineal inheritance, and much of the immovable property could be inherited either way (1974:119–22).

A phenomenon in Ohaffia, which is absent in accounts of patrilineal Igbo areas, is the ritual superiority of the female in the matrilineage. The Ohaffia matrilineage recognized two heads, one male and one female. The male head took care of secular duties involving the general management of property, its allocation and exploitation, and the settlement of disputes. An adult female could play this male role when no male was available (Nsugbe 1974:93). The sacred duties of the female matrilineage head, called 'female king' like the head of the village Women's Association, involved the performance of sacrifices to the sacred pots representing the ancestresses of the matrilineage. This role could never be performed by a male. This was not so in Nnobi, where men sought control over women through their control of ancestral symbols and rituals. Ohaffia female ancestral pots were moved as female elders succeeded female heads of matrilineages. As a result of this very strong matrifocality in the Ohaffia cultural system, matrilineage pots are said to have been better cared for and to 'evoke stronger and deeper emotions of loyalty even today than their male counterparts do' (Nsugbe 1974:111).

Making a distinction between the patrilineage and the matrilineage, Ohaffia is said to state the gender aspect of its culture thus: 'a man's worst enemy is his patrikin' (Nsugbe 1974:94), implying continuous struggle, rivalry and competition within the patrilineage, which constituted the residential group and owned residential land, liable to suffer from population pressure.

But of the matrilineage they said, 'father's penis scatters, mother's womb gathers' (Nsugbe 1974). Here, I believe that what they may be associating with the male role is the tendency towards irresponsibility and lack of accountability for personal action. The penis plants its seed in the womb, perhaps in many wombs, and moves on to do the same elsewhere. Ohaffia men were traditionally head-hunters and warriors employed as mercenaries by other Igbo groups (Nsugbe 1974:21, 25–31; Isichei 1976:81–7; Henderson 1972:499–501). Most social and domestic responsibilities therefore fell to the women. Nsugbe, for example, writes, 'Ohaffia women are considered by other Ibo groups to be the hardest-worked on the farm of any Ibo womenfolk, just as the men are regarded as being among the hardiest travellers' (1974:21). The material experience of an Ohaffia, the primary identification with and centrality of the female in reproduction, production, property and status inheritance, were thus given cultural expression in a strong, matrifocal ideology.

As was shown in the case of indigenous Nnobi society, women derived power and high self-esteem from a matrifocal culture, especially from a goddess-focused religion. Strong matrifocality is also present in the ideological concepts of all other Igbo communities. The centrality of the female role in reproduction and the primary identification of children with their mother is manifested both in their kinship terminology and the domestic structure, irrespective of their classification on the basis of patrilineality or matrilineality.

The primary kinship unit recognized by the Igbo is the matricentric unit of a mother and her children. This is the Igbo *umunne otu afo*, children of one womb, both a farming and an eating unit, which sees itself as those who eat of the same pot (see Nsugbe 1974:94; Henderson 1972:169). The strongest kinship ties and sentiment are expressed within this group and other, wider relationships, real or fictitious, traced through a womb connection. For example, Nsugbe writes of the Ohaffia, 'An Ohaffia person makes a great deal of fuss about "those with whom I share the same womb"' . . . The people are open about their strong bias towards their mothers and mother's own kin group' (1974:93–4).

Of the same sentiments among the patrilineal Owerri Igbo, M. Green, assuming a uniform system for the Igbo, writes, 'clearly matriliny plays a considerable part in Ibo society. Descent and succession are patrilineal, marriage is patrilocal and a man inherits from his father. But the matrilineal principle is there asserting itself both legally and emotionally' (1947:161). This sentiment is epitomized in the special status and privileges given to children of daughters and their mediatory role in linking lineages or villages (1947:152, 160).

Similar sentiments have also been recorded among other patrilineal northern Igbo communities, especially where daughters have structural political and ritual roles in their patrilineages, as, for example, in Onitsha society[2] (see Henderson 1972:140–41, 153–5). Here, too, motherhood has been canonized. Daughters erected personal shrines called 'the mothers', dedicated to series of dead mothers. As daughters married, they took these shrines to their marital homes (Henderson 1972:169). About these shrines, Henderson writes,

Intimately associated with the personal god of every woman is the spirit called *Oma*, objectified in the form of a small rounded conical clay mound set against the wall on the floor of the woman's kitchen called 'the mothers', this symbol represents maternity as a perpetual force which acts upon all descendants of a woman. (1972:193)

A woman was said to sit before the shrine to address the dead in the same way as the patrilineage priest did before the shrine of lineage male ancestors. The only difference was the fact that the woman would not use the *ofo*, symbol of authority, and therefore, according to Henderson (1972) 'the normative component of righteous power associated with males is absent in such ritual communication; instead, the worship of *Oma* evokes associations of maternal indulgence and loving filial dependence.' Yet Henderson himself writes, 'It is believed that through *Oma* a mother's spiritual power can make her children sick, barren or impotent' (1972:194). This punishment would result from any neglect of filial duties (1972:195). The wrath of *Oma*, it seems to me, was therefore more powerful in the social processes of Onitsha people as it governed the sentiments, emotions and actions of everyone, all the time, than the sanctions of ancestors used by a few males in key positions in the society.

The strong sibling emotional tie is further stressed by Henderson, who writes, 'Children born of one mother are expected to behave maternally towards one another as the children of one father are not'. Their relationship of 'mutual nurturance and mutual dependence' on the *Oma* shrine, is what Henderson terms 'being in *Oma*'. This condition of 'being in *Oma*' to a mother is said to last beyond the woman's lifetime and is thus part of a descent relationship. After the funeral of a mother, it was up to her eldest daughter to make her an ancestress by bringing her into her kitchen, as it was the duty of the eldest son to bring his father into the *obi* (1972:113).

The spiritual force of the original mother remained strong, affecting both male and female descendants despite the multiplicity of mounds dedicated to subsequent mothers. As the tie to a shrine gave the participants the status of common motherhood, they remained an exogamous unit; Henderson therefore accepts the ideology of *Oma* as 'matrilineal', since it is a relationship traced through a 'descending line of mothers' (1972:195). This would refute Nsugbe's claim, derived from misinformation from Meek (1937:62), that female ancestors were not represented among the patrilineal Igbo, while the Ohaffia represented both male and female ancestors (1974:102). Green (1947) also makes reference to villages in the southern Igbo areas of Owerri which, in spite of the general rule of village exogamy, could not intermarry as they were in *umunne*, the bond of common motherhood relationship. Here, in fact, the villages involved had common ancestral symbols known as *umunne* (Green 1947:153, 155).

Similarly, in Nri society, typified by its divine kingship system and patrilineal system of descent and inheritance (Onwuejeogwu 1981), the bond of common motherhood known as *Ibenne* was ritualized and symbolized in a cult object (see Akunne 1977). This was an earthenware bowl, which contained sacred sticks thought of as males and females and tied together, signifying the unity of those involved. During sacrifices, the blood of a hen was sprinkled over the bowl and its contents, that is, kola-nuts and wine. This ritual bowl was given a significant place at the ancestral altar of every family and other, wider, lineage organizations (Akunne 1977:60–61).

It appears that in this culture, *Ibenne*, described as 'the true spirit of unity which binds persons through common motherhood' (Akunne 1977:60), was manipulated at other, higher, levels of lineage organization, where trust, unity and solidarity were sought. Even in the contemporary society, in the face of change, this moral force is still effectively applied in certain social and economic sectors, even by non-related individuals. As Akunne put it,

> Christianity has reduced the people's ritual consciousness of *Ibenne*, but the corporate ideology of lineage morality remains. *Ibenne* is still influential in commerce: individuals pool their capital to launch an urban business after taking their *Ibenne* oath, in their rural home, not to cheat one another. *Ibenne* is the foundation for trust and confidence – a ritual agreement with a ritual sanction. (1977:63)

It seems, therefore, that contrary to the general impression, maternal ancestresses or relationships traced matrilineally were ritualized and symbolized in cult objects in most Igbo societies, whether classified as matrilineal or patrilineal. They played very significant roles in governing kinship relationships in traditional Igbo systems. It thus follows that strong emphasis on principles of patriliny and systems of descent and inheritance could have given only a distorted or partial presentation of traditional Igbo social and cultural gender dialectics. That approach simply made women invisible, contrary to social facts.

More importantly, with more data and detailed study from the women's point of view, we can go beyond Tanner's (1974) survey of matrifocality to show how its political implication for women goes deeper than women's importance in kinship systems.

More research is needed into new marriage patterns and family composition in both urban and rural towns. In southern Nigeria, and I believe in the west, there seems to be a widespread revival of matriarchal or matrifocal households. These are autonomous households headed by women who have visiting husbands or lovers. Most of these women are either graduates, traders or business contractors and, therefore, economically independent. It would be interesting to study the effect of such arrangements on gender relations, on the women's economic and political mobility, and on the gender attitudes of their children.

In the religious sphere, the challenge to a male representation of the image of God is growing; so also is the effort to make visible the role of women in religious histories. This can stem only from the fact that women need positive and powerful female models for their own self-esteem, comparable to those used by men to masculinize human languages, histories and cultures.

Notes

1. Nsugbe estimated the population of Ohaffia in the 1960s to be over 65,000 (1974:10).

2. In the 1953 census, the population of Onitsha was given as 76,921 (Ofomata 1975:141).

12. Gender, Class and Female Solidarity

It is my view that a strong cultural bond of female solidarity in traditional Igbo systems overcame the potentially divisive effects of gender and class among women.

It is arguable, however, whether Igbo societies were class societies in the Western sense. Nzimiro, for example sees inequality in centralized Igbo societies in terms of class (1972:24). His Marxist interpretation has been challenged by Onwuejeogwu (1977), who, like Henderson (1972), insists on the use of the term 'political groupings' rather than 'political class', as membership to the qualifying titles was open to all free-born of the particular towns. The Nnobi case showed that not all the titles were open to all free-born; some were restricted to particular patrilineages, e.g., *Dunu, Aho* and *Ezeani*.

Onwuejeogwu has, of course, overlooked women in making his statement: the titles involved are gender linked and mainly exclusively male titles. The standard Igbo bought title, which conferred on the holder political or ritual leadership, is *ozo*. Only men took, and still take, that title in Igbo societies. Some communities, however, had other titles for women, or some categories of women.

In the case of centralized Onitsha, Nzimiro's (1972:23–55) broad categories of citizen (free-born) and non-citizen (slaves and foreigners) to describe the social and ideological framework lack a gender perspective.

A general Igbo principle in gender relations is that a woman, as a daughter, has the status of citizen – an acknowledged member of her natal patrilineage; but as a wife, she is treated as a non-citizen of her marital patrilineage. This was given symbolic expression in burial practices, whereby a wife's body was returned to her natal patrilineage for burial, and in the mortuary rite of seclusion associated with the widow pending the definition of her new status after the husband's death (Henderson 1972:229–30; Basden 1938:278–9, 291).

Igbo women's duality of status is best revealed in the exogamy rules of some Igbo societies, and the indigenous women's organizations of most Igbo societies. From Green's data, for example, the stranger or outsider classification of women as wives is more widespread in the southern Igbo areas of Owerri province, where the rules of exogamy applied at village level. The resulting effect was the concentration of wives in individual villages and the dispersal of daughters all over the villages (Green 1947:149–57). The status of wives as strangers for example, becomes clear from the fact that the 'aggressive medicine' or 'magic' used against strangers could be used by village men against the wives (Green 1947:80–81). On the other hand, spatial separation of wives and daughters appears to have minimized conflicts between both interest groups, or the possibility of manipulation of them against each other by lineage men. This has not been the case in the northern Igbo provinces, where village or town endogamy was preferred. Onitsha, for example, operated town endogamy (Henderson 1972:196–9, 243) to the extent that for those in incestuous or taboo relationships there seems to have been a modified rule, or a compromise solution, enabling them to marry under specified conditions (Henderson 1972:197). This was also the practice in Nnobi.

The preference for village endogamy in these northern Igbo communities encouraged the proximity of daughters to their natal homes, where they had important ritual and political roles to fulfil, whether in the family, or formally, through their very powerful organizations of patrilineage daughters (see Henderson 1972:153–6; Basden 1938:225–7; Okonjo 1976:52).

In the valuation of daughters and wives, all the literature attests to the superior status that Igbo communities, including Nnobi, have accorded their daughters in relation to their wives. Data from other Igbo societies also point out the association of daughters with male roles and status in relation to wives. For example, all Igbo daughters of a patrilineage are addressed as 'husbands' by the wives of the patrilineage. This, among other practices, negates any assumption of rigidity in the association of gender to sex in Igbo culture in general. More importantly, it poses the question of class and gender division of women.

Onitsha appears to be the most stratified Igbo society, therefore data from there are the most relevant in examining how women were able to maintain a strong sense of solidarity in face of the divisive factors of gender and class.

Okonjo (1976) basically sees the role of the Onitsha female monarch, *Omu*, as fulfilling the dual-sex nature of the political system typical of the western and riverine Igbo monarchies. Thus, the *Omu* and her councillors concerned themselves with the female section of the community (Okonjo 1976:47). From Henderson's data, however, we see that the *Omu* and her councillors, who were known in office as the Queen's Council or the Women's Trade Organization, were the major organized élite core of wealthy women, over and above a larger organization called 'women of Onitsha', which included all the married women (Okonjo 1976:309–10). We learn that members of the Queen's Council were patrilineal and clan daughters, while the queen herself

> should be head daughter of her segment of the royal clan, and her titled councillors should be head daughters of their clan or village units. Thus they are tied to the ascriptive base of descent group membership. The queen is handed her *ofo omu*[1] by the king of Onitsha, and the titled councillors receive their own head daughter's *ofo* from their hidden kings. (Okonjo 1976:312).

The relationship of the queen and her councillors to the women of Onitsha was therefore an extension of the relationship of daughters to wives at the extra-descent level of political organization. As those who had undergone rituals of purification like *ozo* titled men, the bodies of the queen and her councillors were also considered holy (Okonjo 1976:212). Therefore, in their ritual duties of performing market sacrifices and other town cleansing rituals (Okonjo 1976:310, 313), they were classed as males, like daughters in the patrilineage.

Despite the distinguishing and divisive factors of gender and class, however, the idea of oneness of gender in terms of sex was manipulated by the queen and her councillors in the management of market affairs and the mass of Onitsha women.[2] The market square and other geographical areas controlled by women were, for example, defined by the queen and her councillors as female zones, to the exclusion of men. All these areas were associated with powerful female medicines and shrines served by women (Okonjo 1976:310–11) and were avoided by Onitsha men, owing to their fear of the female medicines and of the women themselves as witches (Okonjo 1976:311). There was therefore a contradiction in the image of the queen and her councillors as prophets of the community, taking care of sacrifice and driving away evil from the town, for, concomitantly, the same women were seen as witches, trading by day and practising witchcraft by night (Okonjo 1976:311).

These women, however, had both an economic and an organizational base from which to participate in the ideology-making process. For example, they generated favourable gender rules and beliefs associated with their control of the market. Henderson, for example, writes,

> The connection of men with market trade comes mainly through their individual sponsorship of their wives or daughters as traders. Symbolically, the marketplace is defined as outside the sphere of assertion by males, whether human or animal; any cock that crows there during trading hours must become the property of the Queen. (Quoted in Okonjo 1976)

The Queen's Council was also strongly represented in the king's court, so that no trade legislation or transactions were made without their knowledge and consent (Okonjo 1976:313). The queen's power was enhanced by the fact that she was in a position to mobilize the power of Onitsha women. She also appears to have been independent of the king, as we learn that, even though she and her councillors paid annual tribute to him, she was not ritually subservient to him, but to the divine king of Nri, whose female dwarfs crowned succeeding Onitsha queens (Okonjo 1976:314).

The flexibility of gender in this political and cultural system thus favours the presence of women in the highest élite core of the society, whether in the status acquired through titles, or in the position of the kingship itself. This conclusion was also reached by Henderson. According to him, there is 'the tendency for prominent women to accumulate male symbols of prestige. Indeed, the queen has at times so extensively emulated the king that she has threatened his position' (1972:376). That the queen was not the king's wife, but had to be 'genealogically distant from him' (Henderson 1972:310), and the separateness of her palace and council, were all factors which added to her autonomy.

The autonomy of the *Omu* meant that she was not associated with men by the mass of Onitsha women, as both her time and trading activities centred on the market-place, an exclusive female zone. The women thus perceived the *Omu* and her titled councillors as their symbolic leaders, representing their interests in administration and government. Their support could therefore be called upon unquestionably.

Irrespective of gender division, the same sense of solidarity of wives and daughters is true of Igbo women in the less centralized southern Igbo societies, with minimal titled élites. From Green's data, we have an example of how women, though complete strangers in their husbands' villages, could combine power derived from their control of subsistence farming and family sustenance, as they were the food producers and crop owners (1947:172), with their organizational ability, for effective mass action against a particular village or all the village group, until their demands were met (1947:211–14). Their strong economic position made up for their lack of formal political authority. This is also manifested in the general belief that, even though women did not have the real symbol of authority in the form of an *ofo*, their mere gesture of protest, either by knocking the pestle used for pounding food, or their hands, on the ground, could be very effective in causing sickness in the village (Green 1947:175, 209). Women's anger was, therefore, feared. Their custom of swearing loyalty and solidarity before village shrines for the sake of unity (1947:209) and in a common enterprise (1947:221), and their effective sanction against any deviating or disobedient members were other factors that safeguarded the unity of the women (1974: 196, 201–4).

As Green's approach did not incorporate a study of the socio-cultural dynamics of gender ideologies, she is unable, in her conclusion, to relate the supposed ideal female pacific roles, whether as sisters in relation to brothers, or wives to husbands (1947:256), or female to male medicine (1947:255), to other instances or occasions when the 'ideal' gender relations were reversed and women performed 'ideal' male roles. A good example of this is her description of the mass walk-out by the women of the village group during the course of a month-long strike (1947:213). From Green's description of this incident, the men were completely passive compared to the women, who even performed such ritual acts, normally forbidden them, as killing a fowl (1947:213). There had been an unusually high rate of female mortality, for which the women blamed the men (Green 1947:213). The women's suspicions were allayed only by a mass swearing ceremony by the men. The date of this event was put at the period just before the 1919 influenza epidemic. The women had insisted that the men should come to the central market-place and swear before the Earth Spirit *Ala*, a goddess. As Green describes what took place,

> The wives of each village collected together the men of that village and they came in turn to Orie Ekpa, the senior village coming first. The swearing took eight days . . . the women dug a hole in the ground . . . and poured into it water collected from the shrines of two of the most powerful Agbaja deities and made a kind of soup and put it in. And they killed a fowl and poured its blood into the hole . . . They also made fufu of pounded plantain and rolled it into small balls. The main body of women then stood back and the principal ones stood near the hole. And the men came up one by one and had to dip their hands in the hole and wash their faces in the liquid. Each man had then to eat a ball of the . . . fufu . . . and swear on pain of death that he neither had killed nor would kill people or pregnant women or children. Nor had he stolen. (1947:213)

This ceremony, according to Green's informants, had not been repeated since the advent of Christianity in their villages, but they felt that they could revive it at any time if necessary (1947:214).

Other situations described and witnessed by Green indicate village women's strong aggressiveness, especially during all-female ceremonies or occasions, which tended to quickly become rituals of rebellion. The occasion of the women's annual religious rites for the feminine aspect of the male–female guardian spirit of the village, for example, is typified by its bawdiness and the women's unrestrained wildness. They dance with knives, which they clash (Green 1947:193), demonstrating aggression and militancy. Their songs rebelliously reject standard female roles, as Green's statement shows,

> Snatches of their songs – Is it any shame if we do not marry? – Is it any shame if we will not lie with a man? – Is it any shame if we wish to marry a young man? – gave one the impression of a definitely feminist flavour, which was enhanced by the fact that during the whole day hardly a man was to be seen. The women were left in undisputed possession of the village. (Green 1947:193)

Not only did the women possess the village, but on this women's day, men, who, in Igbo society and culture, customarily did not cook, were expected to cook for the women (Green 1947:197).

Igbo women's strong commitment to female solidarity was more advantageous in the period before electoral politics and the forming of political parties when, to a large extent, it could be claimed that there was a unity of purpose in women's struggles. This is in strong contrast to modern Nigerian history, which is typified by the exploitation of women's organizational ability and sense of female solidarity by male-dominated political parties and individual female political careerists (see Mba 1982). Mba's conclusion is supported by the evidence presented here; both show that women in Nigeria had more power under the traditional dual-sex political system, which gave them greater autonomy as women. I have, however, stressed the flexibility of gender construct which modified the traditional dual-sex system. Mba's study also shows that Igbo women are politically disadvantaged by their lack of titles in comparison to Yoruba women, who can still buy chieftaincy titles during a political career, just as men can.

The option of a dual-sex political system requires further research, not only in the context of Africa and the Third World in general, but also of the West. In Britain, for example, Labour-controlled local authorities have for the past few years instituted, in local government councils, Women's Units and Women's Committees which are responsible for women's interests. They have powers to challenge and modify policies and allocate grants. Having worked in one of these Women's Units myself, I know that racism, class and even sexual politics divide the women in the Units and Committees. More importantly, the majority of local women are alienated by the very élitist policies, structures and priorities of the Women's Committees. In comparison to the struggles of African women in local politics, women in the West are privileged in terms of funds and opportunities, which they do not seem to know how to handle. Igbo women will say of them, 'The dog with a tail says that human beings, blessed with buttocks, do not know how to sit.' Assessing the sense and show of sisterhood or female solidarity with Western women, an Igbo woman will find herself asking the question: 'Am I in the company of men or women?'

Notes

1. *Ofo Omu*: symbol of authority.
2. For the life and history of a powerful Igbo woman, a particular *Omu* in the context of Onitsha society and relations with Europeans, see Felicia Ekejiuba's study of Omu Okwei (1872–1943), the Merchant Queen of Ossomari, in *Nigeria* magazine No. 90, September 1966.

13. Conclusion

The Implications of a Rigid Gender System

In this study, I have looked at the ideology of gender in the socio-cultural systems of Nnobi during three historical periods and at the effect of that ideology on the structural position of women in that society. In the indigenous society, the dual-sex principle behind social organization was mediated by the flexible gender system of the traditional culture and language. The fact that biological sex did not always correspond to ideological gender meant that women could play roles usually monopolized by men, or be classified as 'males' in terms of power and authority over others. As such roles were not rigidly masculinized or feminized, no stigma was attached to breaking gender rules. Furthermore, the presence of an all-embracing goddess-focused religion favoured the acceptance of women in statuses and roles of authority and power.

In contrast, Western culture and the Christian religion, brought by colonialism, carried rigid gender ideologies which aided and supported the exclusion of women from the power hierarchy, whether in government or the church in the modern society. This rigid gender system meant that roles are strictly masculinized or feminized; breaking gender rules therefore carries a stigma.

It is my opinion that in the West, as a result of the rigid gender system, women wielding power tend to be seen as reclassified, or present themselves as 'manly' or 'manlike'. This point is also made by Silvia Rogers (1981). She shows how women Members of Parliament entering the British House of Commons, essentially a 'Men's House', are acknowledged only as 'men' or derided if they remain 'female'; for Western women acceptance in a man's world involves a 'reclassification'. This includes a 'reclassification' of Mrs Thatcher, the present British Prime Minister, as the 'Iron Lady' of the Soviets and other 'fantastic' descriptions by herself, her colleagues and the press (Rogers 1981:67). In addition, the tailored trouser-suits worn by some of these women seem to answer part of their need to manipulate male symbols for power. In view of the manliness of women in power, Silvia Rogers concludes that having a woman British Prime Minister has not changed the essential nature of the 'Men's House'.

Significantly, under colonial rule and the influence of Western culture the 'queen' of Onitsha and her councillors thought it necessary to wear male clothes in the bid to identify themselves with the new symbols of power, which were solely male. This

185

was observed by Basden, who wrote,

> In this custom also changes have been introduced. The crown is no longer in the traditional fashion: sad to state, quite probably a man's hat becomes the crown of office . . . In one instance observed, the women were dressed as men. They wore men's hats, and some had coats. Their breasts were bound close to their bodies by cross-over straps and each woman brandished a cutlass. (1938:210)

In Nnobi's traditional cultural system, with the Igbo language's flexible gender construction, the conceptualization of daughters as male in ritual matters and politically in relation to wives, did not imply that daughters should be seen as 'manlike'; nor were 'female husbands' expected to dress or behave like men. There is, therefore, no linguistic or mental adjustment or confusion in references to a woman in a typical male role. Powerful women were not divorced or alienated from 'fellow' women. (In using 'fellow' here, I have suffered a moment of mental strain, as 'fellow' popularly means 'man'. This would not happen in Igbo, since a genderless word, *ibe* (one of the same kind), would be used.)

In examining contemporary women's associations, I noted that politically orientated women's organizations are not church based. They systematically attract economically successful women and restrict the membership of younger women still dependent on husbands and constrained by domestic responsibilities. These organizations are therefore dominated by post-menopausal widows and divorced women, and it is these women who are invited to fill political offices, nominated as possible candidates by political parties, or given honorary titles by towns and governments.

In the new gender realities, such women are still seen and defined as females, even though they are no longer involved in domestic female roles. They are employed in departments and services considered 'feminine', such as education, health, the social services and welfare. Politically, their role is restricted to winning or organizing women's votes for political parties. In practice, to the detriment of women, there is a trend towards rigid Western gender systems, and this is supported by official use of the English language, despite the flexible gender system of the mother tongue, the Igbo language.

More research is needed on the relationship between language and gender relations, especially the effect of Western languages on gender relations in African societies and other Third World communities.

Gender and Power in Other African Societies

It would have been useful to compare my findings in Nnobi with the situation elsewhere in Africa, but I have found no material with the kind of perspective and detail to make such comparison possible. However, Lebeuf's (1963) paper on women in the political organization of African societies gives some valuable insights.

Lebeuf acknowledges the 'very real authority exercised by women in traditional African political systems'. If they lack authority today, it is as a result of policies initiated from Western prejudice which relegates women 'to the sphere of domestic tasks and private life, and men alone are considered equal to the task of shouldering the burden of public affairs.' In her historical reconstruction of the past, like Sweetman (1984), she is able to offer only a sketchy survey of celebrated African ancestresses and queens, their exploits and some of their achievements. About the total systems they operated, we have very little information. With more information, it would have been interesting to make a comparison between some of the societies mentioned by Lebeuf and the system described for traditional Nnobi society.

Material on the Lovedu and their neighbours who inhabit the north-eastern Transvaal (population: 40,000) arouses curiosity about their gender system. They have a recent history of supreme female rule. They are an agricultural people with a patrilineal descent system and patrilocal residence. As in Nnobi, sisters have a higher status than wives; a queen reigns at the capital and is the head of the judicial system; either men or women act as district heads. The queen has supernatural powers: she makes rain. She is given 'wives' and is obliged to keep a 'harem', and is therefore a 'female husband'. Like Nnobi 'male daughters', she may not officially marry a man but may have children. The children of her wives belong to her and through them, she has affinal links with her subjects and consequently mutual obligations in patron–client relationships. She may also marry off her wives and gain more clients. From female representatives of the various districts known as 'mothers of the kingdom', she appoints those who act as intermediaries between herself and the people. She has no military backing – only her divinity. The goddess Idemili in Nnobi also abhorred bloodshed.

There are other southern African peoples where specific women share equal power with the kings, and always participate in rituals. In each case, the maternal attributes of the woman are stressed, though we have no information about their gender roles. Among the Swazi, the king's mother shares power with him, and is described thus: 'She is the Elephant, the Earth, the Beautiful, the Mother of the Country, the King is the Lion, the Sun, the Great Wild Animal' (Lebeuf 1963:100). Among the Lunda, a matrilineal people ruled by a patriarchal aristocracy, the king shares power with his kinswoman, who is regarded as the mother of the kingdom. This woman's husband is 'invisible'.

In West Africa, there are similar patterns in many societies. Among the Bamileke of Cameroon, the chief's mother – who wears masculine attire – is equivalent to the chief. Her domain is outside the chief's authority and therefore a sanctuary. She controls the agricultural work of the community which is a female sphere. In the administrative council she takes precedence over the chief. She presides over the women's secret societies and belongs to those of men which are not military. Under no one's control, she has total freedom. Her children belong to her, not to her husband. She is therefore different from all the other women.

Among the Chamba of Benue in northern Nigeria, a female relative of the king rules over the women and has corresponding duties to the king's. She is in charge of the female cult and participates with the king in the ancestral cult, and is buried in the same manner as the chiefs. Her husband is 'invisible'. Similarly, among the Ashanti of Ghana, the female joint ruler with the king has powers greater than those of any man. Her court, from which she rules in female matters, is separate from the king's. She is the custodian of the consecrated royal stools, and participates in the royal ancestral cult and some other rituals performed by the king. She is involved in the election, presentation and enthronement of a new king, and remains his adviser, guide and critic and in his absence takes his place in war. She is regarded as the feminine and maternal aspect of the Supreme Being: she is the moon, the king is the sun. Among the Bemba of north-eastern Zimbabwe, the Bushongo of the Kasai and the Loango, the king shares power with a woman.

In the region of the Great Lakes, a tripartite rule obtains whereby the king shares power with two women. The women have important ritual duties, and are custodians of the royal crown or the regalia. This is the case in Kitara, in Ankole and with the Bateke.

In Muslim Nigeria and Chad, we find only traces of what Lebeuf calls 'feminine roles' – 'feminine' in the sense that women filled them. Yet the women, though biologically female, could be playing the roles as male or female in a purely gender sense. Among the Nupe, two titles still survive which are taken by women who have shared power with the king. As usual with most of these political systems, one of the women was the king's mother. Among the Bolewa – a Kanuri people – the Kotoko of the Chari delta and the Bagirmians, again two women shared power with the king. In Bagirmi, if a man was appointed to one of these titles, he had to wear women's clothes for the ceremonies. Of the Kotoko, Lebeuf writes, 'the entire political system being conceived as a delicate balance between masculine and feminine, right and left, north and south, that must be maintained in the power relations of individuals, in all their activities, and even in their spatial location' (1963:106).

The class position of these ruling women differentiates them from other women in their societies. It also differentiates these political systems from traditional Nnobi society, where the position and status of the titled women were achieved and not ascribed. Also in Nnobi, a ruling class was less pronounced or distinguished from the rest of the people.

Even in these more centralized states, women below the highest level were also involved in politics. Female leaders were also elected or appointed from among the mass of women at the community level of politics. Thus African women have a tradition of formal or informal socio-political organizing in which they excel. Consequently, most African groups have women's associations, for example, those of the Lunda group, the Ekoi of southern Nigeria, the Bini, the Ube, Gere, Wobe of the Ivory Coast, the Mende, the Yoruba, etc. These associations control or direct agricultural work, trade, the market and female customs and rituals.

Other systems close to the Nnobi institution of 'male daughter' are mentioned by Lebeuf for other African societies such as the Babamba and the Mindossi in the Congo region, the Lovale of Zimbabwe, and the Mende of Sierra Leone. Among the Venda, such women practise woman-to-woman marriage. Also among the Venda, and Mboshi (Congo), Luba (Katanga), Mende (Sierra Leone) etc., some groups chose to have women as hereditary chiefs, as a mark of their reverence for the spirit of female ancestors. Other examples are the town of Njimoso among the Bachama of northern Nigeria, and the Chamba Tsugu town of Debbo. Women there are assigned very important ritual duties. Lebeuf also noticed that the widespread institution of very important roles for women is quite separate from the rule of descent.

Another interesting cultural classification is the Tonga institution called 'the wife of the district'. This woman organizes the other women and is in charge of the women's cults. Some Kwilu and Kasai peoples, such as the Pende, Bundi, Dinga and Lele, have a similar institution called 'wife of the village'. This woman participates in male, not female, activities, and has several husbands.

Lebeuf's general survey and the material I have presented for the Igbo show how erroneous and ethnocentric is the position taken in Rosaldo and Lamphere (1974) and in Young, Wolkowitz and McCullagh (1981), a position which assumes a universal subordination of all women at all times in history and in all cultures. In acknowledging the political importance of women in African history, my aim has not been to add to the long list of individual queens who have ruled at specific periods, for they may have operated oppressive male and patriarchal systems. I have been more interested in the systems or structures which made it possible for women to exercise power or to be part of the power structure as subjects, not objects.

The Implications of this Study for Future Research on African Women

I believe that this study calls for a reassessment of the term 'matriarchy' and of its true place and role in the history of African political systems and cultures. It calls for the recognition of such factors as mother right, matrifocality/mother focus, matricentrism, female orientation, etc., as aspects of a matriarchal culture. We should dismiss the anthropological definition which recognizes as matriarchal only a society completely ruled by women and which claims that such a society has only ever existed in myth. It is only logical that the opposite definition should hold for patriarchy, that is, a society completely ruled by men. New research, which acknowledges women as subjects and reveals women's contribution to society and culture, indicates that the facts contradict the standard definition. Men never ruled completely anywhere. The claim of patriarchy remains valid only if what women do in society and culture is denied and they are treated as invisible. Matriarchy and patriarchy are parts of ideology, patriarchal ideology being oppressive to women, matriarchal ideology being strongly linked with motherliness and love, indeed at the expense of mothers. Any ideology or culture has its contradictions and people may become mystified (Bloch 1976).

This study calls for more positive research which will be of value to women in their various struggles. Sanday stated that one aim of her cross-cultural analysis of female public power and authority was to 'give activist Western women further insight into where to concentrate their efforts to bring about change in the imbalance of power between males and females' (1974:192). But I believe that Sanday's approach to the data is not positive, she has simply juggled cause and effect, in the tradition of male anthropology, and failed to take the bull by the horns and give women the positive message that they need. Her basic assumption is negative as a result of her ethnocentric domestic/public dichotomy and her assumption that motherhood and child-rearing are to blame for the supposed universal subordination of women. Her basic assumption was that originally, women were concerned with reproduction and child-rearing, men with subsistence. Men later moved on to defence, while women moved into subsistence.

I would assume that women were permanently engaged in subsistence but the men only intermittently. Hence, the universal importance of women in household management and how that can be related to power: the mother-focused nature of the household, patriarchy encroaching on it, that is, the imposition of family on household autonomy. This approach is at least true of Africa where it has been proved beyond doubt that women contribute more to subsistence than anywhere else (Boserup 1970).

After evaluating 'maternal and domestic roles' historically, the conclusion of this study does not support Sanday's position, which is also shared by Rosaldo (1974), Chodorow (1974) and Ortner (1974), that what accounts for the universal subordination of women is their definition largely in terms of their maternal and domestic roles. This theory lacks socio-cultural analysis. As values are culturally determined, these roles do not carry the same valuation in all societies. They were highly valued in traditional Nnobi society, but are constraining and unrewarded in modern Nnobi society.

Marxist materialism or economism is limiting in that the role of culture is denied. The equation of power with the control of the means of production, and female high status with the degree of contribution to subsistence, can explain achieved, but not ascribed, power and authority. Friedl's (1975) theory is that it is important to have rights to extra-domestic distribution in order to have power and prestige in society.

This study shows that daughters in general can have a higher status than wives. Nnobi daughters, who had no economic base, had a higher status than wives, whose labour was central to the economy as a whole. The power and authority of daughters were the result of a cultural construct, not of economic achievement or of any rights to extra-domestic distribution. In the case of woman-to-woman marriage, 'female husbands' who did not themselves contribute their labour to the economy had a higher status than the women whose labour and services they controlled. The high status of *Ekwe* titled women, on the other hand, had both a cultural and an economic base.

Again, on the question of the kind of material used to represent African women, Le Vine's (1970) paper on the Afikpo as representative of Igbo women is not a good choice for Sanday to utilize for the purpose of analysing the status of women. If we are to go by the picture painted of the Afikpo by Le Vine and the Ottenbergs, then Afikpo appears to be the Igbo society where women have the least power, in spite of being, in my opinion, matrilineal rather than double descent in their inheritance system. According to S. Ottenberg (1968:103), as much as 85% of the farm land was under the control of the matrilineage. This is another example which indicates that descent system has little to do with women and power. Even though the matrilineage controlled most of the land, a woman received only small portions of land from her husband for the planting of subsidiary crops and vegetables

(S. Ottenberg 1968:62). A man, on the other hand, received farm land from his own matrilineage, his patrilineage and from both his father's and his wives' matrilineages (S. Ottenberg 1968:180–81). Sanday should have used material from another Igbo society, Onitsha for example, or from other African societies where women have been reported to have powerful organizations which have made an input into the political systems of their societies.

Sanday's alternative explanation, that is, the emphasis on 'magico-religious means by which women gain and maintain title to control' may yet prove the most important area for women to investigate. This would call for the analysis of culture and an emphasis on belief systems which have legitimized women's power. Diop (1978) has argued that ancient Africa was matriarchal. We consequently find that maternity is viewed as sacred in the traditions of all African societies. And in all of them, the earth's fertility is traditionally linked to women's maternal powers. Hence the centrality of women as producers and providers and the reverence in which they were held. These are factors of ancient African matriarchal systems, residues of which can still be traced, if sought, even in the most patriarchal African societies today.

This cultural approach is dismissed by Sanday. According to her, 'The problem with this type of explanation is that it can be considered an effect and not a cause of female status. A belief system emphasizing maternity and fertility as sacred may function to legitimize female status that develops because of ecological and economic factors' (1974:204). She consequently sees female deities 'as a means for recognizing and accepting female power' (1974:206). This is juggling cause and effect; like the hen and the egg, which came first? This kind of negative approach stems from a prejudiced position which assumes that women did not have power from the start. Nnobi data prove the contrary. Women were the bedrock of the society which was matriarchal until a patriarchal culture intruded and began to undermine female autonomy and power. Several questions for research on African women are therefore raised by the Nnobi case study:

1. To what extent are the customs of any particular African society indigenous or traditional? This question requires a good distribution of material into appropriate historical periods, taking into account alien factors such as colonialism, racism, imperialism and change.
2. Language and gender ideology: how rigid or flexible is the grammatical gender construction of a particular language, that is, how strictly are nouns and pronouns divided or distinguished on the basis of gender? Are there any neuter particles or pronouns? To what extent are the gender rules reflected in the socio-political organizations of the society and its cultural systems? What are the gender rules in according status, in filling important political positions and in performing roles? Is there any status ambiguity or gender neutrality of expressions and symbols such that members of either sex can step into important political positions or perform important political roles without breaking gender rules or being stigmatized?
3. What was the gender representation of deities and spirits in the indigenous religion? If there is no evidence of female deities, at what point in history could this have been obliterated? Could it have been due to the intrusion of a patriarchal

people, in recorded history, or in myth or legend; or the centralizing tendencies of the pre-colonial state; or missionary and colonial influences – European or Arab; or uncritical post-colonial analysis of local people and a new gender bias? What were considered ideal male and female virtues and how were these celebrated? What sacred duties do/did women have in relation to ancestral cults, rituals, indigenous religion? How were the status and self-esteem of women reflected in beliefs surrounding female deities and female spirits?

4. What was/is the position of women in the economic system? What are the main economic resources and what access do women have to them? To what extent does women's management of economic resources, including land, contradict formal rules of succession and inheritance?

5. How has the particular society classified its men and women? What is the social and cultural significance of the different categories of woman? What are the socialization processes? What is the social and cultural significance of the different stages in the life-cycle? How do they relate to formal and informal power structures amongst women and with men?

6. What is the degree of female autonomy in household and family structures and the relations of production? What are the gender dynamics in terms of power and authority? What is the capacity of members to recruit labour, and what are the economic and political advantages derived?

7. How autonomous are women's customs and other economic and political activities? If there is strong evidence of patriarchal control, is it possible from oral traditions, myth, songs, legends, etc., to date the intrusion of patriarchy on the people? If there is a strong ideology of female subjection, how is this contradicted in women's economic and political activities, and customs and ideologies which still survive from the ancient African matriarchy?

8. What sanctions, economic, ritual, political, could women apply to men? Are there historical events where these are recalled?

9. What were the traditional symbols of wealth for men and for women? What was the degree to which, and what were the means by which, they could accumulate wealth? Which social categories could do it more easily than others and how was wealth related to power for men and for women?

10. In the traditional society, how central were relationships traced through women in linking lineages and villages and in the circulation of goods as in exchanges in marriage, funeral and mortuary rites? In what power position did this place the women involved? How has this been affected by change and the cash economy? What share did women have in goods circulated during various ceremonies? What did the payment or share they had signify in possible loss of old power and autonomy or in the recognition of rights?

11. What were individual women remembered for – wealth, beauty, skill at economic management, management of people including command over their husbands, motherhood or religious/prophetic powers? What role did this play in terms of models for later generations of women?

12. What forms did gender struggle take? How were women involved in the management of meaning? What was their involvement in the communication processes? Through what forms of organizations, ceremonies, songs, folk-tales,

rituals, etc., did women generate favourable gender ideologies and stress the importance of their roles and duties? Did men try to counteract these in other ways?

13. To what extent does a conventional anthropological perspective correctly interpret the consequences of relationships involved in the jungle of anthropological terms, such as, patri/matrilocality, patri/matrilineality, classificatory kinship, role of maternal relatives, affines, preferential marriage patterns, endogamy/exogamy, etc.? To what extent are there conflicting and contradictory patterns of behaviour, relations, organizations, which undermine, sabotage or mediate the consequences of these relationships? Are there any traces, in a society which is supposed to be patriarchal, of earlier matriarchal ideologies or practices?

14. How was motherhood economically and politically rewarded in the pre-colonial society? What were the ideological and cultural components? What were the organizations through which it was expressed? In what ways have these been affected by change?

15. What was the structure of pre-colonial institutions, formal and informal, male and female? Was there sexual dualism? Any mediating factors? What happened to these institutions during and after the colonial period? Which ones have been replaced, incorporated, etc? How did sexual dualism become more rigid and how has it affected the situation of women and their role in the decision-making processes and in local politics? Who continues to manage life-cycle ceremonies? Is it inside or outside formal religious organizations? What new gender realities are being generated and how are they affecting the political consciousness and situation of women?

16. What were the initial female responses to the religions of colonizers, Islam or Christianity? Why, later, were women attracted in larger numbers than men to the Christian religion? What role did Western education play in this? What are the new gender realities and how have they affected the gender status of symbols in divinity?

17. In the situation of plurality of cultures, have interpretation and meaning become a political issue in social relations? What new interpretations of the old culture are those in power seeking to impose? Which aspects of the old culture which legitimize their new positions are they trying to stress? In which areas, in any given society, is this kind of struggle taking place (e.g. over the question of gender identity or in power relations between the sexes)?

18. Did the new sexual politics, legitimized by colonial rule, enable local men to manipulate the very rigid gender ideology on which it is based to monopolize power in the public sphere? If so, this suggests that a) in the pre-colonial period, there was a struggle over gender ideology, and between the sexes since matriarchal and patriarchal ideologies were juxtaposed; b) sexual dualism, whether mediated by gender flexibility or not, enabled women to negotiate from a position of greater strength than they do now. Therefore, what was lost? In the case of Nnobi, for example, it is the whole body of supportive systems derived from pro-female ideologies e.g. the goddess religion, female titles, male or female polygyny, female autonomy in domestic arrangements and in the wider descent and extra-descent women's organizations.

19. What is the character of female urban/rural organizations today? What ideologies are they controlled by? How does this work to their advantage or detriment?

20. What role in undermining matriarchal values was played by pre-colonial centralizing (patriarchal) states?

21. Contrast the old polygynous systems with present-day monogamy from the point of view of women; their constraints, their mobility, supportive systems in the areas of childcare, maternity, autonomy in sexuality, etc. What group of women benefited most from which type of marriage?

22. What alternate choices to conventional concepts of marriage and the family are women making? What are the implications?

Some Practical Considerations

Finally, I feel a strong moral commitment to deal briefly with the practical considerations arising from this study; those with whom I worked in Nnobi expected such a commitment from me. The women especially did not consider me a stranger or a visitor or a scientist divorced from local problems and politics. In Nigeria, unlike the West, recommendations arising from research are formally encouraged. Nigeria is a developing country and everyone's opinion is sought, and there is an Igbo saying: 'You do not see a spring nearby and leave it and go far away looking for water to fetch.' It is, then, as a Nnobi daughter obligated to the women of Nnobi that I include these practical formulations.

This study confirmed the existence of a dual-sex political system in Nnobi traditional society, but showed that divisions and interests of political groups were not only on the basis of biological sex, they also reflected ideological gender and élitist divisions. As a result of Western influence, however, local men now manipulate a rigid gender ideology in contemporary sexual politics and thereby succeed in marginalizing women's political position, or in excluding them from power altogether. This study therefore recommends:

1. The institution of a true dual-sex political system in local administration, with clearly defined spheres of interest. This position assumes that, in practice, the general interests and concerns of the mass of rural women differ from men's. Therefore, the dual-sex political institutions suggested are a modification of those being revived in the western and riverine Igbo towns. In this system, the traditional female ruler's cabinet deals with 'female affairs' and the traditional male ruler's council deals with 'male affairs' (see Henderson 1972; Okonjo 1976).

2. As subsistence in the household and the subsistence economy as a whole are regarded as women's responsibility, both legislative and executive rights over the markets should be regarded as 'female affairs'. This would give women effective power to check male politicians who monopolize the distribution and sale of food items, traditionally a female domain. The Women's Council should retain judicial powers in 'very female affairs', notably those affecting women's health and sanity.

3. Given a separate women's cabinet, it will be necessary and imperative to create female titles parallel to male titles.

4. In order for women and their interests to be represented in the wider decision-making processes, and for politically ambitious women not to be confined in and

constrained by a separate female sphere, it is necessary to create seats for representatives of the Women's Council in the other three organs of local government, namely, the Nnobi Welfare Organization, the local government council and the traditional *igwe*'s council. It is imperative that there should be equal numbers of titled women to titled men in the *igwe*-in-council.

5. The system of voting in the councils should be organized in such a way that males and females have equal numbers of votes in order to reflect the dual-sex political system. Some men may, however, choose to vote with women and vice versa, according to their convictions. The possibility of voting according to sex also allows for collective action by women to check or frustrate male dominance.

6. This system of government makes it imperative that there should be two elected or nominated candidates in local government elections for each ward, a male councillor and a female one.

7. In order that women may participate and be represented in national politics, the community should approach women as well as men when choosing and supporting candidates for general elections to the State House of Assembly and the Federal House of Assembly. Female politicians in hitherto male-dominated political parties would have an opportunity to direct their efforts towards canvassing for female votes for themselves or other female candidates, instead of being used to support male candidates, as they are at present.

8. Finally, the current constitution for Nnobi should be scrapped, the constitution committee dissolved and a new one with equal numbers of men and women set up. New proposals reflecting the dual-sex political system should be put forward, discussed and finally written in the Igbo language.

In January 1986, the President of Nigeria, Major-General Ibrahim Babangida, appointed a Political Bureau to conduct a nationwide political debate. The aim was to search for a solution to the problem of political instability in Nigeria and work out a political dispensation for 1990, when the military would hand power over to a civilian government. The debate lasted until October 1986, and was conducted at federal, state and local government levels. One of the themes was 'Women in Politics' and women participated extensively in the debate. I presented several papers in the debate (see the Bibliography) and was personally involved in mobilizing women to participate, and thus had a rare opportunity to assess the state of Nigerian women's political awareness, their role in development and some of the demands they are making for the improvement of their socio-economic conditions.

In the Muslim communities, especially those in the northern states, an organization of Muslim women has begun to consolidate their organizations under one umbrella. This is in reaction to the National Council of Women's Societies (NCWS), which has served as the umbrella to women's organizations nationwide. Historically, the NCWS has its origin in the Christian south, and the Muslim sisters have accused the Society of not representing the views of Muslim women or taking account of the teaching of Islam.

Generally, in the southern towns and villages, there are various modern women's organizations – 200 to 300 in some states. There are the women's patriotic unions, town unions or improvement unions of various communities, villages or towns.

There are those which have been described as mere appendages, that is, associations of wives of various ranks of the professional élites, including the military; and those of the multiple churches and prayer houses in Nigeria. There are organizations and associations of women traders, market women, contractors and those in industry. There are also those of the people's clubs, the Lionesses, the old girls' associations of various secondary schools and universities; and there are the clubs of the wealthy women.

Unfortunately, all these modern women's organizations see themselves as non-political and concern themselves primarily with welfare and charity work. By clinging to the stereotyped role of women as unpaid carers, taking over the state's social welfare responsibilities, they are counter-productive in the struggle for a true socialist transformation. This is because they are unwittingly propping up capitalism by saving the government billions of Naira which should be allocated towards the welfare and development of the destitute, the handicapped and the majority poor, especially those in the rural communities. This counter-productive aspect has received very little attention from researchers.

The involvement of women in development efforts in the various states is minimal indeed. The only governmental bodies mentioned as assisting rural women with funds or supervision are the Federal and State Departments of Rural Development and the Federal and State Ministries of Agriculture. They have either supplied equipment or trained personnel, as a token gesture. Most development projects come, therefore, from the self-help efforts of local women's organizations in the very few communities where they are being set up.

The types of projects these women are setting up and which most other women would like to set up are: home economics centres, adult education schemes, multi-purpose centres including nurseries, vegetable gardens, demonstration farms, poultry farms, small-scale industries for manufacturing soaps, pomade, snacks, etc., health centres, rural electrification, electricity plants and pipe-borne water, bore holes, pharmacies and dispensaries, maternity homes, fish ponds, home management units, craft centres, etc.

Some of the problems highlighted as affecting existing projects or the setting up of new ones were: lack of funds, inadequate accommodation, the need for trained personnel to teach the use of machines and technical equipment and fix them when they break down, lack of teachers, teaching aids and equipment, access to agricultural fertilizers at government controlled price, government assistance in equipping projects, lack of electrification and pipe-borne water, government's approval for setting up fish ponds, the need for extension staff, technical advisers, and seedlings for their farms. The rural women expressed the need for government to assist them set up money-yielding projects to generate skills, improve living standards in the rural communities and promote unity and solidarity among women.

What came out very clearly from the national political debate is the political frustration of grassroots women. They had so much to say about the poor state of the nation's economy, the political chaos in terms of corruption, the exploitation of women, especially the incessant demands for huge levies from women, etc.; once given a microphone to speak, it proved very difficult to take it away from them!

Among the points stressed was the need for unity among women. Even though women were aware of class contradictions in terms of the privileges of the rich and powerful, differences and diversity appeared threatening to most women. The general call was for all women to unite by 1990 when they would elect a woman president! The general opinion of women was that men have failed in ruling the country; it is now time to try women! In order to sharpen women's awareness of such concepts as class interests, class contradictions and class conflicts, a great deal needs to be done.

The responsibility of educated élite women and organizations to their rural sisters was identified as providing information, education and leadership. In my opinion, any organization truly committed to the achievement of economic and social justice for women must be guided by a socialist ideology. Such an organization cannot, therefore, be an umbrella or a miscellaneous organization representing women with conflicting and varied ideologies and orientations. It cannot be an organization working for or always in harmony with whatever government is in power. As we know, like male politicians, on the platform of umbrella organizations, many women have used the services and support of the majority of women, especially at the grassroots, to enhance their own political careers. They have either ripped off existing women's organizations or have organized women to serve their own self-interest rather than that of the women they claim to represent. The result is that women's organizations which previously directed themselves began to wait for directives.

Some women's organizations are already involved in development work, or have plans for projects for which they need advice and funds to implement. It is, therefore, important first to set up a de-linking process, to minimize the dependency and subservience of the exploited classes of women. This process can be achieved by a measure of women's economic independence through co-operatives, and other forms of co-operation in income and employment generating ventures.

Several articles revealing the growing concern about the situation and rights of women in Nigeria have appeared in the press at home and abroad. A report by Women In Nigeria (WIN), a progressive national organization with potentialities as a national vanguard, was submitted at the United Nations Nairobi conference (1985). The *WIN Document* has policy recommendations for the improvement of women's conditions in the various social, economic and political sectors. WIN combines a gender and class awareness. For this reason, it can offer Nigerian women leadership in the struggle for political change, while the women's wing of the Nigerian Labour Congress can champion the struggle for economic justice. Their roles should be complementary.

In a way, the dialogue has already begun. My contribution is the proposal that Nigerian women should make the ultimate demand for total equal opportunities for men and women and full representation in government as of right.

During the election campaigns of 1979, Alhaji Aminu Kano, leader of the People's Redemption Party (PRP), pledged to have a woman Vice-President. Major-General Muhammadu Buhari's regime, which in 1983 toppled the civilian government of Alhaji Shehu Shagari, recommended one seat for women in the state cabinets. But Buhari himself shared power only with men in the Supreme Military

Council (SMC). The regime led by Major-General Ibrahim Babangida, which toppled Buhari's government in 1985, has further ruled that one of the five councillors for each of the local government areas must be a woman. Again, Babangida rules the nation through an Armed Forces Ruling Council (AFRC) comprised solely of men.

Why should Nigerian women accept half-measures or tokenism? Why should women have only 'Vices' and 'Deputies' dangled before their eyes? Tokenism is divisive to women. It leaves individual women vulnerable to red-tape from men, isolated from other women, and therefore at the mercy of the men who have appointed them. This is why contributions to the political debate stressed the need for comprehensive legislation to restore women's rights, and the creation of institutions to serve as watchdogs to ensure proper implementation of such legislation. Such institutions should include a Ministry of Women's Affairs as the central co-ordinating body, Women's Committees and Women's Units at all levels of government and within key ministries. I also called for the creation of a strong and effective grassroots democratic local government system to which a much larger share of the Federation Account Revenue should be allocated.

In such a system, the local government Women's Unit and Women's Committees would effectively consult with and mobilize rural women for development. Such committees would give the badly needed firsthand information, education, guidance and enlightenment to the mass of illiterate, uninformed and marginalized rural women and thus integrate them into government development efforts and strategies. This way, there can be a link between the lone female councillor in the new Local Government Council, the Women's Unit, the Women's Committee and local women.

An important resolution which came out of the UN Nairobi conference (1985), to which member nations, including Nigeria, are signatory, is the setting up of a Ministry of Women's Affairs in each country. Nigeria still has not set up this ministry, but has set up a National Committee on Women and Development under the Federal Ministry of Social Development, Youth and Sports. The states have been instructed to do the same in the appropriate ministry. The Babangida regime, as I have argued, is a male-exclusive government and, as such, lacks the machinery or forum for consultation with women. What information we have on the Women and Development Committee is heard only through the 'grapevine'. Open and extensive discussions and dialogue on these committees is essential. For example, what is the rationale for the very élitist composition of the committee, given the fact that special attention is to be given to rural women? Why are the committees located in the state capitals, instead of forming an integral part of a Local Government Council?

In the history of Nigeria, to the present day, the representation of women in any government, civilian or military, has remained at the behest of individual men in power. Exclusively male federal cabinets have gone on running a nation, the majority of whose population are women who are highly politicized and a sizeable number of whom are extremely well educated and in every way more competent than the collection of men ruling them without consultation or representation. No doubt, this state of affairs calls for the institution of equal opportunities for men and women in all sectors of the administrative machinery, at home and abroad, and at all levels of government, local, state and federal. The majority of rural women might not see the demand for equal opportunities as an immediate priority, but it must be argued that they have growing daughters whose choices they hope will be wider and better than their own.

Among the more immediate demands should be the institution of legislative checks on the practice of keeping girls away from school in some local government areas and on early marriage for girls; there should be some form of central policy on prostitution in order to prevent arbitrary action by religious fundamentalists and patriarchal state governors, and the kind of action taken by a northern state which outlawed rented accommodation for single women, considering them all to be prostitutes against whom punitive action should be taken; there should also be some form of policy regarding the provision of childcare facilities.

The debate concerning women is now a matter of urgency, since the Chief Judge of the Federal Republic of Nigeria joined in the public protest against the condition of modern women especially regarding aspects of our traditions and customs which are applied out of context in a different, modern environment. As reported in the popular press in February 1985, the Chief Judge called for a review of our customary laws. More than just reviews, we need some controlling legislative measures with prosecution powers to check the excesses of oppressive patriarchs all over the country.

Other areas where change and improvement are needed would best be tackled through campaign work and massive adult education programmes in health care, childcare, workshops on such economic activities as, for example, running co-operatives, starting small businesses and crafts, political education, even religious debates which reveal to women the positive and powerful roles which women have played in Islam, Christianity, etc., in order to arm them against conservatism, etc.

Finally, I remain convinced that in the drive for change and improvement, the momentum and specifications must be left to individual local areas. Women outside such areas should give information and support only when invited to do so.

Appendixes

Appendix 1

Chief Edmond Eze Okoli, *Igwe* II of Nnobi (reading from a document left by his father, Chief Solomon Eze Okoli, *Igwe* I of Nnobi),

Nnobi means ancient or traditional or the popular tribal *obi*. There is no self-evident decree available to enable us to review the past records of the history with regard to the origin of Nnobi. All that might have been had, is an intelligent observation from the past, from known to unknown. The elders say, '*E fe Nshi, e fe Adama, Nnobi aha efe Nshi, kama o bu Adama ka a n'ebulu ihu.*'[1] This statement is open to various interpretations. Nshi refers to the traditional Nri of Agu Ukwu. Although the present elders of Nnobi maintain intimate contact and communication with Nri Oreri, they recognize the Nri of Agu Ukwu and that of Oreri as one. They also hold that Nnokwa had some intimate relationship with Nri Oreri. The Nri was regarded as the highest authority in pagan priesthood in Igboland. In the ancient system of political leadership, there were various adaptations to comply with the needs of the time. It is very likely that Nri hegemony conferred the leadership of Nnobi to the pagan priest of Aho. But the actual day-to-day rituals and administration of justice were offices of the Ukozala priesthood. The changeover of leadership of the town came about under the Aho regime which superseded the Nri quasi-religio-political mandate.

Ihu consists of homage originally paid to the family ancestors through their particular living representatives. A stranger or slave or indentured servant brought *ihu* to the head of the family or to his master. A farmer also sent *ihu* to his landlord. *Ihu*, therefore, is a sign of homage given to a superior person. In a large family, the descendants and wives observe *ihu* occasionally to the head of the family. Why did the ancients of Nnobi pay *ihu* to the *Adama*(s), the Nri king-makers?

The *Adama*(s) were special title holders in Agu Ukwu Nri, and in Oreri. They are called the *Okpala*(s). In both places, they enjoyed the extraordinary privilege of touching the person of Eze Nri for his installation and burial ceremonies. It is difficult to explain this relationship between the *Adama* and the people of Nnobi – '*Nnobi aha efe Nri*' ('Nnobi does not revere Nri'). There are small villages in Nnobi that are known to be of Nri origin, i.e. Umunshim and Aghaluogu in Ebenesi, Ihunshi in Umuagu in Ngo. The ancestors of these three villages used to engage in the pagan rite of *ikwu ahu* in Nnobi [see Chapter 6]. This *ikwu aha* (pagan ritual of reconciliation) was the prerogative of the Nri throughout the Igbo-speaking area. Some guess may be made about the relationship between the Nri and Nnobi people in the pagan days.

In 1924, after the official outing parade of Eze Nri Oreri, Eze Okonkwo (who died in 1944) visited the River Niger. On his return journey via Nnewi, he called at Ani Nnobi shrine (shrine to the Earth Spirit of Nnobi) and worshipped. He received a metal staff from the head of a village in Umuagu in Ngo called Ikpuotutu village. The significance of this is difficult to assess. The evidence of this visit was offered by Mr I. C. Amadi, a tutor and an Oreri citizen who knew Eze Okonkwo intimately and who discussed with him his journey and return to Oreri in 1924. Dr Achukoson, the Dean of the Faculty of Arts, Nsukka, has found that by 3000 BC, the Nri hegemony had spread far beyond the Igbo country. With this contact with Nri in the early years, one is inclined to suggest that the origin of Nnobi must be sought in the year 3000 BC or earlier.

The Idemili pagan cult is the cult that made Nnobi town popular throughout the Idemili, Ana Edo and parts of Awka divisions. Personal contacts confirm that the Idemili Nnobi is the head of all Idemili(s) wherever the cult is observed in Igboland. In Aga Ukwu Nri, Idemili shrine is located in Diodo. The Ezu lake in Agulu is the traditional source of the Idemili River. In all the localities through which the river passes, it is called by different names. For example, it is called Okogba around Abagana. To be the head of Idemili cult, which is intimately bound up with the River Idemili, Nnobi must have settled originally around the Ezu lake. This suggestion brings us nearer to the traditional contact between the *Adama*(s) and ancient Nnobi people. The possibilities were that Nnobi people must have settled somewhere around Agu Ukwu, but moved away as the Nri Agu Ukwu people arrived in the locality. The history of the journey of the ancestors of Nri indicates that when the Nri came to the Agu Ukwu site, they met people who already dwelt on the land and they negotiated with them for good neighbourliness. Hence Nnobi people could not give *ihu* to their neighbours.

With regard to the *Adama*(s), it may be speculated that the people of Nnobi owe their pagan priesthood leadership to the *Adama*(s), who must have conferred on them the pagan *ozo* title. Hence the *Adama*(s) were superior to Nnobi people on the issue of rank of pagan title. We notice that the *ozo* title is of Nri origin. In those days, the handing over of *ozo* stick was part of *ozo* initiation. We notice that, in the latter years, the *ofo* stick for the *ozo* title in Nnobi was obtained from Nnokwa, the cousin of Nri. The head of the Ukozala cultural *ozo* rank was at Nnokwa. Again, the ceremony of splitting the kola-nut was the official duty of the priesthood. Nri, being superior in this respect, presided over the kola-nut rites. Nnokwa being the cousin of Nri used to chair this ceremony when the people of Nnokwa and Nnobi met. One can therefore infer that Nnobi are aboriginal, but culturally, they owe allegiance to the Nri.

The goddess Edo is regarded as a descendant of the mother goddess, Idemili Nnobi. This consideration is widely held in Nnewi, the head of the Ana Edo area. The elders of Nnewi hail Nnobi people as *ndi nna ochie*, 'ancient-parents' [see Chapter 3]. This fact was established during my visit to the head of the Edo shrine at Nnewi. The Edo cult also brings Nnobi people into contact with the Abatete and the Ichida people. The Ezemewi of Nnewi, the Omaliko of Abatete and the Otoogwe of Ichida reportedly canvassed the marriage of Edo. But eventually, the Ezemewi of Nnewi won [see Chapter 1]. The episode might not be mere human marriage relations. Nnobi played a senior role in the ancient days over the rest of these towns. This is one of the aspects of local history which the future generation may have to tackle.

Note

1. 'One reveres Nshi, then Adama. Nnobi does not revere Nshi, but pays ritual homage to Adama.' The order of reverence indicates the superiority of Adama to Nri.

Appendix 2

Figure 1

Minor Patrilineages of Umuona and the Genealogical Position of Nwajiuba

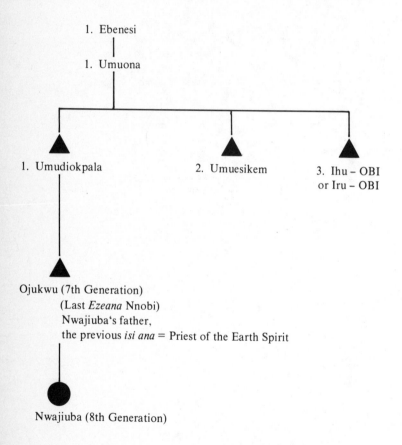

1. Ebenesi

1. Umuona

1. Umudiokpala

2. Umuesikem

3. Ihu – OBI
or Iru – OBI

Ojukwu (7th Generation)
(Last *Ezeana* Nnobi)
Nwajiuba's father,
the previous *isi ana* = Priest of the Earth Spirit

Nwajiuba (8th Generation)

Figure 2

Minor Patrilineages of Amadunu in their Ranking Order

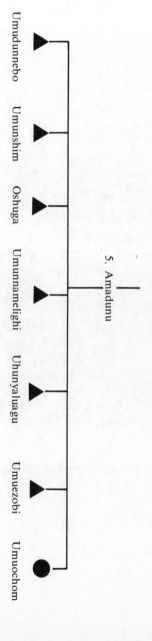

5. Amadunu

Umudunnebo Umunshim Oshuga Umunnamelighi Uhunyaluagu Umuezobi Umuochom

Figure 3

Minor Patrilineages in Ifite

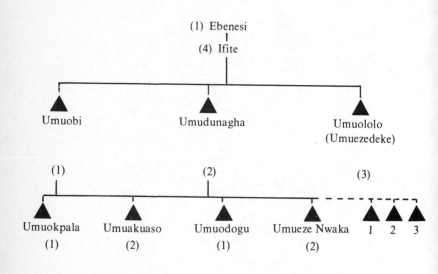

(1) Ebenesi
(4) Ifite

Umuobi   Umudunagha   Umuololo (Umuezedeke)

(1)   (2)   (3)

Umuokpala   Umuakuaso   Umuodogu   Umueze Nwaka   1   2   3
(1)   (2)   (1)   (2)

1. Umuugobuodo
2. Umuezesie
3 Aghaluogu (Nshi Strangers)

Umuokpala as first son of Obi should provide priests of Idemili, but they do not. Explanation for this is in the Myth of Domestication of Idemili (see Chapter 6). Umuakuaso, last son of Obi, provided the priest of Idemili shrine, but receive the *ofo* of authority from Umuokpala, who, some claimed, also give *ofo* for *ozo Aho* (Ogidiuche Obi does this). They were also said to have given *ofo* symbol of authority to all other *ozo* titles. This contradicts the impression given to the first anthropologist in Nnobi (see Appendix 1) that Nnobi received *ofo ozo* from neighbouring Nnokwa people, the said cousins of Nri. It also confirms the antiquity of Ifite as the ritual centre of Nnobi, and the Idemili religion as the indigenous religion.

Appendix 3

Plan of the *Obi* of Eze Okigbo

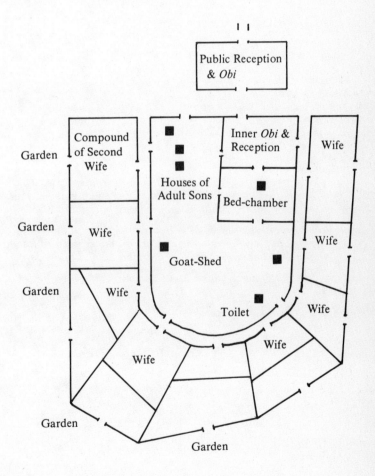

(This three-tier plan is typical of the family compounds of the very wealthy and powerful. Ordinary people has a two-tier system; an *obi* compound in front and female sub-compound units behind.)

Appendix 4

24th August, 1982.

Messrs. U. C. D. Okoye
Messrs. Richard Anoliefo
Messrs. Michael Ezike
Messrs. Ben Ewelugo
Mr Solomon Amadi Ume
Hon. Justice M. O. Nweje

Chiefs/Gentlemen,

I have the pleasure to inform you that it is the wish of Igwe-in-Council and Nnobi Community to confer on you an honorary title in appreciation of your great contributions towards the upliftment of our beloved town Nnobi.

The title if accepted, shall not, repeat not be associated with any pagan rites. If accepted please let us know the title you may like to choose and forward same to the Igwe of Nnobi on or before the 5th of September, 1982.

The title shall be conferred on you on 25th September, 1982, being Nnobi Afia Olu Festival day.

Thanks for your usual Co-operation.

Yours,
(Signed) HRH Igwe E. Ezeokoli, II

Ichie Edozie Okonkwo
Secretary.

cc
Ebenesi Brothers Meeting
Ngo Brothers Meeting
Awuda Community Meeting

Bibliography

Achebe, Chinua *Things Fall Apart* (Heinemann Educational Books Ltd, London, 1958).

Adamolekun, L. and Rowland, L. (eds.) *The New Local Government System in Nigeria* (Heinemann Educational Books (NIG) Ltd, Ibadan, 1979).

Afigbo, A.E. *The Warrant Chiefs: Indirect Rule in South-Eastern Nigeria, 1891-1929* (Longman Group Ltd, London, 1972).

Akunne, B. M. 'Ibe Nne: Bond of Common Motherhood at Nri', *Odinani* (Journal of the Odinani Museum, Nri, Nigeria), No. 2, September 1977.

Amadiume, Ifi 'The Local Government System: The Institution of a Women's Committee' (Paper delivered at the National Political Debate, organized by the Nigerian Union of Journalists, Anambra State Council, NUJ Press Centre, Enugu, 14 May 1986).

—— 'Women and the Political Debate', *The Guardian*, 19 May 1986.

—— 'Conditions needed to Ensure Women's Awareness and Participation in Development' (Paper presented at the National Political Debate Symposium 'Women and Nigeria's Political Development', organized by Women In Nigeria (WIN), Anambra, Imo, Rivers and Cross River States, Alvan Ikoku College of Education, Owerri, 23-24 May 1986).

—— 'Town/Community Unions or a Grassroots Democratic Local Government System for a Relevant and Even Rural Development in Anambra State?' (Paper presented at the IDS Forum, Institute For Development Studies, University of Nigeria, Enugu Campus, 15 July 1986).

—— 'Women and Political Development: Mobilization and Awareness in Anambra State' (Case study and situation analysis of women's mobilization in Anambra State, presented at Women In Nigeria (WIN) training seminar on awareness and mobilization, at WIN 5th Annual Conference, University of Benin, Benin, 22-26 July, 1986).

—— 'Women and Development: Another Development with Women in Nigeria' (Paper presented at the National Political Debate Seminar on The Nigerian Economic System and Political Order, organized by the Institute for Development Studies, University of Nigeria, Enugu Campus, 9-11 September 1986).

—— 'Unitary System of Government VS Grassroots Democracy' (Paper presented at the National Political Debate, Forum on Nigeria's Political Order: In Search of a Viable Popular Democracy, organized by the Department of Political Science, University of Nigeria, Nsukka, 23-24 September 1986).

Amadiume, M. E. 'Sex Differences in the Career Choice of University Students: A

Case Study of the University of Jos'. Unpublished research report submitted in partial fulfilment for the Master's Degree in Education, University of Jos, Nigeria, July 1982.

Amos, Valerie and Parmar, Pratibha 'Challenging Imperial Feminism', *Feminist Review*, No. 17, July 1984.

Anene, J. C. *Southern Nigeria in Transition 1885–1906* (Cambridge University Press, Cambridge, 1966).

Ardener, E. 'Belief and the Problem of Women' in Ardener, S. (ed.) 1975.

Ardener, S. (ed.) *Perceiving Women* (Dent/Malaby, London, and Halsted, New York, 1975).

—— *Defining Females – The Nature of Women in Society* (Croom Helm Ltd, London, 1978).

Asad, Talal (ed.) *Anthropology and the Colonial Encounter* (Ithaca Press, London, 1973).

Association of African Women for Research and Development (AAWORD) 'Document', *Development Dialogue*, Nos. 1–2, 1982.

Bailey, H. 'The Role of Anthropology in Colonial Development', *Man*, Vol. 44, 1944.

Barrett, Michele *Women's Oppression Today: Problems in Marxist Feminist Analysis* (Verso Editions, London, 1980).

Barrett, Michele and McIntosh, Mary 'Ethnocentrism and Socialist–Feminist Theory', *Feminist Review*, No. 20, June 1985.

Basden, G. T. *Niger Ibos* (London, 1938). (New impression by Frank Cass & Co. Ltd, London, 1966).

Baxter, Paul and Sansom, Basil (eds.) *Race and Social Differences* (Penguin Books, Harmondsworth, 1972).

Bloch, M. 'The Past and the Present in the Present', *Man*, N.S. 12, 1976, pp. 278–92.

Boserup, Ester *Women's Role in Economic Development* (St Martin's Press, New York, 1970).

Bujra, J. M. 'Introductory: Female Solidarity and the Sexual Division of Labour' in Caplan, P. and Bujra, J. M. (eds.) 1978.

Caplan, P. and Bujra, J. M. (eds.) *Women United, Women Divided – Cross-Cultural Perspective on Female Solidarity* (Tavistock Publications, London, 1978).

Carby, Hazel 'White Woman Listen! Black Feminism and the Boundaries of Sisterhood', in Centre for Contemporary Cultural Studies (Race and Politics Group) *The Empire Strikes Back, Race and Racism in 70's Britain* (Hutchinson, London, 1982).

Carmen, Gail, Shaila and Pratibha 'Becoming Visible: Black Lesbian Discussions', *Feminist Review*, 17, Autumn 1984.

Chodorow, N. 'Family Structure and Feminine Personality', in Rosaldo, M. and Lamphere L. (eds.) 1974.

Cutrufelli, Maria Rosa *Women of Africa: Roots of Oppression* (Zed Press, London, 1983).

Davis, Angela *Women, Race and Class* (Women's Press, London, 1982).

Diop, Cheikh Anta *The Cultural Unity of Black Africa: The Domains of Patriarchy and of Matriarchy in Classical Antiquity* (Third World Press, Chicago, Ill., 1978).

Douglas, Mary *Purity and Danger: an Analysis of Concepts of Pollution and Taboo* (Routledge & Kegan Paul, London, 1966).

—— *Implicit Meanings: Essays in Anthropology* (Routledge & Kegan Paul, London, 1975).

El Saadawi, Nawal *The Hidden Face of Eve* (Zed Press, London, 1980).

Evans-Pritchard, E. E. *The Position of Women in Primitive Societies and Other Essays in Social Anthropology* (Faber & Faber, London, 1965).

Ezeani, C. I. 'Afor Nnobi Market as a Central Place'. An unpublished special research project submitted to the Department of Geography, Anambra State College of Education, Awka, in partial fulfilment of requirements for NCE, June 1980.

Ezeokoli II, *Igwe* of Nnobi 'What Manner of Men?', *Abalukwu*, Vol. 1, September 1975.

Forde, D. and Jones, G. I. *The Ibo and Ibibio-Speaking Peoples of South-Eastern Nigeria* (Oxford University Press, London, 1950).

Friedl, E. *Women and Men, An Anthropologist's View* (Holt, Rinehart & Winston, Stanford, Calif., 1975).

Godelier, M. 'The Origins of Male Domination', *New Left Review*, 127, May/June 1981.

Green, M. M. *Igbo Village Affairs* (1947). (2nd edn, Frank Cass & Co. Ltd, London, 1964).

Greer, Germaine *The Female Eunuch* (Paladin, London, 1971).

—— *Sex and Destiny: The Politics of Human Fertility* (Secker & Warburg, London, 1984).

Hafkin, N. J. and Bay, E. G. (eds.) *Women in Africa: Studies in Social and Economic Change* (Stanford University Press, Stanford, Calif., 1976).

Harris, Jack S. 'The Position of Women in Nigerian Society', *Annals of the New York Academy of Sciences*, 2, 1940.

Henderson, R. N. *The King in Every Man: Evolutionary Trends in Onitsha Ibo Society and Culture* (Yale University Press, New Haven and London, 1972).

Hooks, Bell *Ain't I a Woman: Black Women and Feminism* (Pluto Press, London, 1982).

Hymes, Dell (ed.) *Reinventing Anthropology* (Random House, New York, 1969). (Reissued by Vintage Books, 1974).

Ifeka-Moller, C. 'Female Militancy and Colonial Revolt. The Women's War of 1929, Eastern Nigeria', in Ardener, S. (ed.) 1975.

Isichei, E. *The Igbo People and the Europeans: The Genesis of a Relationship – to 1906*, (Faber & Faber, London, 1973).

—— *A History of the Igbo People* (Macmillan, London, 1976).

Jones, G. I. 'Agriculture and Ibo Village Planning', *Farm and Forest*, 6, 1, 1945, pp. 9–15.

—— 'Dual Organisation in Ibo Social Structure', *Africa*, 19, 2, April 1949, pp. 150–56.

—— 'Ibo Land Tenure', *Africa*, 19, 4, October 1949, pp. 309–23.

—— 'Ecology and Social Structure among the North Eastern Ibo', *Africa*, 31, 2, April 1961, pp. 117–34.

—— 'Ibo Age Organization with Special Reference to the Cross River and North Eastern Ibo', *Journal of the Royal Anthropological Institute*, 92, 2, July–December 1962, pp. 191–211.

Kuper, Adam *Anthropologists and Anthropology: The British School 1922–72* (Penguin Books, Harmondsworth, 1973).

Leach, E. *Rethinking Anthropology* (Athlone Press, London, 1961). (Paperback edition 1966.)

Lebeuf, Annie M. D. 'The Role of Women in the Political Organization of African

Societies', in Paulme (ed.) 1963.

Leith-Ross, S. *African Women* (London, 1939). (Reissued by Routledge & Kegan Paul, London, 1965).

Le Vine, Robert A. 'Sex Roles and Economic Change in Africa', in Middleton, John (ed.) *Black Africa* (London, 1970).

Little, Kenneth *African Women in Towns* (Cambridge University Press, Cambridge, 1973).

Lloyd, P. C. *Africa in Social Change* (Penguin Books, Harmondsworth, 1967).

Lorde, Audre *Sister Outsider, Essays and Speeches* (The Crossing Press, 1984).

MacCormack, C. and Strathern, M. (eds.) *Nature, Culture and Gender* (Cambridge University Press, Cambridge, 1980).

Mama, Amina 'Black Women, the Economic Crisis and the British State', *Feminist Review*, No. 17, July 1984.

—— 'African Women Fight Back', *West Africa*, 10 December 1984.

Mathieu, N. 'Is Man–Culture and Woman–Nature?', *L'Homme*, 1973.

Mba, Nina Emma *Nigerian Women Mobilized: Women's Political Activities in Southern Nigeria, 1900–1965* (Institute of International Studies, University of California, Berkeley, 1982).

Meek, C. K. *Law and Authority in a Nigerian Tribe: A Study in Indirect Rule* (1937). (2nd impression, Oxford University Press, London, 1950).

Needham, R. (ed.) *Rethinking Kinship and Marriage* (Tavistock, London, 1971).

Nelson, Nici 'Women Must Help Each Other', in Caplan and Bujra (eds.) 1978.

Nsugbe, P. O. *Ohaffia: A Matrilineal Ibo People* (Oxford University Press, London, 1974).

Nwabara, S. N. *Iboland. A Century of Contact with Britain 1860–1960* (Hodder and Stoughton, 1977).

Nzimiro, I. *Studies in Ibo Political Systems: Chieftaincy and Politics in Four Niger States* (Frank Cass & Co. Ltd, London, 1972).

—— 'Anthropological Briefs on Eze-ship in Ibagwa Ani', *Odinani*, No. 2, 1977.

Oakley, Ann *Sex, Gender and Society* (Temple Smith, London, 1972).

Obiefuna, J. 'The Origin of Nnobi', *Abalukwu*, Vol. 5, December 1976, p. 34.

Ofomata, G. E. K. *Nigeria in Maps: Eastern States* (Ethiope Publishing House, P.M.B. 1192, Benin City, Nigeria, 1975).

Okigbo, P. 'Social Consequences of Economic Development in West Africa', in Van den Berghe (ed.) *Africa, Social Problems of Change and Conflict* (Chandler Publishing Company, San Francisco, 1965).

Okonjo, K. 'The Dual-Sex Political System in Operation: Igbo Women and Community Politics in Midwestern Nigeria', in Hafkin and Bay (eds.) 1976.

Okoye, T. O. 'Traditional Urbanization', in Ofomata, G. E. K. (ed.) 1975.

Onwuejeogwu, M. A. in *Odinani*, Journal of Odinani Museum, Nri, 1, 1972.

—— *An Igbo Civilization: Nri Kingdom and Hegemony* (Ethnographica Ltd, Ethiope Publishing Corporation, London, 1981).

—— 'Review: Studies in Igbo Political System', in *Odinani*, No. 2, September 1977.

Ortner, S. B. 'Is Female to Male as Nature is to Culture?', in Rosaldo and Lamphere (eds.) 1974.

Ortner, Sherry B. and Whitehead, Harriet (eds.) *Sexual Meanings: The Cultural Construction of Gender and Sexuality* (Cambridge University Press, Cambridge, 1981).

Ottenberg, P. V. 'The Changing Economic Position of Women among the Afikpo

Ibo', in Bascom, W. R. and Herskovits, M. J. (eds.) *Continuity and Change in African Cultures* (The University of Chicago Press, Chicago and London, 1959).

Ottenberg, S. *Double Descent in an African Society: The Afikpo Village-Group* (University of Washington Press, Seattle and London, 1968).

Palmer, M. D. *Henry VIII* (Longman Group Ltd, Harlow, 1971).

Paulme, Denise (ed.) *Women of Tropical Africa* (University of California Press, Berkeley, 1963).

P'Bitek, Okot *African Religions in Western Scholarship* (Kenya Literature Bureau, Nairobi, 1970).

Perham, M. *Native Administration in Nigeria* (Oxford University Press, Oxford, 1937).

Reiter, R. *Toward an Anthropology of Women* (Monthly Review Press, London and New York, 1975).

Report of Rural Economic Survey of the East Central State of Nigeria, Official Document No. 3 of 1977, Ministry of Economic Development, Statistics Division, Enugu, Nigeria.

Rogers, Barbara *The Domestication of Women: Discrimination in Developing Societies* (1980). (Reprint Tavistock Publications Ltd and Methuen, Inc., London, 1983).

Rogers, S. 'Women's Space in a Men's House: The British House of Commons', in Ardener, S. (ed.) *Women and Space – Ground Rules and Social Maps* (Croom Helm, London, 1981).

Rosaldo, M. Z. 'Woman, Culture and Society: A Theoretical Overview', in Rosaldo and Lamphere (eds.) 1974.

Rosaldo, M. Z. and Lamphere, L. (eds.) *Woman, Culture and Society* (Stanford University Press, Stanford, Calif., 1974).

Sanday, P.R. 'Female Status in the Public Domain', in Rosaldo and Lamphere (eds.) 1974.

Statistical Digest 1973, East-Central State of Nigeria, Statistical Division, Ministry of Economic Development and Reconstruction, Edition 4, Official Document No. 2 of 1978.

Steady, F. C. 'Protestant Women's Associations in Freetown, Sierra Leone', in Hafkin and Bay (eds.) 1976.

Stevenson, R. F. *Population and Political Systems in Tropical Africa* (Columbia University Press, New York, 1968).

Sweetman, David *Women Leaders in African History* (Heinemann Educational Books Ltd, London, 1984).

Tanner, Nancy 'Matrifocality in Indonesia and Africa and among Black Americans', in Rosaldo and Lamphere (eds.) 1974.

Uchendu, V. C. *The Igbo of Southeast Nigeria* (Holt, Rinehart & Winston Inc., New York, 1965).

Uzuagu, E. J. 'The *Ima Ogodo* Ceremony in Nnobi', *Abalukwu*, Vol. 8, September 1978.

Van Allen, Judith 'Sitting on a Man: Colonialism and the lost Political Institutions of Igbo Women', in *Canadian Journal of African Studies*, 6, 2, 1972, pp. 168–81.

―――― '"Aba Riots" or Igbo "Women's War"? Ideology, Stratification, and the Invisibility of Women', in Hafkin and Bay (eds.) 1976.

Weideger, Paula *Female Cycles* (The Women's Press, London, 1978).

Women in Nigeria, the WIN Document: *Conditions of Women in Nigeria and Policy Recommendations to AD 2000* (Women in Nigeria, Ahmadu Bello University,

Zaria, 1985).

Young, K., Wolkowitz, C. and McCullagh, R. (eds.) *Of Marriage and the Market: Women's Subordination in International Perspective* (CSE Books, London, 1981).

Glossary

This is a glossary of Igbo words which have been used more than once in the text. Some Igbo words and expressions have been explained more fully in the text. Tones and vowels have not been marked.

ada: first daughter
agba: tall pole
Agba Ekwe: the chief *Ekwe* titled woman
agbogho ofe: maidens of the bed-chamber
aghota eke: picking and sharing
agu: a leopard
Agwu: a spirit which possesses and afflicts inadequate men; the associated title
aha acho ndu: one who does not try to survive, one who is not industrious
ajadu: a widow
aja uke: ritual for warding off evil spirits
ajo nwanyi: bad woman
ajo ofia: evil forest
aka n'ato: three hands
akara: fried bean cake
akpa nwa: afterbirth
aku nkpi: double-seeded palm nut
akwukwo nnuno: bird's letter, that is anonymous letter
akwukwo ukpum: traditional dish cooked with vegetables, plantain and banana, with no water added and without meat or fish. It was therefore regarded as food of the poor
alu: sacrilege
Alusi: deities and other supernatural spirits
ani obi: ancestral compound with surrounding lands
ani okpu: original ancestral land
chi: deity
di: genderless prefix word which means specialist in, or expert at, or master of something
dibia: ritual specialist
di-bu-no: family head
di-okpala: first son
egbugbu: tattoos
eghu chi: ritual goat
ego: money

217

Eke Okwu: day holy to Idemili
Ekwe: title taken by women and associated with the goddess Idemili
ekwu: mother's pot
Etedenaghu: traditional yearly ceremony performed by women. It involved the giving of gifts to a woman by her daughters' husbands; a nurse-maid is also given gifts
Eze/eze: King; or kingly when it is a prefix to an epithet or name of an *ozo* man
Ezeani/Ezeana Nnobi: Priest of the Land or Earth Spirit of Nnobi
Eze Nwanyi: female king; queen
ezigbo nwanyi: good woman
Ibenne: ritualized and symbolized supernatural sanction applied to relationship among siblings and other relations. Among Nri Igbo people, it is referred to as the bond of common motherhood.
ibu ihu: paying homage to a superior
ibu nkwu: 'carrying palm-wine' ceremony in the series of ceremonies associated with getting married
ibu nne amu: gift to the mother of maternity
ichi: facial markings of ritual purification
ichie: titled members of the *igwe*'s council; the traditional ruler's council
ichi Ekwe: the taking of the *Ekwe* title
ideyi: flowing wet sand
idi uchu: perseverance and industriousness
igba agboghobia: coming into womanhood
igba ohu: woman-to-woman marriage
igbu udud oma: a ritual which separated blood tie before those related could be married
igo nmuo: (same as *ilo nmuo*)
igo oji: saying blessing and incantations before the breaking of kola-nut
igwe: title of the traditional ruler of Nnobi
igwo ajo ogwu: indulging in bad sorcery
ihe isi: headship share
ihu: the gift given in the paying of ritual homage
ika: to surpass
ikenga: a ritual object kept by men of independent status
ikolo: war drum
ikolobia: manhood
iko ugwu: give prestige and honour to someone
ikpa nku: picking wood
ikpa omu: yellow palm-leaf
ikpo ji: the call for the Eating of New Yam Festival
ikpu mmanwu: masquerade group
ikpu okwa: the annual festival performed for the deity Aho
ikwu ahu: the festival in which cows are slaughtered for the goddess Idemili
ikwunne: one's matrilineage, that is, one's mother's patrilineage
ili ji: Eating of the New Yam Festival
ilo chi: women's religious worship of the goddess Idemili
ilo nmuo: remembrance of the ancestors
ilu aka: pointing at a thing
ilu ji: tending the yam plant
ima ogodo: the ritual process of becoming a woman and a mother

ima upo: discovery that a bride was pregnant before the marriage ceremonies were complete; the groom is then fined

imenne: inner-mother circle; closer relationships traced through the mother

inyom di: patrilineage wives and also the name of their formal organization

inyom Nnobi: the collective of all adult Nnobi women and also the name of the Women's Council

isi ahihaa, isi nta: picketing

Isi ana: same as Ezeani/Ezeana

isi nmili: the source of the spring – the mother

ite ogwu: pot of medicine

ite uba: the pot of prosperity

ito ogodo: to untie a woman's wrapper

itu ji abani: yam given to wife by husband as his contribution to household food

itu mgbele: selling and buying, buying and selling

mgba Ekwe: the staff of authority carried by an *Ekwe* titled woman

mmadu: humankind

mmuo: spirit; spirits of the incarnate ancestors

na awa awa: involuntary action

ndi be: family

ndi nna ochie (plural): male members of one's mother's patrilineage, whom I have called ancient-fathers

ndi nne ochie (plural): female members of one's mother's patrilineage – ancient-mothers

ndi odinani: custodians of the original culture

ndi ushe: respected elders

ngiga: a basket of seasoning ingredients and other food items, always hung above the fire in a woman's kitchen

ngu: potash

nhayikwa/nhanye: officially placing a daughter in the position of a son, that is, making her a male

njada ukwu: string anklet worn by the titled

nkpuke: wife's sub-compound unit which was a matricentric household

nkwu ana: palm tree pointed out to a daughter by her father as a wedding present

nma ekwu: kitchen knife

nma eneke: small knife

nmuo: (same as *mmuo*)

nna: father

nna anyi: our father

nna ochie (singular): ancient-father

nne: mother

nne nwanyi: fully fledged woman

nne ochie (singular): ancient-mother

nni ocha: pounded cocoyam

nso ani: crime against the land

nwa: child

nwadiana/nwadiani: child of a daughter

nwanne: sibling; classificatory brothers and sisters

nwanne otu afo/nwanne afo: siblings

nwanyi: woman

nwoke: man

nyi: female
nzu: white clay
oba ji: yam store
obi: ancestral house or compound
obi okpu: original ancestral *obi*
ochie: ancient one; short for ancient-father or -mother
odinke: (same as *ikwu ahu*)
ofe: bed-chamber
ofe ukpum: similar to *akwukwo ukpum*, but is thickened with cocoyam and cooked without salt
ofo: a symbol of authority held by the titled and those in positions of authority
ogbenye nne: the state of being motherless
ogbuefi: title taken by men and women who have killed a cow for the goddess Idemili
ogili: fermented oil-bean seeds, used for flavouring sauce
ogwu ji: ritual medicine eaten before new yam can be cooked for food
ogwugwu: title taken by daughters after spirit possession
oke: male
Oke Nwanyi: the Great Woman
oke opi: an exclusive dance traditionally danced by titled men and women
oke ozo: high *ozo* titles
oku nmuo: hell fire
okwa: the mask worn by the masqueraders during the *ikpu okwa* festival
okwu chi: personal shrine
oli aku: wife
Oma: personal shrines erected by Onitsha daughters and dedicated to series of their dead mothers
ome-na-ani: customs of the land
omu: young yellow palm-leaves
Omu: of Onitsha title of the 'queen' of Onitsha women
onye be: wife
onye isi: head, leader
osisi uzo: food and cash-crop trees
osu: a social outcast or cult-slave dedicated to the shrine of the goddess Idemili and the goddess herself
ozo: a title taken by Igbo men which introduces them into both ritual and political élites in their various villages or towns
ozo Aho: title taken for the deity Aho
udala: a fruit tree
ukozala: the men so titled acted as the police in the indigenous society
umudiana/umudiani: plural of *nwadiana*
umunna: children of one father; the collective of patrilineage men and also the name of their formal organization
umunne: plural of *nwanne*; and also the spirit of common motherhood which compelled love and trust
umu okpu: patrilineage daughters and also the name of their formal organization
upiti: fertility ritual mud dance during marriage ceremony
ushe/ushie: red paint; camwood dye
ushie or *ufie:* an exclusive dance, performed only by *ozo* titled men

Index